About the author:

Tanner Lagasca is an American actor, writer, director, member of SAG-AFTRA, and author of The Portable Acting Coach. He studied acting under the guidance of Elizabeth Kemp, Ellen Barkin, Arthur Storch, and Ron Leibman from Actors Studio Drama School. He also attended Roosevelt University, and the Pacific Conservatory for the Performing Arts for his theatre and acting training.

He has been involved in theatre for over 40 years and has participated in almost every aspect of the business both on stage and behind the scenes, including acting, directing, stage managing, script writing, and Artistic Director of the theatre department in South Korea's multi-million dollar "English Village" where he developed a three-week theatre training program for non-native English speakers. It's success is still continuing to this day.

He has performed across the country with touring shows of *Robin Hood*, *The Barber of Seville*, and *Tom Sawyer*. He was seen on the Chicago stage in productions of *The Birds*, *Prometheus Bound*, *Balm in Gilead*, and *Seven Dates with Seven Writers*. He was also part of a staged reading of the original yet ill-fated *Psycho: The American Musical*.

He performed in the outdoor drama *Unto These Hills* in the Smoky Mountains before moving to New York and showcasing his cabaret shows *Reflections of a Dream* and *Can You Hold, That's My Life Calling?* at Danny's Skylight Cabaret Room.

He is featured in the 2015 web series *The Super Femmes* and as the head gentleman in the fan-based web series *Doctor*

Who: The Ginger Chronicles' episode *A Loud Lush*. He can be seen on screen as a featured extra in *You are Here* with Owen Wilson and as a A.I.M. employee in *Iron Man 3* as well as *Remnants* and *The Remaining*. His body of theatrical work is extensive and diverse, performing in numerous musical productions including *Once Upon a Mattress, Jesus Christ Superstar, Evita, Guys and Dolls*, and *Hello Dolly!* He has toured extensively with many professional children's theatre companies including National Theatre of Arts and Education (New York), National Theatre for Children (Minneapolis), and Poetry Alive, Inc. (Asheville, NC).

Other acting credits include Arnold Wiggins in *The Boys Next Door,* Daniel Corban in *Catch Me if You Can,* Seymour in *Little Shop of Horrors*, and Garry in *Noises Off!* His directing credits include *Bobby Gould in Hell, The Lesson, Heartland, Safe, Ladies in Retirement, Shrek Jr. the Musical, I Hate Hamlet*, and *Little Shop of Horrors.*

In 2020, he produced his short film, *The Portraits of Lillian Gray.* He teaches acting classes year-round at Actors Training Ground and also works as a private acting coach.

The Portable Acting Coach

ACTORS TRAINING GROUND
TANNER LAGASCA

EDITED BY TANNER LAGASCA AND JENNIFER L. ANDERSON

The Portable Acting Coach
3rd Edition
Copyright © 2013, 2015, 2020 by Tanner Lagasca

Printed in the United States of America

Cover and book design by Tanner Lagasca

This book is dedicated with much love to my mother, Doreen. Her constant support in my career has given me the strength to strive to be the best I could be. I love you, Mom. This book is for you.

Special thanks to the following teachers who shared their knowledge during my theatre education and showed me that with passion, inspiration, and perserverance I can believe in myself. Without their training, this book would not have been possible.

Kitty Balay	Jack Greenman
Karen Barbour	Peter Kjennas
Ellen Barkin	Christian Leban
Paul Barnes	Gene Lasko
Keith Buhl	Ron Leibman
Brad Caroll	Jeremy Mann
Jon Daly	Paul Rudd
Jim Edmonson	Arthur Storch
Patricia Fletcher	Nova Thomas
Gale Fury-Childs	Theresa Thuman

Very special thanks to Jennifer L. Anderson and David Henderson for the feedback during the editing of this book.

The Portable Acting Coach
ACTORS TRAINING GROUND

Preface	**13**
Foreword	**17**
CHAPTER 1: GETTING STARTED	**21**
What is Acting?	22
Keeping a Journal	26
Stage Directions	28
Stage Terminology	30
Before You Step on Stage	34
Memorizing Lines	36
CHAPTER 2: THE BASICS	**43**
Acting Overview	44
Objective/Intention	46
Obstacle	49
Tactic	51
Vocal Gesture	55
Ultimate Verb List – Intention and Tactic Verbs	57
Ultimate Verb List – Suggested Vocal Gestures	65
Relationship	66
Status	69
Trust	71
Listening	73
CHAPTER 3: ADDING TO THE BASICS	**75**
Subtext	76
Action	78
Inner Monologue	80
Given Circumstances	82
Beats and Pauses	86
Justification	88
CHAPTER 4: BEYOND THE BASICS	**93**

Relaxation and The Green Light 94
The Magic "If" 99
The Moment Before 101
Moment-to-Moment 104
Emotional Tones 107
Emotional Chart 108
Arcs 109
Endowment 114
Substitution 116
Sense Memory 119
Emotional Recall 123

CHAPTER 5: VOICE **129**
Voice Overview 130
Warming Up the Voice And Exercises 131
Relaxation 132
Posture and Alignment 135
Respiration and Positioning 140
Phonation 143
Support 146
Registration 149
Resonance 151
Articulation 153
Articulation warm-up 158
Your 30-Minute Vocal Warm-Up 161

CHAPTER 6: SPEECH **163**
Speech Overview 164
Honing Speech Through Listening Skills 165
Rhythm And Tempo 166
Utilizing Patterns of Speech 169
Freeing the Voice Through Singing 173
Pitch Exercises and Drills 174
Musical Terms in Sheet Music 176
Theatre/Acting/Music Terms 183
International Phonetic Alphabet 211
Vowel Placement 215
Regional, Neutral, & Standard American 217
Removing A Regional Dialect 219
Quick Dialect Reference Guide 220

CHAPTER 7: MOVEMENT — 223

Movement Overview — 224
Leading — 225
Weight — 227
Laban — 231
Warm-Up: Basic Structure — 233
Warm-Up Exercise #1 - Relaxation — 235
Warm-Up Exercise #2 - Stretching — 241
Warm-Up Exercise #3 – Relaxation and Voice — 245
Warm-Up Exercise #4 - Thirty-Minute Warm-Up — 249
Additional Warm-Up Stretches — 252
Massages — 254

CHAPTER 8: CREATING A CHARACTER — 257

Character Analysis Overview — 258
Research — 259
Character Analysis – From a Play — 261
Character Analysis – Not from A Play — 263
The Nine Questions — 265
Observations — 267
Slice of Life — 270
Animal Work — 272
Meet Your Ancestor — 277
Portrait Exercise — 279
Private Moments — 281
Loss and Betrayal — 283
Character Analysis Sheet — 284

CHAPTER 9: WORKING ON MONOLOGUES AND SCENES — 285

Monologues Overview — 286
Cutting and PastingCutting and Pasting — 287
Choosing the Monologue — 293
Analyzing the Monologue — 295
Marking the Monologue — 296
Exploring the Monologue — 297
Blocking the Monologue — 300
Scenes Overview — 304
Fair Verona — 305
Preparing — 306
Working with a Partner — 307

Blocking a Scene 308
Using Props and Set 309

CHAPTER 10: AUDITIONS — 311

Auditions Overview 312
Scheduling an Audition (Agent Or Agency) ... 313
Scheduling an Audition (Casting Notice) 314
Preparing for the Audition 315
What to Wear 320
Headshots 324
Resumes 326
Arriving at The Audition 329
Entering the Audition Space 331
Presenting Your Pieces 333
Callbacks and Cold Readings 337
After the Audition 339
Self-Taping Overview 340
The Set-up 341
Following Directions 343
Readers 344
Slating and Performances 345
Costumes and Props 347
Staying Proactive Between Auditions 348

CHAPTER 11: REHEARSALS AND PERFORMANCES — 349

The First Read-Through 350
Making Choices 352
The Rehearsals 353
The Role Of The Director 354
Working With A Director 355
The Role Of The Stage Manager 357
Tech Week 358
The Performances 359

CHAPTER 12: SHAKESPEARE   361
     Shakespeare Overview   362
     Rhythmic Patterns   363
     Scansion   367
     Script Detective   368
     Exploring Shakespearean Verse   369
     Learning To Scan The Text   371
     Physicalizing the Text   378

CHAPTER 13: SUZUKI   381
     Suzuki Overview   382
     Using Text   383
     Ich Ni Sum   384
     Stomping   386
     Shakuhachi   388
     Ten-Te-Ke-Ten   390
     The Walks   391
     Statues And Jumping   393
     Speech And Fights   394

CHAPTER 14: STAGE COMBAT   395
     Stage Combat Overview   396
     Rules of Stage Combat   397
     Hospital And Non-Hospital Zone Chart   399
     General Guidelines   400
     Knaps   402
     Pushing   403
     Stumbles, Trips, and Falls Overview   405
     Stumbles   406
     Tripping   408
     Falling   411
     Kicks   414
     Punches/Slaps   417
     Grabbing And Choking   420
     Running into Walls and Other Objects   423

CHAPTER 15: GAMES AND EXERCISES   425
A FINAL WORD   441
Bibliography and Sited Works   443
Index   445

PREFACE

Seven years ago, I published the first edition of *The Portable Acting Coach*. At that time, I had just started Actors Training Ground with summer scene study classes. Every year the classes I offered increased and now in 2020, we have classes year-round, and two acting intensives for the more experienced actor.

I've used my book in every class and as I taught from it, I noticed that I was mentioning many things to do with acting that weren't in my book. Every time I would bring up these tenets of acting in class, I would remind myself to add it in my new revision.

This went on for a few years, until I finally decided, in 2017, that I would start the revision for my third edition of the book. Though I had good intentions, I also knew that it would be a long journey for me and the idea of adding new content seemed a bit overwhelming.

At first, I made a valiant attempt to start what soon would turn out to be longer than I anticipated. I created the new chapter titles, set up the sections I wanted to add, and began putting the words onto paper. I soon realized I was right, it was going to be a long and arduous project.

I put the revision on hold as my classes took most of my time and life kept throwing things at me making it difficult to concentrate. My mom and I finally decided to invest in a small house, and at the closing of the deal, my mom had to travel to California to help my cousin take care of my aunt who was in home hospice. Just two weeks after my mom had flown over there, my aunt passed away. I lost my favorite aunt to cancer at the end of that year. I spent the first two months of 2018 in the house alone while dealing with our loss so I didn't feel like writing. When my mom returned from California, we had to grow accustomed to owning instead of renting, there was a lot of work to be done, that took up much of my time and I didn't have the patience to sit for hours, staring into a computer screen trying to put my thoughts into words.

I was still intent on doing this update and every time I spoke to my classes about my idea to write the revision, I would say, "It should be done in three months". But as the founder of a new acting studio and not having the resources to hire people to help, I was in charge of everything: marketing, updating the web site, creating the graphics, designing logos, making the class schedules, hiring the guest artists for the intensives. it was a lot and so three months turned into a year.

In March of 2019, I once again decided I would sit down and finish this revision. I slowly starting completing new sections and updating the older ones. I was making a little progress and I had hopes I would finish by that December.

However, summer put a halt to that when the mother of one of my closest friends had passed away. I was so completely taken back by this unexpected event that again, I couldn't find the time to sit down and finish this book.

Weeks turned into months and before I knew it we were into 2020. I knew that I had to finish this book revision soon or I would never do it but then I had the opportunity to produce a short film script that I wrote. This took up most of my time since I had to hire the actors, secure the locations, hire a film crew, start a fundraiser to pay everyone and be on set to coach the actors.

This happened two weeks before the coronavirus hit the world and the pandemic began. My classes came to a halt and two weeks later, we were issued with stay-at-home orders. I was at a loss for words. I had to come up with a way to keep my classes going during all this. But from this unprecedented event in our lifetime, my creative juices started flowing. I decided to hold my classes online.

In doing this, I moved my website over to an easier platform, designed a newer logo, and came up with the idea to create a virtual acting studio for people who didn't have the time or schedule to take classes during my regular sessions. It will have pre-recorded classes, interviews, and acting webinars. If everything goes to plan the virtual acting studio should launch in September 2020.

With all this creative energy flowing, and the start of my summer online classes, I was suddenly filled with the drive to complete my revisions so I could have a new book to go with the evolution of Actors Training Ground. And within one month, I did it.

Along with the new content and revisions, I designed a new book cover and added this preface to show you the journey it took to update *The Portable Acting Coach*. I kept the foreword the same because I want people to also know the story of how this book first came to be.

I hope you enjoy what *The Portable Acting Coach 3.0* has to offer and that you grow and flourish as an actor. Me updating this book will be like most of you in this business: you have the dream, you know what you want to do but something always gets in your way, but if you keep pushing yourself and overcome those hurdles, you can accomplish anything. – Tanner :)

FOREWORD

Wouldn't it be great to have a private acting coach at your fingertips whenever you had a question or wanted to refresh your memory on a technique or exercise? That's exactly what I set out to do when I started writing this book in 2010. It contains the numerous notes I meticulously took while in school, the handouts, and the knowledge I accumulated over the years throughout my career.

This book doesn't cover all the schools of thought on acting nor every exercise actors use to hone their craft. If it did, it would be volumes upon volumes of information: too much to comprehend or take in. This book is how I teach, how I coach. And like any class, you take from it what you find helpful and discard those ideas that you don't need.

Originally, I set out to preserve my notes for my own use when I needed easier access to them. As this book evolved it became more than just a book taken from notes. It turned into a book about techniques and skills that I teach in my acting classes and how I talk to my students whether in a classroom setting or in a private coaching: a book I felt would benefit other actors.

There are so many views on acting styles, which school of thought is the best, and so on, that many times we lose sight of the real goal: to produce believability in our performances whether on stage or in front of a camera. I tell all of my students, "it doesn't matter which process you use as long as it gets you where you need to go", both emotionally and truthfully.

I define acting as "the art of creating reality on stage". This statement can also be applied to film. No matter where you study

17

acting, which techniques you use, or who you hire as your private acting coach, they all share a common bond: to get the actor to open up and share themselves truthfully with the audience and engage them for a few hours, bringing them into the actor's world. That's the simplicity and complexity of acting.

Actors have many obstacles to overcome when they start out: getting out of their head, over-thinking ideas, over-internalizing, body movements without purpose, stagnant or colorless patterns of speech, stage fright, lack of vocal support, lack of connection to text, character or self, the list goes on and on. Not every actor suffers from all of these fixable problems but at one time or another could face any one of them. The actor overcomes these obstacles by diligently working in class, having an acting coach, or working on sets and stages with competent actors who know what they're doing.

Acting is "living in the moment" whether on stage or screen. An actor who isn't "living in the moment" will not hold the audience's attention. Their movements, speech, lines, blocking, connection to other actors, and such, will appear lifeless, false, mechanical, and pretty much uninspiring. Even if an actor doesn't go to school because they have a gift or are labeled a "natural" at it does not mean they cannot benefit from a class or coach to serve as a second pair of eyes.

This book is ideal for both the beginning and advanced actor. For the beginner, this book can serve as a stepping-stone: to whet your appetite for the wonderful world of acting. Read it. Absorb it. It is not meant to replace a theatre education but to inspire you to act. Continue to read different types of books on acting until you find the right style for you.

For the advanced actor, it can serve as a refresher course: to remind you of techniques and tools you may have forgotten along the way. Use it as a quick reference guide when you need a push in the right direction. It is also perfect for the acting teacher or coach needing a handy reference guide when teaching.

As I stated earlier, this book is a culmination of the notes I took, the experience I've gained, and the lessons I've learned. It is meant to help you and inspire you. The chapters on Shakespeare, Suzuki, and Stage Combat are meant to be an introduction and not to replace a class, book, or training that specializes on these subjects.

I hope you find this book useful in developing or refreshing your acting skills and that it helps you appreciate the art of acting and creating life on stage.

The Portable Acting Coach

FOREWORD

CHAPTER 1: GETTING STARTED

What is Acting? 22

Keeping a Journal 26

Stage Directions 28

Stage Terminology 30

Before You Step on Stage 34

Memorizing Lines 36

WHAT IS ACTING?

One of my most influential professors, Elizabeth Kemp, who unfortunately passed away in 2017, called her students "warriors". I've adopted using this word when I'm teaching because actors are perseverant, continually opening themselves up to others, revealing their vulnerabilities, exposing their souls, and enduring the countless waves of rejection throughout their career. These traits are indicative of a warrior.

Every actor is different. Some never get training. They may have a natural ability and grow every time they perform. Other actors take acting classes in their community to improve themselves, using the learning environment to push them in the right direction. And then there is the actor who goes the way of higher education. Training under various teachers in their profession to hone their skills and ability.

There is no right or wrong path when it comes to approaching the art of acting. My belief is that an actor should take a class even if they do have a natural ability. They should understand the principles behind acting. The choices they make when creating a character and performing are exactly that…choices. It should not be through sheer "chance" from their natural ability.

Another aspect you should be aware of is that an actor's training can be a very frustrating one. It's one thing to understand the principles behind acting but it's another thing to put it into action. When we act, we are creating a real emotion through fabrication. That's not something that people normally do, yet actors create these emotions and make use believe that they are experiencing them for the first time.

When you begin the process of learning to act, you may feel frustrated. You may cry or scream because you aren't grasping the technique and feel like you aren't getting anywhere. This is perfectly normal. Don't compare your progress to others. Everyone has ups and downs in their craft. We learn at our own pace and you will get there when you get there.

One more point I want to make about acting: every actor has a technique and a set of tools they use. No technique is better than another. There is no "one way" to do it. We try, we fail, we succeed, we learn. It's what makes each actor's style so unique. The techniques and styles you use will shape you as an actor and hopefully make you do what you do best: act truthfully. The tools that you find in this book are to help you along your way. Pick the techniques you like and discard the ones you don't.

The tools and techniques that you find in this book are to help you get to where you need to be emotionally, mentally, and physically when you are unable to achieve this organically. They are tools, nothing more. Just as a carpenter uses various tools to shape his woodwork, so are you, using various acting tools to shape your craft.

Allow yourself time to grasp the ideas contained in this book. Try them out. Experiment. Actors succeed because of their perseverance and tenacity. Don't be too hard on yourself when you find yourself up against a block or you are trying something that makes you emotionally uncomfortable. It's a natural occurrence. In class, Ron Leibman told us, "If it makes you feel uncomfortable, that's where you need to head."

Playing it safe is not the way of a warrior. You need to push through your blocks and achieve those breakthroughs that will strengthen you and help you become the warrior that is inside you.

In acting class, one of my students asked me to define a character actor, in the process, I expounded on Ron's words adding, there is a difference between something that doesn't feel comfortable and something that doesn't feel right. Usually something that doesn't feel comfortable involves emotions or feelings that we haven't felt or acknowledged and trying to gain access to these emotions puts us in a vulnerable state, making us feel uncomfortable. If something doesn't feel right, it usually involves something that affects us either morally, ethically, or just who we are as people, which doesn't allow us to feel "right" doing that part. The trick is to know the difference and being able to act on it accordingly.

FOUR RULES TO REMEMBER

Because acting is subjective and sometimes it's easy to fall into the trap of feeling unworthy as an actor. As you read and work through this book, remember these four important rules to live by as an actor:

1. Never apologize for your work – Your work is yours, good or bad. We learn from our mistakes. If you apologize for your work it is showing that you are not worthy to be watched and people will start to expect less from you. Be proud of what you do, maybe you didn't succeed but you put yourself out there and that in itself is an achievement.

2. Don't compare yourself to others – Everyone learns and grows at their own rate. As actors it's easy to fall into the trap of comparing ourselves to other actors, i.e. This person is making it, I'm not, they always get cast and I don't, everyone understand this concept, why can't I? Comparing yourself will subconsciously keep you back and deter you from growing as an actor.

3. Give yourself permission to fail – No matter what we do in life, we have to learn. We can't succeed at everything the first time. By giving yourself permission to fail, you are allowing yourself to make mistakes or fall flat on your face. When that happens, pick yourself up, brush yourself off, and do it again. Only by failing can we grow as an actor.

4. Keep your secrets – **Never** disclose to another actor or director the personal choices you use for substitution, emotional recall, sense memory, or anything that gets you in the mindset that you are aiming to achieve. It weakens that choice for you and makes it unusable. It gives them power over you as an actor. Instead of them thinking about what you are giving them, they will be thinking subconsciously, "He told me

24

he's using this tactic on me", or "He's thinking of this person", etc. Your personal choices should remain secret during the entire rehearsal and run of the show. If, after the show, you choose to reveal what you used, you may, but I wouldn't. You want to keep your secrets exactly that: secret.

Above all, be patient and open. Always be observant. Always be aware of your surroundings: the people, the objects, the smells, what you hear, see, touch, and taste. You will never know when something that you encountered in your life will be used and re-created on the stage.

KEEPING A JOURNAL

Before you begin your journey into acting you need to have a journal to keep track of your progress. You can use a standard notebook or a blank diary. I don't recommend using a binder filled with paper. It is too bulky and not conducive to the role of a journal.

Your journal should be with you whenever you are in class, at a coaching, or working at home on your acting skills. You should carry your journal with you at all times. Inspiration and breakthroughs can happen at any moment. It is a great way to keep track of the character traits of other individuals, sensory perceptions, and observations you may notice throughout the day.

You will also use your journal to keep track of your work and progress. I can't tell you how many times I've gone back to look through my notes and remembered an exercise or experience. Re-reading it reminded me where I've been or even techniques I may have forgotten.

I recommend spending at least 15 minutes writing in your journal after attending an acting class, private coaching, rehearsal, or performance. Let your thoughts flow. It can be stream-of-consciousness writing or carefully thought out. Whichever way you choose to use your acting journal, don't stop using it.

As you become more experienced on stage, you may find journal work isn't as important or vital to your needs as an actor but as a beginning actor it is crucial to have one. Be as specific as you can be when writing in your journal. Notate everything you remember, experienced, and retained. Don't wait too long to write in your journal after your class, doing an exercise, meeting with your acting coach, etc. You want the journal entry to be as fresh in your mind as possible. Too much time elapsed could result in forgetting a vital piece of information you may find helpful later.

Your journal and your journey as an actor are unique, remember you are joining that elite and special breed of person: the performer, the actor, and the warrior. Be brave, be true to yourself and let your journal tell your story of challenges and successes.

STAGE DIRECTIONS

Every actor should know his way around the stage and the terminology associated with it. It is important to know these directions since every director uses them when blocking actors or telling them where to stand during an audition.

Back in the early days of theatre, the stage was raked. This means that the back end of the stage was raised. When an actor moved towards the back of the stage they were moving up or upstage. When the actor moved closer to the front of the stage they were moving down or downstage. The terms upstage and downstage remained after stages were built parallel to the ground and no longer raked.

Also, remember that moving on stage is always from the actor's point of view. So when facing the audience, stage right is to the actor's right side and stage left is to the actor's left side. Upstage is behind the actor and downstage is in front.

On the next page, I've included a diagram of a stage with all the points of a stage that you should be familiar with as an actor. Learn these terms and positions as soon as possible. This will make your job moving on stage and taking direction much easier.

One more thing, I'd like to point out: not all stages are created equal. There are stages in ¾ thrust, which means the stage is shaped like a baseball field with one of the corners of the stage thrust towards the audience. There is also theatre in the round, which means the audience completely surrounds the stage area. The diagram I'm using is for a basic proscenium stage.

Bolded stage directions indicate more commonly used stage directions by directors. The stage directions in parenthesis are rarely used.

BACKSTAGE					

	USR	(URC)	USC	(ULC)	USL	
BACKSTAGE / WINGS / WINGS	SR	(RC)	C	(LC)	SL	WINGS / WINGS / BACKSTAGE
	DSR	(DRC)	DSC	(DLC)	DSL	

USR – Upstage Right	**SR – Stage Right**	**DSR – Downstage Right**
URC – Up Right Center	RC – Right Center	DRC – Down Right Center
USC – Upstage Center	**C – Center**	**DSC – Downstage Center**
ULC – Up Left Center	LC – Left Center	DLC – Down Left Center
USL – Upstage Left	**SL – Stage Left**	**DSL – Downstage Left**

House – The area where the audience sits

Wings – The side areas off the main stage area

Backstage – The area behind the stage

Also, remember that there are strong and weak points on a stage. Knowing these basic principles will help give you a stronger presence on stage and also prevent you from being upstaged by another actor either unintentionally or deliberately.

Downstage is stronger than Upstage.

Center Stage is stronger than Stage Right/Left.

Stage Right is stronger than Stage Left.

STAGE TERMINOLOGY

Not only is it important to know where to move on stage, it is equally important to understand how to move on the stage. Below is a short, simple glossary of common terms for moving on stage. In addition, I've also included acting terms you may hear when being directed. The movements for stage are underlined.

Ad-lib – Any unscripted dialogue spoken by an actor on stage.

Beat – A slight pause. Can also indicate a change of emotion, objective, or thought from the character.

Blocking –
1. To prevent an actor from being seen on stage by standing in front of them or to prevent yourself from being seen on stage by the audience by standing directly behind an actor.
2. The movements and/or staging for a scene given to an actor by a director.

Business – An action the actor does on stage that may or may not be related to the main focal point of the stage, i.e., folding clothes, making a drink, reading a book, etc.

Cross – To move on the stage from one place to another. Start with upstage leg. Turn downstage when ending cross unless otherwise directed. A cross is written as an X when you mark your script for blocking.

Counter-cross or Counter – To adjust yourself when an actor crosses in front of you or blocks you on stage. Start with your upstage leg. Slightly move SR/SL of the actor that is crossing you. Turn towards actor, ending in a ¼ profile to the audience unless directed otherwise. A counter-cross is written as CX when you mark your script for blocking.

Note: Countering is defensive acting. It keeps you open to the audience and prevents you from being blocked or upstaged.

Cue – The previous line said by another actor before your line.

Dialogue – The words a character speaks in a play.

Delivery – The way the actor speaks his lines.

Gesture – To make a movement with your arm, hand, or head towards someone or something on stage. Using your upstage hand or arm will prevent you from blocking your face and body to the audience. This also applies to picking up objects on stage.

Hand prop – Any object that is hand-held by the actor on stage such as a mirror or fan.

Kneeling – Use your downstage leg to kneel. This will keep your body open to the audience.

Off-Book – When you are no longer allowed to use your scripts in rehearsals and expected to have your lines memorized.

Pace – The rate of speed at which dialogue, pauses, and actions are measured on stage.

Pause – A period of silence. It is longer than a beat. It usually is filled with objective, thought, or action by the character.

Positioning –

1. This relates to the way the actor's body is angled on stage. Imagine that you are standing in front of an audience on stage. You are the center of a large clock. 12 o'clock is directly in front of you (downstage) and 6 o'clock is directly behind you (upstage).

    a. Front – When you are facing the audience completely. You are facing 12 o'clock.

    b. ¼ profile – When your body is facing 2 or 10 o'clock on stage allowing the audience to see your face and body.

    c. Side Profile – When your body is facing 3 or 9 o'clock, allowing the audience to see your side profile.

    d. ¾ profile – When your body is facing 4 or 8 o'clock, cutting off most of your face and body to the audience, revealing most of your back.

    e. Back – When your body is facing 6 o'clock and completely turned away from the audience. Your back is facing the audience.

2. It is also used in voice to describe the placement of the soft palate for producing a proper air channel for breath and sound.

Pick up cue – To remove a pause between your line and the previous line said by another actor.

Pick up pace – To increase the speed or tempo of the dialogue, pauses, or actions on stage.

Prop – Any object used on stage in a play by any actor. This can also include furniture.

Projection – The amount of sound the actor produces when speaking his lines on stage.

Set – The fixed stage scenery such as walls, doors, platforms, etc.

Set piece – Any individual part of the set scenery, it is usually freestanding, such as a table.

Turn out – To face towards the audience more, so your face and/or body is visible to the audience.

Upstage – To block yourself or another actor through movement on stage or stage positioning.

Before You Step on Stage

There are some basic but vital rules you should follow when you are acting in theatre. These rules should be embedded in your core and never forgotten. These are things that every actor knows and adheres to when acting for an audience. Learn these and implement them every time.

1. NEVER TURN YOUR BACK TO THE AUDIENCE.

   Nothing appears less professional than an actor who turns his body to the audience while acting. They didn't pay to see your back, they paid to see your face, your body. There are three ways you can stand on stage: ¼ or ¾ angle, profile, and front. This is the order of preference. However, I will say though I mentioned that you should not act with your back to the audience, this rule can be broken if the director has explicitly blocked you that way for purposes of the scene.

2. PROJECT YOUR VOICE

   Unlike film, a theatre actor must learn to support and project your voice to be heard. You may be asked to perform for an audience of 20 or 2,500, or if you're lucky Broadway and then that number greatly increases. And

3. DON'T DEPEND ON MICS

   Even though theatres these days use mics to help the actors be heard. They don't increase your voice they amplify it. So if you're speaking in a whisper it will amplify a whisper, it can't create a fuller sound. Learning to use your voice effectively will increase your chances of getting work as an actor.

4. DON'T GIVE OTHER ACTORS NOTES

   You are not the director and it not your job to tell another actor what they are doing wrong or advice on how to act. If they're supposed to pick it up something with their right hand and not their left, don't correct them if they do it wrong. Don't tell them how to say a line, or where their mistakes are in a scene. Nothing is more annoying than an actor telling another actor how to act.

However, if someone comes to you first and ask your advice, you can help them if you feel comfortable talking to them (such as a close friend or peer) or you can suggest they talk to a director first. I've seen many actors talking and giving others advice but it's because it was a mutual collaboration on the help being given. Think of it like this, you can help other actors if they want your help on the "how to do something" but don't tell them "what to do".

5. COMMIT YOUR ALL

From the first audition, to the closing night, you should give 100% of your talent and skill to the process. From the very first rehearsal you should give your all. Don't hold back the creative process. You may be thinking, "I'll just wait till we're further in the rehearsals", but you're only cheating yourself, the director, and other actors.

6. RESPECT

Everyone working in the theatre plays a part; the actor is not the most important one. Don't fool yourself into thinking you're better than someone else. You should treat everyone with the same respect and I mean everyone: the set designer, prop master, costume designer, lights designer, stage manager, house manager, box office staff, the ushers…everyone.

In fact, I tell all my students that they should work every aspect of backstage to understand what makes a production work. You'd be surprised at what you learn. I've worked almost all aspects of tech and I understand and appreciate every individual involved with the process. As my student, you should as well.

MEMORIZING LINES

One of the most monotonous and time-consuming areas of acting is the memorization. Some of you reading this book may or may not have a monologue or scene to work on yet. Never-the less, it is important to know the proper way to memorize as well as a few techniques that will help you accomplish this task.

There are many ways to approach memorizing a monologue. I've included the ones that I have used over there years. Ever actor has their preferred way to memorize. There is not one cut and dry way of doing it. However, whichever method you prefer, remember to continue to practice. Remembering lines takes time and patience. Don't be too hard on yourself as you are starting the process. If you do, you will only frustrate yourself and make it harder for yourself.

Also, the goal of memorizing a monologue or scene is to know the lines word for word. In the beginning of the process it is okay if you paraphrase a line or replace a word here or there, it's only natural when first starting out, however, don't memorize the paraphrasing. The playwright wrote every word for a reason and your job as an actor is to say these words the way the playwright intended.

Speaking of the words a playwright put in a script. Students ask me all the time is it okay if they replace a word they feel uncomfortable saying, usually this is a curse word. My reply is "No, you may not". While it is a common practice to cut and paste a monologue together, this means shortening a long monologue to fit the time constraint of an audition, or taking a scene and turning it into a monologue by removing the other characters words, it is not okay to change the actual words the character says. Changing what a character says changes that character. This book covers cutting and pasting a monologue in CHAPER 9.

I will use a very generic curse word as an example since this book is available to all ages. Suppose your character has to say the word "Damn!" or a more derogatory variation of that word but because of your beliefs or ideals, you cannot say that word, you cannot change the word to "Darn!", or "Shoot!", or "Fudge". The character may be having an epiphany or reaching an emotional level that requires that word. Changing that word softens the character and in turn, changes the way the character was written.

If there is a monologue you want to perform or a play you want to be in and the character does or says something that you don't feel comfortable doing, don't audition for that show or pick a new monologue. While there are times a director will change a word due to the audience they are performing for, they will not change it because as actor doesn't want to say that word. Now does that mean changing these words are not done. No. Actors do it all the time but it is not a habit that you want to get in and that's why I'm discouraging you from starting.

There is one steadfast rule that you must uphold at all times when memorizing: **do not set your vocal pattern in stone**. This is the death of a monologue. You must allow the voice of the character to come through and have the freedom to say the words the way they want to say it.

When you first start the memorization process, begin by saying the words simply without any major vocal inflexions. Avoid adding the vocal objective into the words of the monologue at this stage, as much as you want to. If you do, you will fall into the trap of teaching or conditioning your body to speak the words the same way every time. This is only the initial memorization process. Once it is memorized you may add the "acting" into it.

Finally, I find that memorizing lines in a scene easier than a monologue. Partly because your lines are a reaction to what is previously said or what is happening in the scene. Avoid the need to memorize the lines right away. Instead, work with your partner and allow yourself to learn the words as you rehearse.

As with monologues, when you first start to memorize, do not add objective or tactic when you are saying the words out loud. Let your mouth, tongue, and lips get used to what you are saying. It's all about muscle memory. Once you have gone through the scene a couple of times, (saying the lines as I've described), you are ready to begin the actual memorization process.

MEMORIZATION TECHNIQUES

DON'T MEMORIZE SITTING STILL

When you begin the process of remembering your lines, try not to stay in one place. Move around the room as you are doing this task. Memorizing lines is muscle memory. Our brain remembers what we are doing when lines are being put into our memory. If we memorize sitting down, when we stand up and start to act, the brain freezes, the lines are forgotten because we memorized them while sitting still. If we move around while memorizing our lines, it will be easier to recall the lines.

Also, try looking at different areas of the room you are working in as you put your lines to memory. This will train your brain to be able to focus on different things while speaking and will enable you to recall your lines when it comes to blocking or when things happen on stage that are unexpected.

WRITE OUT THE WORDS

Look at the first sentence and write it out as you say it. Say the sentence again and write it out. After you have written it five times. Go on to the next line. Repeat this process until you have completed the monologue. Now go back and try to write out the monologue as best as you can. See how much you have retained. When you have forgotten a line, read it out loud and write it out again. Continue this process until you have the monologue memorized.

THE COVER UP

Take a sheet of paper and cover your script, allowing only the first line to be seen. Say the line and then move the sheet of paper to reveal the next line. Say it a few times and then cover the script back up and say the first two lines. Repeat this process for your monologue. Memorize one line at a time. When you get the lines right move on to the next one, if you get it wrong, look the line over, repeat it and then return to the beginning of the monologue.

THE COVER UP (SCENE)

Take a sheet of paper and cover your script, allowing only the first line (if it's not yours) to be seen, read the previous line and then say your line that follows it. You would repeat this process for your scene. Memorize one line at a time. You start with one line, and once you have it you move on to the next line. When you think you have the next line, start at the beginning and work down. If you get the lines right, move on to the next one. If you get it wrong, look the line over, repeat it, and then return to the beginning of the scene.

VOCAL RECORDING

Record your lines into a recording device. Try not to add too many of your acting choices into the recording. You don't want it monotone but you don't want it to be fully acted out either. Play the recording and after you've heard it a few times, try to say the monologue with the recording. Once you have done it a few times, try to do the monologue without the recording. When you get stumped, play back the recording and repeat the words with the recording and try again.

VOCAL RECORDING (SCENE)

Record the other person's lines into a recording device. Then you play their line, pause the machine and respond with your line. If you get it right, press play and continue. If you got it wrong, you would look over your line and then play the recording from the beginning of the scene. Some actors find that listening to their cue line helps them memorize quicker and easier.

PERFORM AN ACTION

As you get more of your lines in your head, pick an action that makes your body move, i.e. washing dishes, cleaning a room, exercises, etc. You may notice that you may forget your lines easier but that's okay. If you forget your line, continue to do the action while trying to remember your line. If you can't, stop your action and look over your monologue, then return to your action and start the monologue over. Eventually, through practice you will be able to do your entire monologue while performing a primary action. This is a great way to get out of your head and make your lines seem like second nature.

MEMORIZING THROUGH BLOCKING (SCENE)

Personally, I like to block a scene and then start to memorize. The movement helps me associate the lines to the blocking because, (as I've stated before): everything becomes muscle memory in acting. I'm not recommending that you completely memorize your lines through the blocking but more as a starting point just to help jog your memory as you are learning them.

GET A FRIEND

Have a friend come over and read the scene with you. Use them to correct the mistakes you make when saying your lines. Have them say the line for you and then you repeat it back. As with the previous examples, go to the beginning of the scene and work through it. Make sure that they do not help you remember what you have to say unless you say the word, "line". By doing this, you enable yourself to think for the line or allow acting moments such as pauses to happen during the scene without your memorization partner prematurely interrupting.

You may choose one of these techniques or may have others that work for you. Whichever way you choose to memorize your lines, stay diligent and focused and the lines will come in no time.

Remember this mantra and you will succeed in memorization: "Repetition, repetition, repetition!" The more you practice and rehearse, the more you will feel comfortable with the monologue or scene and it will sound natural.

CHAPTER 2: THE BASICS

Acting Overview 44

Objective/Intention 46

Obstacle.. 49

Tactic 51

Vocal Gesture 55

Ultimate Verb List – Intention and Tactic Verbs 57

Ultimate Verb List – Suggested Vocal Gestures 65

Relationship... 66

Status.. 69

Trust 71

Listening.. 73

ACTING OVERVIEW

Every day we act without knowing it. We play practical jokes on our friends or colleagues, pretending and fooling them to believe something before we say, "We're joking" or "April Fools", etc. While my definition of acting is the art of creating reality on stage or screen, you must realize that acting is not "pretending", this form of pretending doesn't necessarily fall under the category of acting for the stage.

Unlike children pretending to be someone or something else, acting is a heightened art form. The words, the movement, the voice, the emotions, everything is in a heightened form and as an actor we must be able to do all of this and make it look natural and realistic as if it is real-life, a feat hard to do.

The common misconception by non-actors is that acting is easy; anyone can do it. If it <u>was</u> easy everyone would be an actor and it wouldn't be seen as such a lucrative endeavor. However, it is not easy, not everyone can do it, and it takes a special person to be able to convey his or her emotions honestly and openly while living in a heightened state both physically, mentally, and emotionally.

A question I always pose to a group of new students is: What is Acting? While the answers may vary and it may seem a bit harder for some to answer than others, I find that generally I hear the same responses and only a few are from my list of what I believe acting is. So here are my thoughts on acting. Acting is the art of creating reality on stage and screen. Acting is being connected to your character. Acting is expressing emotion openly and honestly. Acting is observation, communication, and listening. Acting is being in the moment. Acting "is".

There is a recurring argument among actors between two principles: acting is reacting and acting is doing. Actors will debate this for hours, making their cases and trying to prove the other principle wrong. I don't believe in either of those single principles as being correct. In fact, I believe that acting is a combination of both principles: reacting <u>and</u> doing. You cannot do something before you've reacted to what has happened or been said, and you can't react to something and not do anything. Even standing still and not moving or saying anything is doing something.

You, the actor, are choosing to stand still, or move towards something/someone, or say a line. You observe, you listen, you react, you do. "Reacting" and "doing" go hand-in-hand. You cannot do one without the other. This is acting.

Now that I've shared my semantics on acting, it's time to get down to the nuts and bolts of it all. There are three basic principles that drive a character: objective, obstacle, and tactic. Without these firmly in place and fleshed out, your character will seem stiff, unconnected, and stale. Once an actor learns how to flesh these out, they will be unstoppable in creating a living, breathing character. They will be full of life, believable, and living "in moment" on stage. You must have emotional connection to the text to make it happen.

Other acting tools I will talk about in this chapter are relationship, status, trust, and listening. These basics will focus on you and the other actors on stage, aiding you in creating a strong foundation for your acting skills and help you when you proceed to CHAPTER 4.

Objective/Intention

Objective and intention are interchangeable and mean the exact same thing. These two words will be used throughout the book. Objectives or intentions are the driving force for every character. Each and every one of them, down to the smallest role has a purpose on stage. Their purpose drives them throughout the play. It doesn't matter if they are there for the entirety, are in one scene, have one line, or no lines. All of the characters have one thing in common. They want something. Your job as an actor is to discover what it is they want.

Objectives can be put into three categories: Super Objective, Main Objective, and Immediate Objective. The Super Objective is what a character wants throughout the entire play. The Main Objective is what a character wants throughout a scene. The Immediate Objective is what the character wants right now within the scene. Learn and understand the difference between these three categories and be careful not to confuse them with each other.

To help you define your objective easier, phrase it with "I want", "I" need", or "I must have". Phrasing your objective in this manner creates a playable and accessible objective for your character. Every character wants something that propels them through the play/film. Examples of objectives are "I want acceptance", "I need power", "I must have freedom", etc. When you phrase your objective try not to use "to be" verbs. "To be" verbs are a state of being and not always playable by an actor. Examples of "to be" verbs are: to be happy, to be sad, to be angry, etc.

Let's look at *Oleanna* by David Mamet. John, a teacher at a University, wants to secure his tenure and is in the process of buying a house. His wife, (who John talks to on the phone but is never seen), is worried about losing the house and his ability to gain the tenure. His super objective is to resolve the crisis in his life

In the opening scene, Carol, a student who is having problems in John's class, approaches him at his office while he's on the phone trying to calm his wife. His main objective in the scene is to reason with Carol and help her understand so he can get back to his super objective. As the scene continues, he struggles to make Carol comprehend what he is talking about. His immediate objective changes within the scene; acknowledging her concerns, defending his teaching ability, reasoning with Carol, all in attempts to complete his main objective: to make Carol understand so he can get back to his super objective: to resolve the crisis in his life.

Sometimes it can be difficult to find the super objective in a play or the main and immediate objectives in a scene. If you can't hone in on them, keep reading the play or scene. Maybe you are missing something that another character is doing to your character. Possibly the way they are talking to them or physically encroaching on them will lead you to discover what your character wants. It could be a case of maintaining the status quo for that character, which becomes their main objective in the scene.

Let's look at the example from *Oleanna* again. If you gave John the super objective "I want to be happy" or "I want to be successful." You placed his objective as a state of being and set yourself up for an unplayable need. You could, however, rephrase it and give him the objective "I want happiness" or "I want to succeed."

Also keep in mind that you want a strong, specific objective for your character. Try to dig deep so you can find the strongest choice possible. If you were analyzing John and couldn't think of anything but "I want to be happy" then take it a step further. Ask yourself, "What would make John happy?". You might answer with "I want to buy this house", "I want to secure my tenure", or possibly "I need to get my life back in order". Keep asking yourself questions about the character and eventually you will come up with a stronger and more specific "want".

One last thing to remember: keep it simple when working with intentions. Don't over-complicate it. This will make it too confusing and impossible to act. Using our previous example, let's look at the wrong way to approach an intention and over-complicate it. Instead of a simple intention of "I want Carol to leave my office" the actor decides to use "I want Carol to leave so I can calm my wife down and concentrate on getting my tenure so I can be happy and have peace of mind."

You can see how this overly complicated sentence would be extremely hard to act out. You put three or four intentions into one and they cannot be played all at once. This is why we use the super, main, and immediate intentions. It separates them and makes it much easier to act.

OBSTACLE

For every objective our character wants, there is always something that prevents them from obtaining it. If there were no obstacles to overcome, the action would stay status quo and there would be no reason for them to exist. Without obstacles, everyone would be happy and that would make for a pretty boring play.

An obstacle can be a person, an object, a state of mind (emotional), a state of body (physical), natural (weather), a society (laws, morals, ethics, etc.), time, or anything that makes it impossible to continue unless it is removed or overcome. Obstacles can range from easily handled to extremely difficult. No matter the difficulty of the obstacle the character **MUST** keep fighting to overcome it. The minute they give up, the hope of achieving their goal is lost.

Let's examine how obstacles work using a fictional scene about Bob Jones. Bob is an executive who has an important meeting to go to regarding his job. This meeting will determine if he keeps his job or not. He's wearing a suit and about to leave the house. He doesn't have a car and has to walk to work. He opens the door and it's raining, pouring down hard. He can't go out like that and get his suit wet.

His super objective is to keep his job. His main objective is to get to his meeting. Nature is his obstacle. The rain is a simple obstacle to overcome. He needs an umbrella. His immediate objective is to find an umbrella. He looks around and can't find it. He looks at his watch and realizes he's going to be late. Time has become an obstacle in addition to the rain. Now he must make a decision. Does he walk to work in the rain to get there on time and in the process getting drenched, making a bad impression at the meeting or does he take time to search for his umbrella and being late but dry?

Bob's obstacle has switched to panic. Panic is a state of mind. The playwright has written that, eventually, Bob leaves for work without the umbrella. He overcomes all obstacles in order to get to the meeting, although when he arrives at the meeting, he will have a new obstacle to overcome: explaining why he is late, soaking wet, and why he should keep his job.

There can be more than one obstacle in a scene. Find all the obstacles and find ways to overcome them. Even though you, as the actor, know that the character does or doesn't beat the obstacle, you must make it life or death for the character. They must continue to fight for what they want even if it means negative consequences resulting from the decisions made.

TACTIC

The way a character approaches an objective or obstacle is called a tactic. Characters use tactics to get what they want. Tactics are action verbs that can be played by the actor. It is necessary to pick verbs that you can put into action. When approaching a tactic use the phrase "I am going to..." followed by the verb of your choice. Avoid using "to be" verbs. Instead of using "to be manipulative" replace that with "I am going to manipulate". By turning the "to be" verb into a playable verb you have more freedom and flexibility to explore your character both physically and vocally.

There are two different ways to look at tactics: what you are doing and how are you saying it. The "doing" is referred to as "tactic" and the "saying" is referred to, as I like to call it, the vocal gesture. Let's look at the "doing" tactic first. While the intention is "what you want", the "doing" tactic is "how you are going to get what you want." If you choose the verb "to convince" as your intention, you may pick the verb "to sweet talk" as your tactic. This tactic works with the objective you've chosen.

As in real life, if you aren't getting what you want, change your tactic. If you find that "sweet talking" isn't working, you may try "to seduce". Remember that your tactic should support what you want. Keep exploring and don't settle for the first tactic you choose. Acting is made up of choices. Play around with different tactics until you find the right one.

You can use numerous tactics to get what you want. Your choice of tactic is dependent upon what your character wants to accomplish in the scene or do to the other characters. Sometimes your first verb choice isn't always the best choice. One line can have many tactics to choose from using the actor's arsenal of verbs. Your job as an actor is to fully explore your options.

Tactics also change throughout a scene. There is a well-known phrase that defines insanity as "doing the same thing over and over again, but expecting different results." This is actually from Rita Mae Brown's mystery novel, "Sudden Death"[1]. This concept applies to tactics as well. You can't keep playing the same tactic with everything your character says and expect anything to change. We, the actor, know what is happening or is going to happen in a scene but our character doesn't. They would not continue to do the same thing over and over again, (unless the character is written that way) and expect anything to change. That is why it's important to change up your tactic when you find your character isn't getting what they want.

Let's revisit the *Oleanna* scene with John and Carol. When Carol accuses John of calling her stupid, he replies, "I did not say that." His main objective of making her understand is blocked by her tactic of attacking him. He can choose many verbs to push his line "I did not say that." He could choose "to attack", to defend", to push back", "to put up a shield", to recoil", to laugh off", "to shrug off", etc. Each of these verbs will affect the actor in a different way when responding to Carol. They are all acceptable and there are more that the actor could choose from if he wanted.

Be careful when choosing your verb to use for your tactic. It must fit the objective that you are trying to accomplish in the scene. Don't be afraid to try different tactics when analyzing your monologue or scene. Never settle for the first tactic you choose. Doing this will stall your creativity. You will find yourself in a rut and unable to follow your impulses and instincts because you will find yourself wanting to play your thoughts and actions the same way every time. Often in a scene, a character may say or do many things to get what they want. If you play the same tactic or verb throughout the scene it will become flat and predictable.

---

[1] The Business Insider, 12 Famous Quotes That Always Get Misattributed, Article, Christina Sterbenz, 2013

TACTIC EXERCISE #1

Take the phrase, "I won't do it." Say it once without any tactic (verb) attached to it. Now try it with these vocal tactics in mind: "to tickle", "to slap", "to mock", and "to rally." How do these tactics affect the way you say that line? How does this inform your choice for an objective?

Suppose your main objective is to flatter a character on stage and your line is "I love that dress". If you use the tactic "to mock" or any tactic that would have an imposing or attacking nature to it, the tactic would not suit the objective. Instead you might try "to melt", "to cajole", "to embrace" or even "to stroke."

You can add to the verb as well. Let's say you are using the verb "to twist" but you want it to be more potent, you can adapt it by saying, "to twist his arm." You aren't actually twisting his arm but you are using your words to vocally do what the action of the verb is implying.

The words you say are like wet clay and the tactics you use are your sculpting tools. Finding the right tool for the clay will produce the effect that you are looking to achieve. Keep exploring. Wet clay can be sculpted over and over again until you are satisfied with the result.

TACTIC EXERECISE #2

This needs to be done in a group or with a friend. You should have your monologue at least half if not all memorized. Perform your monologue as you normally do. The tactics you chose should be integrated into your monologue. After you finish your monologue, perform it again.

This time you will give your friend the Ultimate Verb list. As you are performing your monologue this time, your friend or the other actors in your group will shout out verbs from this list. Your job is to evoke these verbs as best you can using your voice or voice and body.

Once you have established the verb and said a few lines with it, someone should yell out another verb. Keep doing this until the end of your monologue. If you don't know what a verb means, do your best to portray it, even if it is wrong. It's about getting out of your head and saying things different.

The verbs that are yelled out don't have to match with what you are saying. But you will discover that sometimes a verb you would have never thought of using actually works with what you are saying. This is a great way to open up your palette and have more options to color your tactics to achieve your intention.

VOCAL GESTURE

The vocal gesture is a little different than the "doing" tactic and it works underneath your tactic. To use the vocal gesture, pick a verb that is a physical action and imagine that your voice is doing that action. Let's say that you are using the intention "to convince" and your "doing" tactic is "to manipulate". Your vocal tactic may be "to entwine. The words might come out slower and more controlled. You may imagine the words are slowly twisting around like a vine. The vocal gesture is used to help shape the words you say and the way you are saying them. This, in turn, should support what it is you are doing to get what you want.

Sometimes it helps to physicalize the verb you are you using for your vocal gesture. This will help get the action in your body and hopefully, expressed through the voice. However, when using a vocal gesture, there should be no physicalizing of the actual verb, unless it helps support the movement for your character (See CHAPTER 7).

Using the same example, if you chose the verb "entwine", besides using your voice to explore this verb, you may choose to move your body slowly, in order to get the feel of what you want your voice to convey.

Once you have found your tactic and the vocal gesture, you can put the two together. You may find that the vocal gesture helps inform you in regards to the character's movement. This, in turn, might lead to some physical discoveries, such as, wrapping your arms around them, or bringing your mouth close to the side of their face and whispering into their ear. The tactic and vocal gesture could lead your character to circle them like a predator around its prey. A verb can have many interpretations and options so play around with your choices and see where it leads you.

Also, be aware that the vocal gesture doesn't have to be in the same family of verbs as the tactic you've chosen. For instance, when using the same verb "to manipulate", the vocal gesture "to twist" would work and it could fall under the same category as manipulation. However, what if you are trying to manipulate them but don't want to use a strong approach, you might implement the vocal gesture "to tickle". The high-pitched rise in your voice with the slightly quickening of your vocal tempo might provide a different way of using the tactical verb "to manipulate". Tickling is not normally associated with manipulating but the sound of tickling in your voice can.

Explore your vocal gesture with different verbs, even those you might not think would work. You may very well surprise yourself and make a whole new discovery for yourself and your character.

ULTIMATE VERB LIST – INTENTION AND TACTIC VERBS

Intention: I want to _____ .
Tactic: I am going to _____ .

Abase	Anger	Beat
Abet	Animate	Beckon
Abolish	Annihilate	Bedazzle
Absolve	Annoy	Befriend
Abuse	Antagonize	Befuddle
Accept	Anticipate	Beg
Acquaint	Ape Appeal	Beguile
Acquit	Appeal	Belittle
Activate	Appease	Berate
Addle	Appraise	Beseech
Address	Approach	Bewitch
Admonish	Arouse	Bid
Affirm	Arrange	Bind
Afflict	Assert Power	Bite
Affront	Assess	Blame
Aid	Assist	Bless
Ail	Assuage	Block
Alarm	Astound	Bluff
Alert	Attack	Boost
Allow	Authenticate	Brainwash
Allure	Awaken	Bribe
Ally	Baby	Bruise
Alter	Badger	Buck
Amaze	Baffle	Bully
Amend	Bait	Burden
Amuse	Bear	Bury

Bushwhack	Clip	Court
Butt	Cloak	Cover
Butter	Coax	Crack
Buy	Coddle	Crank
Cajole	Coerce	Criticize
Calculate	Coil	Crucify
Call	Collude	Crush
Calm	Comfort	Cuddle
Captivate	Command	Curse
Carry	Commend	Curse
Carve	Compress	Cut
Castrate	Con	Dab
Catch	Conceal	Damn
Caution	Concern	Dare
Censure	Conciliate	Debase
Challenge	Condemn	Deceive
Change	Condescend	Declaim
Charge	Confide	Deduce
Charm	Confirm	Defame
Chastise	Confound	Deflate
Cheat	Confuse	Defraud
Check	Conjure	Defy
Cheer	Conquer	Defy
Cheer up	Consider	Delight
Chew	Consign	Delude
Chide	Contest	Demean
Chide	Contradict	Demoralize
Chill	Convert	Denigrate
Chip	Convince	Denunciate
Chop	Convince	Deny
Circumvent	Correct	Destabilize
Clarify	Corroborate	Destroy

Detect	Duck	Entangle
Deter	Ease	Entertain
Detour	Edify	Enthrall
Devalue	Educate	Enthuse
Devastate	Effuse	Entice
Devour	Elate	Entrap
Dictate	Elevate	Entreat
Dig	Elicit	Entrust
Direct	Eliminate	Eradicate
Disarm	Elucidate	Eschew
Disconcert	Embarrass	Estimate
Discourage	Embrace	Evade
Discredit	Embroil	Evaluate
Discredit	Employ	Exasperate
Disencumber	Empower	Excite
Disgrace	Emulsify	Excuse
Disgust	Enchant	Execute
Dishearten	Encourage	Exploit
Dispirit	Endure	Facilitate
Displease	Energize	Fascinate
Disrobe	Enfeeble	Feed
Dissuade	Enflame	Flatter
Distress	Engage	Flirt
Divert	Engross	Fold
Divine	Engulf	Fondle
Dodge	Enkindle	Force
Dominate	Enlighten	Fortify
Dramatize	Enlist	Foster
Draw	Enliven	Frame
Draw blood	Enmesh	Freak-out
Draw-out	Enslave	Free
Drive	Ensnare	Freeze

Frighten	Ignite	Josh
Frustrate	Ignore	Judge
Fuddle	Imitate	Juice
Gag	Immerse	Justify
Galvanize	Impair	Kick
Gash	Impassion	Kill
Gauge	Impel	Kindle
Gladden	Implicate	Kiss
Gnaw	Impress	Knock (down)
Goad	Incite	Knot
Grab	Indict	Lambast
Graft	Indoctrinate	Lampoon
Gratify	Induce	Lash
Guide	Indulge	Lather
Guilt	Inflate	Lead
Gull	Infuse	Lecture
Hack	Insinuate	Libel
Hallow	Inspire	Liberate
Hammer	Instill	Lick
Harangue	Insult	Loosen-up
Hassle	Interlock	Love
Help	Interview	Lull
Henpeck	Intimidate	Lure
Hold	Intoxicate	Lust-for
Hoodwink	Intrigue	Magnetize
Hug	Intubate	Malign
Humble	Invigorate	Maneuver
Humiliate	Invite	Manipulate
Humor	Involve	Marshall
Hurt	Jab	Mask
Hush	Jiggle	Massage
Hypnotize	Jolt	Masticate

Melt	Ostracize	Pray
Mend	Overlook	Preoccupy
Mess with	Overrun	Press
Mimic	Overwhelm	Press
Mislead	Pacify	Prevail
Misuse	Palliate	Prick
Mobilize	Panic	Prime
Mock	Parrot	Prod
Modify	Patronize	Prod
Mold	Perforate	Promise
Mortify	Perform	Promote
Motivate	Perk-up	Prompt
Move	Perplex	Propagandize
Muffle	Persecute	Propel
Muster	Peruse	Propose
Mystify	Pet	Propound
Nag	Petrify	Prosecute
Nail	Pick	Prove
Nauseate	Pinch	Provoke
Needle	Placate	Psyche-up
Negotiate	Plan	Publicly Humiliate
Nibble	Play	Pull
Notify	Plead	Pump-up
Nourish	Please	Punch
Nullify	Pledge	Punish
Obliterate	Poke	Purge
Offend	Polish	Purify
Oppose	Pontificate	Pursue
Oppress	Pop	Push
Organize	Pose	Quash
Orient	Pound	Quench
Orientate	Praise	Query

Rack	Revolt	Slander
Rally	Rib	Slap
Ratify	Ridicule	Slash
Ravage	Rip	Slaughter
Rave	Rub	Slice
Read	Sanctify	Slur
Ream	Satisfy	Smash
Reassure	Save	Smooth
Rebuke	Savor	Smother
Rebuke	Scar	Smush
Recreate	Scatter	Snare
Rectify	Scheme	Soak
Reduce	Scold	Sober
Refuse	Scold	Soften
Reiterate	Screw	Somber
Reject	Scrutinize	Soothe
Rejoin	Sedate	Spellbind
Relax	Seduce	Splay
Release	Sell	Split
Relegate	Settle	Spoil
Relieve	Shackle	Spur
Remedy	Shake	Spurn
Renege	Shale	Squash
Repel	Shame	Squeeze
Reprehend	Shine	Squelch
Repress	Shock	Stab
Reprimand	Shove	Stamp
Reprove	Showoff	Startle
Repulse	Shroud	Stick
Resist	Shun	Still
Retract	Sicken	Stimulate
Reveal	Simplify	Sting

Stir	Terrify	Win
Stomp on	Thank	Wind
Strangle	Threaten	Wind-up
Strengthen	Thwart	Woo
Stretch	Tickle	Worry
Strike	Titillate	Worship
Strip	Tolerate	Wound
Stroke	Torment	Wrangle
Study	Torture	Wrestle
Stymie	Touch	Wring
Substantiate	Trade	Zap
Subvert	Train	Zing
Succor	Trammel	
Suffer	Transform	
Suffocate	Trick	
Suggest	Trip	
Summon	Trouble	
Supplicate	Turn-on	
Support	Tyrannize	
Suppress	Unburden	
Surprise	Understand	
Swallow	Uproot	
Swindle	Urge	
Tame	Vacillate	
Tangle	Validate verify	
Tantalize	Victimize	
Tarnish	Vilify	
Taunt	Vindicate	
Teach	Warn	
Tear	Warp	
Tease	Weave	
Tempt	Wheedle	

ULTIMATE VERB LIST – SUGGESTED VOCAL GESTURES

Attack	Pet	Squeeze
Bind	Pinch	Stab
Bite	Poke	Stamp
Carve	Pop	Sting
Chop	Pound	Stir
Coil	Press	Strangle
Compress	Prick	Stretch
Crack	Prod	Strike
Crank	Pull	Stroke
Crush	Pump-up	Tear
Cuddle	Punch	Tickle
Cut	Push	Weave
Dab	Rip	Wind-up
Devour	Rub	Wring
Dig	Savor	Zap
Ensnare	Scold	Zing
Entangle	Screw	
Gash	Seduce	
Gouge	Shake	
Grab	Shove	
Hug	Slap	
Jab	Slash	
Jiggle	Slice	
Jolt	Smash	
Kick	Smooth	
Kiss	Smother	
Lick	Smush	
Massage	Snare	
Nibble	Squash	

RELATIONSHIP

Family, friends, acquaintances, and strangers: these are all types of connections and relationships that we have with the other characters on stage. We interact with them on different levels and terms. Who your character is and what their relationships are will play an important part in your interactions with these characters.

Each character you interact with on stage should be defined. Creating and building your relationships takes time and an in-depth exploration. Even the characters that are on stage, in which you don't have direct interactions or contact, contain a relationship and deserve some exploration. This also applies to characters that your character may talk about but are never seen in the play or in the same room as your character.

One way to examine your relationships in a play is to examine the dialogue. Dialogue between characters contains a tremendous amount of information to help you define the relationship. However, it's not enough to examine what you say but how you say it. How we speak to a friend is different from how we speak to a family member or a stranger. Look at all aspects. If you have difficulty creating a relationship, try finding a relationship in your life that mirrors the one you want to create on stage.

Your relationships will also play a part in the tactics that you use. How you interact and handle your character's relationships on stage will also strengthen the tactics you choose to get what you want. This will result in a further understanding and deeper definition of your relationships. You can see that as we start to add additional acting elements to your palette they will intertwine and work together, producing a stronger specificity to your work.

Status plays a role as well when it comes to relationship. Every person we know or encounter has an established status. That relationship when we perform is shaped by how we treat, respond to, and interact with the other characters. You'll start noticing that certain aspects of acting require other aspects in order to be flushed out. And because we use these to help develop our relationship, in turn, it develops our character which is why our characters are ever-evolving. Relationship plays a big part of that.

In addition to status you also have to include the subtler but equally important roles of body language, eye contact, and listening. How you react to a stranger giving you bad news is different from a family member giving you the same news. How is your body positioned? How often do you make eye contact? Are you really listening to them and letting it affect you or are you just going through the motions? Everything you do on stage should be from choice, not from habit.

Below is a list of some questions you should ask yourself to strengthen your relationships to the other characters around you on and off stage.

1. Who are they to me?
    a. Relative?
    b. Friend?
    c. Stranger?
    d. Teacher?
2. How do they make me feel?
    a. Status Quo
    b. Current situation
    c. How is it different, if at all?
3. What is my status to them?
4. Do I let them into my personal space?
5. How do I talk to them?
    a. Like a child?
    b. Like a crazy person?
    c. Like a confidant?

          d. Like an equal?
6. How do they talk to me?
7. Who controls the relationship?
          a. You?
          b. The other character?
          c. Does it shift?
8. Why do I like/love/hate them?
9. What are their traits that draw/repel me?
10. Would I tell them a secret?

You now have the basic understanding of what to do to build and begin your exploration of relationship. The more you explore your relationships on stage the more you will connect with the other actors on stage and create believable inter-personal exchanges.

We will cover another way to create and strengthen your relationships on stage with the technique "Substitution" found in CHAPTER 4.

STATUS

Status is the position that your character holds amongst himself and other characters around him/her. Your status can change throughout the entire course of the play. Using a scale from 1-10, read the script and determine the starting status of your character with 1 being the lowest and 10 being the highest.

The status you have can dictate how you talk, move, and interact with the other actors on stage. Status can also help define more clearly the established relationships with other characters. A higher status might indicate boss, parent, president, or bully. A lower status could indicate employee, child, or weakness. Status also helps define the tactics you use in your scenes. A high status might use manipulation, threatening, persuasion, or affirmation. A lower status might use begging, bargaining, flattery, or confirmation.

A higher status does not necessarily mean a dictator-like personality or one that always gets the final word. It can also represent confidence, assertiveness or comfortability. The same can be said for a lower status. Besides representing someone that is weak or poor it can also indicate shyness, low self-esteem, or youth, just to name a few.

Let's examine status with the Amanda/Laura scene from *The Glass Menagerie* by Tennessee Williams. At the start of the scene, Amanda has a high status, first because she's Laura's mother and second because she just learned something that Laura has been hiding, giving Amanda an upper hand. Laura, on the other hand, has a lower status. First, she is younger and the daughter of Amanda. Second, she is self-conscious about her disability, and third, she has been hiding something from her mother. The actor playing Laura may choose to give Laura a higher status to hide how she really feels about herself. These two statuses define the relationship between Amanda and Laura as mother and daughter.

Throughout the scene Amanda goes through a wide range of emotions and tactics: disappointment, being realistic, stating facts, guilt, and boosting confidence. Laura, on the other hand, seems to shrink in status as the scene progresses until she starts to talk about Jim, her high school crush. As she speaks to Amanda about Jim, she shows her yearbook to her mother. Laura's confidence begins to build and Amanda seems to relate to her daughter more. The statuses seem to be equalizing, as they grow closer together. As the scene ends, Amanda has used her status to build up Laura's confidence and in return, raises her status as well.

So as you can see from the example above: intention, tactic, relationship, status, everything is connected in acting and affects the choices you make.

TRUST

Trust is one of the elements of acting that we as actors take for granted. Trust usually means that you believe a person is trustworthy, honest, and they won't lie to you. But when it's applied to theatre it goes beyond that concept. It also means trusting the other actors will be emotionally open to you, know their blocking, lines, and give you something to work with on stage. You are relying on them to give you 100% of their creativity to the play and to you, just as they are relying on you for the same thing.

Our job as an actor is to make the other actors look good on stage and vice versa. We are not on stage to steal focus, upstage other actors, or make another actor look bad. When we are on stage we trust the other actors to uphold to this belief and not let us fall. When you trust the other actors in a production you are putting your faith in them that they will not let you down.

It's not just about making the other actor look good but also handling situations that happen on stage when you are performing live: missed lines, broken props, missed entrances, music not starting, just to name a few. The goal of the actor is to keep the show moving and appear seamless to the audience no matter what "mistakes" happened during the show. Everyone is relying on each other to make the show succeed and that is the essence of trust.

When, or if, you take a class or go to school for acting, there may be a unit that focuses on trust. Your professor or instructor will conduct trust exercises to help build a bond between you and the other students in the class, creating confidence and self-esteem. I remember one trust exercise when I attended the Pacific Conservatory of the Performing Arts in Santa Maria, CA. that was truly amazing.

It was in Movement 1 class, one of my most inspirational teachers, Karen Barbour, who unfortunately passed away in 2011 to cancer, had the entire class split into pairs. One person put on a blindfold.

The other person, using only their voice, led their partner around a room about half the size of a school gym. As the exercise progressed, she encouraged the person leading to walk faster and make their partner follow them. In the course of 10 minutes, she had the blindfolded partner running around the room being led only by their partner's voice. It was a sight to behold and truly even better to experience. Not only were we running around in circles but through each other. We placed our trust in our partner when we were being led and vice versa.

Once during a production of *Arsenic and Old Lace* at the Santa Rosa Players back in the 80's, I played the role of Officer Brophy. There was a scene where Reverend Harper is talking to Brophy. The other actor and I were sitting at the table and the scene was progressing as usual when suddenly he stopped talking. At first, I didn't know what was going on and then he looked at me and gave me this wide-eyed look like a deer caught in the headlights. I realized that he had forgotten his line. I quickly made up a line to get him back on track and he continued where he left off. Because I was "present" with him in the scene and focused, I was able to help him and no one in the audience was the wiser. Afterwards he thanked me for helping him and I simply replied, "That's my job. It's part of the business."

This, to me, is the epitome of trust and reflects what we expect on stage: 100% commitment from the other actors, working and helping each other to succeed. Trust is integral to theatre; it's trusting the other person will not let you fail (or crash into something) and sets you up to succeed. So when you are in a show, always strive to be the person who you would want to be on stage with when you are performing. If you do this, you will always succeed in being an actor who the other actors can trust, and in turn, give you the trust you need.

LISTENING

The art of listening on stage is another one of those "easier said than done" techniques. It's more than just listening for your next cue line. It's "active listening," allowing what the other actors are saying to affect you. It's not about giving facial expressions of understanding but genuinely letting it inform your body and, in turn, creating a true listening moment. What are they saying? How are they saying it? What is your body language? These are elements that you must be aware of when engaged in active listening. There is a fine line between "active listening" and acting like you're listening. Your job as an actor is to do the former.

When we listen to someone, we don't only look into their eyes and nod. We watch them. We look at their nose, their mouth, maybe their body language. We may glance away and look at something in the room but we are still listening. Occasionally, we may look down in order to process what we are hearing. Listening is reacting: not thinking about what we're going to say next, or thinking about what we should be feeling, but merely reacting as their words affect us and reflecting that back to them.

⌈ The next time you listen to someone tell a story notice what you do and how you respond.⌉ Do you fidget when they say something that makes you feel uncomfortable? Do you lean in when they say something intriguing or that catches your interest? Is there body contact? Do you take a drink? Do you lean back? Do you look down or away and let what they are saying to you be processed? You'll notice that most likely you may do all these things. As you listen, don't try to take in every word. In fact it's almost impossible to do. We may hear everything they are saying but our ears tune in and process certain words.

LISTENING EXERCISE:

Have a friend tell you a story with many details and specifics. After they have finished, repeat the story back to them. Try to incorporate the body language, and their use of the voice. How much did you remember? How much did you embellish? How accurate were you to the original? It's not important if you don't say it exactly like they said it. What's important is that you get in as many of the details as possible, delivering the essence of their story back to them with the same commitment and emotional integrity.

Listening is one of the simplest to understand yet hardest techniques to accomplish on stage. Just keep this in mind: If you find yourself "checking out" or "being distracted" then you aren't truly listening. Stay engaged and you will find that you are even more a part of the scene than you realize.

CHAPTER 3: ADDING TO THE BASICS

Subtext 76

Action.. 78

Inner Monologue 80

Given Circumstances... 82

Beats and Pauses 86

Justification 88

SUBTEXT

Now that you have a better understanding about intention, obstacle, and tactic, it's time to strengthen your choices and add something a bit more to your meaning. Often, what we say and what we mean are two different things. In fact, many times, we have an ulterior motive behind the words we say. This is what we refer to as subtext.

Think of your text in your monologue or scene as the main dish in a meal and your subtext as the spices you add to flavor it. Whenever I work with my students in acting class, I'm constantly posing this question to them, "What do you mean by what you're saying?". It's not enough to say a line. Anyone can speak a line of text but there has to be meaning behind what you're saying.

Sometimes the subtext supports what the line is implying and other times there is a hidden meaning that is flavored by the subtext you have chosen. The subtext you use depends on the choices you made as an actor with your text, including: intention, tactic, relationship, status, etc.

Another way I like to approach subtext is to say the line with a different line in your head. For instance, your text might be "Leave me alone?" It can be said just as a simple question. But what if you're subtext was, "You've got to be kidding me". The way you say your line will be flavored by your subtext. You say your main text the way you would say your subtext.

Subtext also relies on the relationship between you and the other character as well as what your character wants. That's why it's important to read a play thoroughly and not just skim through for your lines only. Also, when you read the entire script, another character may say something about your relationship, that is never mentioned anywhere else in the script. If you, the actor, don't know your relationships in the script, how can you possibly make choices about how you would talk to them? You can't.

The more you understand the complexities of your character, the more you can make choices regarding subtext and any other acting element when developing your character. Subtext can also help with the inflection of your voice. Inflections are just as important to your acting as anything else.

Below is a vocal inflection exercise that works great for understanding subtext. Speak the sentences out loud, not in your head.

SUBTEXT/INFLECTION EXERCISE
Read the following with the subtext provided.

Snow (Look! It snowed last night!)
Snow (Are you kidding?)
Snow (No, come see for yourself.)
Snow (Oh, no!)
Snow (Isn't it beautiful!)
Well (Is he well?)
Well (I'm not sure.)
Well (I'm not surprised.)
Well (After all, what can you expect?)
Lazy (You're lazy)
Lazy (I'm not lazy!')
Lazy (Yes, you are lazy.)

This is a great tool to use to help your understanding of the use of subtext. Finding the subtext in your lines can help strengthen your choices for intentions and tactics. Remember, it's not what you say, it's how you say it.

ACTION

Action has many interpretations in acting. It can be said by a director to start filming a shot, it can mean movement, or it can mean something you are doing or performing. In this particular instance it refers to the latter: performing an action. An action is something the character is doing. This action can be either primary or secondary in nature depending on the circumstances surrounding you. When an action is primary, it is the thing that is at the forefront for the character. This action is more important than anything else and everything else including character interaction and dialogue becomes secondary. When an action is secondary it means that character interactions and dialogue are taking precedence over the action being completed.

So how does one decide if an action is primary or secondary? This depends on what is happening in the scene and can be connected to relationship and status. Intention and tactic can also play a part in an action's placement. When approaching an action in a scene remember two things: a character performs an action because they need to do it not because the actor is trying to find something to do and the second, an actor continues to perform this action until either something stops the action or the action is completed. In either case, a new primary action is introduced.

To better explain this theory, let's look at Rhoda and Leroy's scene from *The Bad Seed* by Maxwell Anderson. The plot of this script revolves around Rhoda, a 9-year old girl with a dark nature. She is a vengeful, hateful, and murderous little girl hiding behind the façade of innocence.

The scene between Rhoda and Leroy, the family's groundskeeper, starts off with Rhoda setting up a tea party for her dolls. This is her primary action. Leroy enters and confronts her. Rhoda does not have much regard or respect for Leroy, and while he is talking to her she continues to set up her tea party. She responds to him while continuing her primary action. Thus, her dialogue becomes her secondary action. As Leroy begins to cause concern for Rhoda, she stops setting up the tea party and start talking to him directly. Her primary action has stopped and her secondary action becomes her primary action. However, since she is no longer concerned with setting up the tea party, that does not become the secondary action.

You don't always have a secondary action but you will always have a primary action. Your primary action is what your character is doing amidst their intentions. Furthermore, the primary action may reflect the main or immediate intention. It depends on the scene. In *Laundry and Bourbon* by James McLure, two women are doing laundry while talking, gossiping, and drinking bourbon. The laundry is the secondary action while the drinking and gossiping are the primary action.

It's important to remember that your character's actions are a result of what they want to accomplish at that moment, whether it's making a drink, folding laundry, tying someone up, having a discussion, etc. You cannot do two actions with equal importance. One must take precedence over the other. This creates your primary and secondary action, and in turn should change throughout the scene if needed, depending on what your character wants at that moment.

Inner Monologue

A technique you can use when approaching a scene is to create a monologue within yourself that will set-up how you approach your movement, your lines, and your actions in a scene. By doing this, you help strengthen the reasons behind your actions. This inner monologue is not to be spoken out loud nor revealed to the other actor or actors in the scene. It is a secret that only you should know about.

I'm going to create an imaginary scene from a play. You are required to go to a work party. Since it is mandatory, you have no choice but to attend. As you are looking around the room you think to yourself. "I don't know why I'm always coming to parties. They aren't exciting and the people are so boring. All I do is drink and watch people. It depresses me and I'm not enjoying myself. I should leave. I don't want to be here but I have to be polite." From your inner monologue it is clear you don't want to be there.

Now that you've expressed your inner monologue, you must now socialize with the people around you. With your inner monologue very clear, your intention becomes clearer: To survive this party. The inner monologue can also strengthen your tactic: To avoid everyone. Because your inner monologue, intention, and tactic are now in place, you know how your character will act. You put on a false front of pleasantries. Engage in polite conversations. Laugh at jokes you don't find funny. A few things that you do in order to achieve your intention.

However, even though your inner monologue expressed your need to leave the party, this does not mean that it has to end that way. Maybe throughout the scene your character warms up, meets someone new, drinks too much. The scene could end differently than how it started out. The inner monologue does not dictate what will happen in the scene. It is what you are thinking prior to the words, movement, inflections, and actions, of your character in the scene.

The inner monologue can also help with finding the subtext for your character. Everything works in tandem when it comes to acting and your choices are based off how your character lives and thinks in the imaginary world of the playwright.

GIVEN CIRCUMSTANCES

If someone were to ask you about your life. You would be able to tell them everything in detail: past, present, and future (things you know were coming up). These details are the same things that you should know about your character. This is called the given circumstances.

You get the given circumstances for your character by reading the play and paying very close attention to what your character says about themselves, what other say about your character, and what the playwright says about your character (through dialogue and stage descriptions.) You should know your character as well as you know yourself.

When developing your character, the best way to incorporate what you know about him or her is to write a bio for them. Their bio should cover from the earliest moment that they talk about up to the present, including any future events coming up. You can also fabricate information about them as long as it does not contradict anything that is said about them in the play nor changes who they are. The bio is also a good way to include secrets about your character that no one knows and will never find out. The given circumstances and bio should cover everything prior to the start of the play. Or if you are doing a scene or monologue should cover up to when the monologue or scene start.

Your bio for your character is not written in stone. After you have written a bio, if things change, feel free to alter it. This is for you and you alone. No one is going to read the bio you've written for your character and don't' feel obligated to share it with anyone.

When writing your bio, you may include other characters in the play if there is a history between them and your character but you cannot change anything about those characters. You may not fabricate any additional information about that character to help enhance yours. Your character may have opinions about these other characters but that is it.

Sometimes your relationship with another character is closely tied. If that is the case, sit down and talk to the other actor portraying that character and decide on the facts that both characters share in their history. This way you don't get conflicting information as you are developing your character. Examples of closely tied relationships that could share history in your bio include: brother/sister, husband/wife, best friends, mother/daughter, past camp buddies, etc. These are just a few examples.

Below is my bio for Seymour from *"Little Shop of Horrors"* based on the given circumstances from the musical.

> I was born in Skidrow in 1925. My parents were unable to raise me and placed me in the Skidrow Home for Boys. There was nothing very special about me but I always hoped that one day someone would adopt me.
>
> When I was 8, I was taken from there by Mr. Mushnik. I thought he was going to adopt me but he just took me in. He taught me how to be a florist. I didn't go to school and wasn't very educated. Growing up in the florist shop wasn't too bad, I had a warm place to sleep and food to eat. I was kind of lonely though since Mr. Mushnik wasn't the warmest of individuals and wouldn't allow me to have a pet. Not that I could have afforded it anyway. I was very shy and not very confident so I kept to myself.
>
> As I got older and more experienced with plants, I began to work more with them, trying to create new plants but they never survived. Mr. Mushnik would always yell at me when a plant died but I think that was just his way of talking to me. But I don't like it when he yells at me.

When I was 28, Mr. Mushnik hired Audrey. The minute I saw her I fell in love with her. I thought she was so pretty. But I could tell by the way she dressed and her taste in clothes, that she would never date anyone like me. I was not in her league. I was just a slob, a nobody, so I never told her my feeling for her. We would have nice conversations though but I could never get my nerve up to ask her out for fear of rejection.

About a week ago, I found a strange little plant at Mr. Chang's corner store. It was so cute and never saw anything like it. I bought it and took it home. I did research on the plant but couldn't find anything on it. It seemed to be one-of-a-kind. At first it grew nicely, but lately it doesn't want to grow. I've tried everything from pot ash to rain and nothing seems to help. One day its thriving and the next its drooping and wilting. I'm such a failure.

I really want to figure out how to help the plant grow so I can cultivate it and make more of them. Mr. Mushnik's business isn't doing too well, and if I could make more of these plants, his business would be more successful and maybe Audrey would finally like me. And if I could successfully grow more of these plants, I would finally be able to get out of Skidrow and have a shot at a decent life.

I'll keep working on the plant and maybe I'll have a breakthrough. In the meantime, back to work.

As you can see, this bio is the start for my character. It stays true to how the character was written by the playwright. I also included things that I actually say in the script to build a connection for me. I included my important relationships in my bio and the emotional and personality traits that my character outwardly shows as well as a secret or two, that no one knows.

This was my starting point for my character using given circumstances. The more in-depth you are about your character, the more you can create a well-rounded, living, breathing entity on stage and in doing so build a stronger connection between you and your character. Remember that finding the given circumstances is key to any well-developed character.

BEATS AND PAUSES

As in real life, no one speaks non-stop without taking a breath or a moment of silence to add drama, suspense, or thought to what is about to be spoken. These moments of silence are referred to as beats or pauses. Even characters who speak non-stop or quickly must take beats even if it is only to catch a breath.

Let's look at beats first. As defined in the Stage Terminology section in CHAPTER 1, a beat has two definitions, let's look at the first definition, a short silence. Beats can add dramatic or comic effect. The short silences may increase the dramatic tension. Keeping the audience engaged with what is happening with your character. In comedy, it can set up a punch line or a comedic moment. However, a beat is more than just silence. A beat or a pause is **always** filled with thought.

The length of the beat is usually a snap of a finger.   In class, I use this example. Take the interaction "How are you?", "I'm fine." With a friend or by yourself, you will say each exchange in the following ways:

1. No beat
2. One beat (one snap)
3. Two beats (two snaps)
4. Three beats (three snaps)

How did the alternating beats inform you? Ask yourself what kind of situation would someone use that number of beats or lack thereof. Since a beat contains thought, what is going through the mind of the character during that time. Are they being contemplative? Are they restraining themselves? Are they feeling stressed? Are they excited? It is not enough just to have a beat. Without the thought behind it, a beat will feel empty and unneeded or simply gratuitous and actor-driven.

The other definition of a beat refers to a change of thought, emotion, or tactic. This type of beat can contain a small silence or pause as well but not always. Often when working with a coach or director, they will have an actor start their monologue or scene prior to a beat so they can sense that change and shape it.

As you are examining your character you will be able to tell what kind of beat they are using. One of my favorite movie clips that is an excellent example of this is Sally Field's performance as M'Lynn in "Steel Magnolias" with the funeral speech. She goes in and out of emotions continuously. Sometimes there are silences and sometimes not. She creates an emotional journey with using the two types of beats that I talked about. Watch that clip and see if you can recognize the difference between the two.

The pause is used for a long silence. Pause are usually more than three snaps. This can denote many things: dramatic tension, action happening during the pause, an awkward silence. These are just a few reasons for using a pause instead of a beat. Using the phrase from earlier, what does a pause do to that simple exchange? Is the character doing something before they respond? Are they distracted? Are they considering what to say? The possibilities are endless and you as the actor must make those choices to why. However, and you will hear me say this continuously throughout this book, everything we do must be character-driven or our acting will be self-serving and not organic.

To help me identify and separate a beat meaning silence and a beat for change of thought when I am marking my script, I use these marking that I borrowed from my Shakespeare chapter. When indicating a change of thought, emotion, or tactic, I use this mark **/** . When I want to indicate a beat or pause, I use this one **//**. If the beat is a combination of both I use this symbol **#**.

JUSTIFICATION

Whether a director blocks us or we use organic blocking, one thing remains the same: all characters move. The movement or non-movement of your character is not a random or careless action. It is a choice. Your character moves because they need to move not because the director told you to. It is your job as an actor to give reason why your character is moving and justify your actions. To not do so will create an ambivalent action for your character and not seem realistic or believable.

Often a director will block you to move someplace on stage and it is up to the actor to justify that blocking. Usually the blocking makes sense but, when it doesn't, that's when we need to use justification. If you don't justify the movement with an action, objective or tactic it will look as though you are moving because the director told you to and not because your character needed to move.

Your character moves for a reason not because you (the actor) are bored or tired of standing in one place. There is an objective or tactic behind each movement. Action is filled with movement and the movement justifies the action. They go hand in hand. There should never be meandering around the stage for the sake of movement. There must be a reason. Superfluous movement or non-movement can prove to be distracting, not only to the audience members but also to you or the other actors on stage.

Adding justification behind an action is simple to execute. Remember though, that the justification has to match the intention, tactic, or action. If it doesn't, you will look awkward and the action will seem unrelated to the reason. Example: Someone tells you to hop up and down on the floor, alternating between legs. To do this without reason would look silly and not get any positive reactions. However, by adding the simple idea of hopping from leg to leg on the floor because the floor is hot suddenly empowers the action and gives it meaning.

What other ways can you justify the above action? Stand up and try it yourself. Write down your justifications in your journal. As you begin to explore your movements, you will become more adept at placing reasons behind the actions so they don't look meaningless and superfluous.

Another way to justify your movement is to look at the dialogue you are speaking. This is what I tell all my students when they are blocking themselves. Most of the time, the dialogue in a scene can inform us of what we are doing. Action can be written into our dialogue without realizing it and can be overlooked with an untrained eye. I will often ask them when they are working on a scene, "Why are you moving on this line?" and I'm expecting an intellectual and justifiable reason.

When I was working on *Oliver Twist*, Fagin had the line, "How do you do Oliver. I should be honored with your intimate acquaintance." Oliver was positioned on stage left and I was on stage right. When I spoke my line, I felt the instinct to cross to Oliver and shake his hand, and so I did. The line indicated to me, by its greeting style, that I should move. This movement also supported my objective "to welcome my new guest" and my tactic "to befriend".

Now if the director had told me not to move when I say that line then it becomes my responsibility to figure out why Fagin doesn't move to greet Oliver. If that was the case, I might use friendly but distant or friendly but cautious. I could have chosen the objective "to assess the situation" and the tactic "to evaluate. This acting choice would support my reason for not moving.

Whatever choices you make for your character including moving or speaking, you **MUST** have a reason for doing so. Nothing is arbitrary when it comes to your character. If you do not have a strong and valid reason for the choices you make or cannot support the choices you make based on research, dialogue, and/or their current emotional state then your choices are actor-based and not character-based which is something you want to avoid at all costs. It's their life you're creating not yours.

JUSTIFICATION EXERCISE

Two actors (A and B) stand opposite each other. A gives B an action to do either by showing or doing the action, i.e., put right hand on ear. B must justify that action with a sound or voiced remark, i.e., "Ow, my ear infection is getting worse." Once A is satisfied with the justified reason, reverse the roles and start again.

MUD EXERCISE

This exercise is best if lead by an instructor but can still be done if you are working on your own. I will describe this exercise as if it was led by an instructor with a group of students.

This exercise works best if you have a monologue fully memorized. First, prior to starting, the instructor will assign a number of moves you may use once you start your monologue. I like to use 5, 3, and finally 1.

You will use the same formula as described in the CHAPTER 7. Move through the space visualizing the thick mud-like consistency. Explore the space vertically, horizontally, incorporating all of your body, arms, legs, back, etc. At some point, the instructor will randomly say "Freeze." Everyone will freeze and the instructor will choose one person to do their monologue. At that point, the rest of the group and sit and watch.

As you perform your monologue, you may use the number of movements the instructor has allowed. Remember, that a movement is any shift of your body including head and eye movements. Example, if your eyes are looking straight ahead and you look to the right, that is a movement. If you lower your arm, and twist your body at the same time, that would be considered two movements. Be aware of rule for this exercise.

Once the student has completed their monologue, everyone moves around the room in the same fashion and the instructor will repeat the process until everyone has gone. As soon as all monologues have been performed with the set number of movements allowed, the instructor will reduce the number of movements the student can do. Continue this exercise until everyone has done their monologue with the new number of movements allowed.

On the last round of movements allowed, the instructor will only allow 1 movement. Everyone will perform their monologues for the last time. If you are watching, you may notice that those performing their monologue usually will make their one movement on a sentence or word that is key to their monologue.

When I conducted with exercise in my Character Development class, the movements in the monologues occurred in the following places: Anne Frank – "I love you, father.", Peter from *Anne Frank* – "I wanted to hit him.", Shelley from *Buried Child* – "I don't know what I'm doing here." It was clear from this exercise that these were the underlying key ideas for these monologues.

Ideally, once this exercise is done using whatever number of movements allowed, you will find the key ideas, words, and sentences that are most important in your monologue will present themselves.

CHAPTER 4: BEYOND THE BASICS

Relaxation and The Green Light 94

The Magic "If" 99

The Moment Before 101

Moment-to-Moment 104

Emotional Tones..107

Emotional Chart 108

Arcs..109

Endowment 114

Substitution 116

Sense Memory...119

Emotional Recall 123

Relaxation and The Green Light

I learned this relaxation technique in Elizabeth Kemp's acting class at Actors Studio Drama School. It is used to get you into a state of readiness and allows your mind and body to be totally relaxed and ready to work. You will use this for many exercises in this book: learn it well so you won't have to keep referring to this chapter.

I should point out that it is easier to have someone lead you through this exercise. It's a little difficult to get all the nuances and specificity required when typing it out. However, I will do my best to relay the information to you.

Find a place in your home where you won't be disturbed by people or too many outside noises. If you want, you may put on some new age music without lyrics. I like to use Enya or any relaxing new age sound. We will use a shortened form of the relaxation exercise from CHAPTER 7 and add a pure green healing light at the end of it.

PART 1 – RELAXATION EXERCISE[1]
1. Take off your shoes, loosen your belt (if you're wearing one), and lie down on the floor with your knees up.
2. Relax your arms at your sides with your palms facing up.
3. Close your eyes and let your legs slide down.

Be aware of which parts of the body are in contact with the floor. Is the contact the same on each side? Be aware of the floor touching the tailbone, between the shoulder blades, elbow, fingers, upper arms, back of the head, calves, buttocks, and shoulders. Look down at yourself from above the whole body.

---

[1] Barbour, K. (1991-92). Movement I. Pacific Conservatory for the Performing Arts, Allan Hancock College

4. Picture the bones of the toe. Imagine they could drop off the feet.

5. Release the feet from the ankles as if they were not attached. Think of them being an immense distance from the torso.

6. Let them warm up and melt.

7. Put your attention in the calves of the legs. Let the mind massage the muscles of the calves so they melt and the shinbones seem to fall on the floor.

8. Imagine a space where the knee joints are and with the mind, melt the joints of the thighs and let the knee joints drop to the floor.

9. Put your attention in the thighs. Let the mind massage the muscles of the thighs so they melt and fall on the floor.

10. Imagine a space where the hip sockets are and let the legs travel away from the body. Put your awareness in the buttock muscles and let them melt.

11. Relax the lower stomach muscles.

12. Imagine the pelvic girdle to be wider than it is so it flows out toward the hands on either side. Imagine it really wide with great spaces that the breath inhabits.

13. Let the breath move down into the lower spaces.

14. Soften the diaphragm and imagine melting the bones of the ribcage so it doesn't feel rigid, but can be moved by the breath that exists inside the ribcage.

15. Imagine the shoulder girdle to be wider than it is.

16. Let your arms move out across the floor from the shoulder sockets.

17. Get an image of space in the wrist sockets.

18. Get an image of the hands miles away from the shoulders.

19. Send attention back up the arms to the neck.

20. Feel the throat melt.

21. Feel the back of the neck give into the floor.

Let there be a large space between the shoulders and the skull so the head is very far from the torso.

22. Melt the jaw muscles so the jawbone drops toward the floor.
23. Let the face muscles melt so you can feel the skin lying on the bone. Feel the weight of the eyelids on the eyes.
24. Relax the scalp muscles.
25. Relax the tongue inside the mouth.
26. Feel the spaces behind the nose.
27. Feel the space behind the cheeks.
28. Feel the space under the eyeballs.
29. Feel the weight of the head on the floor.
30. Take in a nice, long deep breath of positive energy and exhale any negative energy you may have.

Be aware of the whole weight of the body lying abandoned on the floor. You are now ready to add the green light.

:PART 2 - THE GREEN LIGHT[1]

Throughout this entire exercise I want you to think of your breathing as this…in with the positive energy and out with the negative. I will name several bodily areas in each numbered sequence that the light is filling up but visually see the green light filling each area completely before moving onto the next area. This part of the exercise should take between 15 – 20 minutes at least.

31. Picture a green healing light above you. This green light is filled with a healing light and will strengthen the warrior that is inside you.
32. As you breathe in, let the green light slowly fill your body, starting at the head, and gently warming the forehead, eye sockets, nose, mouth, cheeks, jawbone, tongue, and lips.

As you do this, keep reminding yourself that you are a warrior and allow the healing green light to give you strength.

33. The green light gently continues to flow down and warm your neck and shoulders. Remember about your breathing.
34. Let the green light travel down to your arms and fill up your hands and fingers.
35. The green light fills up your chest, the rib cage, your back, and travels down to your stomach and lower back.

Again remind yourself of the warrior within and continue letting the green light fill you.

36. Feel the warmth in your upper torso as the light continues to travel and filling up your pelvic region, your buttocks, groin,

---

[1] Kemp, E. (2002-2003). Acting I. Actors Studio Drama School, New School University

quads, and thighs.

As the light travels through your body, be aware of the parts of your body that the light is already filling and allow it to continue to strengthen and heal you.

37. Now the light is traveling to your knees, calves, shins, down to your ankles filling everything up with the pure green light.
38. Finally, it reaches your feet, heels, and toes, filling up all the spaces in between.
39. Allow the feeling of the warm green light to warm your entire body and energize it.

Feel the green light strengthening you and the warrior being able to come out.

40. Take a few long, deep, cleansing breaths, exhaling out any negative energy.

You are ready to begin any exercise that requires you to be in a physically and mentally relaxed state before starting.

THE MAGIC "IF"

There are moments when an actor may have a difficult time reaching an emotional level. They may struggle connecting with a partner, connecting with their text, identifying with their character's situation, or maybe, not being able to relate to what the character is experiencing. We find ourselves trying the same things within the scene, or unable to come up with other ideas. When these moments occur the actor can use the magic "if." The word "if" is a powerful tool used by the actor to engage their imagination and help them to connect to problems that they are struggling with in their process.

Whenever you use "if" you put yourself, not your character, in the question. You use it like this: "What would I do if I...?" or "How would I feel if I...?" By using these phrases or any phrase regarding "if", you let go of any preconceived notions or mental blocks you may have. You are free to explore. You are allowing yourself to be put in your character's position and react naturally. Once you have explored what you are trying to achieve with the magic "if", you can return to your character and ask questions pertaining to them.

. When asking yourself as your character, do not use your character's name. This will place you outside of your character. Instead continue using the pronoun "I" but remember you are asking it as your character not as yourself. If you find that you are still having a hard time identifying with your character using "if" refer to the character analysis sheet found at the end of CHAPTER 8. Once you have fleshed out the essences of your character, try using the magic "if" again.

As an example, let's look at "John", an actor who has been cast as Richard III. While excited about the role, he is unable to identify with the disability that Richard has and, as a result, finds that he is unsure of the choices to make in regards to the physicality of the hunchback. John decides to use "if" by phrasing this question to himself, "What would I do if I had a hunchback?". This, in turn, would open up other questions such as: "How would it make me feel?", "How would I perceive myself?", "Would I be self-conscious?", "Would I have a chip on my shoulder?"

Once he has explored his questions fully, now he becomes his character. He's already read the play so he knows who Richard is as a person. As Richard, he will ask himself this question, "How would I feel if I didn't have a hunchback?". After he has answered this, he continues asking questions to himself along the same lines with the realization that he does have a hunchback. In order to explore and delve deeper into his character, he may ask himself these follow-up questions, "How do I feel about my hunchback?", "How does this hunchback make me feel about being king?", "Would Anne be able to love me with my deformity?", "Would my subjects trust in my leadership ability?", "Would I be able to lead a war as good as anyone else?", and so on.

This acting tool can help any actor over a stumbling block that they encounter. The magic "if" is endless and can be used with any character in any play: "What if I was unsatisfied with my marriage?" (*Who's Afraid of Virginia Woolf?*, Edward Albee), "How would I feel if I had a slight handicap?" (*The Glass Menagerie*, Tennessee Williams), "What would I do if I couldn't get a student to understand?" (*The Lesson*, Eugene Ionesco), "What would I do if confronted by an angry student?" (*Oleanna*, David Mamet). As you can see the word "if" has endless possibilities and can be very beneficial.

THE MOMENT BEFORE

The life of your character doesn't begin when you first make your entrance. It begins the moment before. Your character has been living before the play has started. When you enter a scene, you aren't coming from the wings or backstage; you are coming from somewhere else in the world of the play. Before you enter your scene, do a bit of analysis with these questions: "Where am I coming from?", "What did I do?", "Did I talk to anyone?", "What was the weather like?", etc. Your answers should reflect your character and maintain the reality that the playwright has structured within the script.

The "moment before" will affect the way you enter a scene. It will affect the way you react to other people in the room and how you talk to them. It may inform you about blocking and status. You should ask yourself as many questions about the "moment before" and be very specific with your answers. These questions will help to strengthen your choices as an actor and give your character greater depth.

In *Oliver Twist*, Fagin comes into a room and discovers Nancy dead. As an actor, I could have just entered the room, noticed her on the floor, immediately crossed over to Nancy to see if she was hurt, fall to my knees, and reacted to her death. The audience would accept that for what it was. However, I could strengthen that choice by building upon the "moment before."

Here is how I prepared for that scene using my "moment before" technique: I just finished having a fight with Bill. My adrenaline is already pumping and I'm in an excited state of mind. I'm not thinking clearly. I want to kill Noah, who betrayed Nancy . .. but I don't have time to deal with him. It's 1 am in the morning. I chase Bill through the cold, dark streets of London. I'm worried for Nancy's safety. After running many blocks and hoping to stop Bill from doing something terrible, I enter the room and stop, catching my breath. I look around for Bill and instead, I see Nancy on the floor, dead. I'm stunned and run to her, hoping that I'm not too late. As I get to her body, I realize she is no longer alive. I take a few beats to let her death register, blaming myself for her death because I didn't get there sooner, and then I fall to her side and cry at my loss.

As you can tell from my "moment before", I have increased the stakes for my character while giving Fagin a strong sense of where he was coming from and something to use when entering the room to stop Bill. I didn't need to discuss my choices about my "moment before" because it doesn't affect anyone else in the scene: Bill has already left the premises and Nancy is dead.

The same rule applies to your "moment before" choices. You don't need to discuss your "moment before" with anyone else <u>unless</u> it directly involves another character, for instance, coming into a room together. An example of this would be George and Martha from *Who's Afraid of Virginia Woolf?*

As Martha, you have decided that you have just come back from a party where you laughed, drank, and made jokes. You walked about a ¼ mile from your father's house, it is late at night, no one is around, and the air is a bit chilly. You enter and start your scene, however, the actor playing George while agreeing with the first part of your "moment before" has decided that the distance is ½ mile from the house, it is warm, and surrounded by neighbors. Since you haven't discussed the "moment before" together, you are going to have different entrances into the house and not match, in turn, causing an inconsistency within the scene. If you discuss and agree upon the "moment before" together, your individual choices will reflect that.

Don't underestimate the power of the "moment before". It can be very helpful, enlightening, and add depth to your choices that you make as an actor.

MOMENT BEFORE EXERCISE

While working on your lines from a show, scene, or monologue, imagine different scenarios before you come on stage. Example: You just stepped on a burning coal, it's raining outside, you ran two miles on a hot day, you bit your tongue, etc. It doesn't matter what you choose, this is only an exercise but it will show you how your entrance and, in turn, your lines, reactions, and relationships are affected by what you encountered before you entered the scene.

After you have explored the different scenarios for your "moment before", go back to your script and figure out what your character might have experienced before entering the scene. Keep the "moment before" true to the script and the character's situation.

MOMENT-TO-MOMENT

One of the biggest mistakes that an actor can make is to anticipate the events that happen to their character in the play. The actor knows what happens in a play but the character does not. As actors, we cannot allow that information to cloud our judgment when making choices for our characters.

To prevent our knowledge of the events in the play from filtering into our character, which could result in playing the end result of a scene, you must approach each moment as it occurs. This is also known as "living in the moment" or "living moment-to-moment".

Start at the beginning of the play and find the first moment for your character. Most likely this is the first time they enter the stage with all the given circumstances that you have unearthed from reading the play. The first moment is filled with the objectives and tactics. You learned about those in CHAPTER 2. Remember that each moment is filled with a super objective, main objective and immediate objective. A new moment happens when the beat changes within the scene. It can also happen when the objective or tactic changes for your character. It all depends on the situation that your character is facing.

It is important to let each moment in your character's life build on the previous one. By allowing this to happen, you are permitting your character to live on stage "in the moment", letting each event affect them, and making choices to move forward to the next moment in their life. When a moment isn't fleshed out or filled with clarity, it can cloud the moments to come and confuse the audience, making it hard for them (or even you) to believe what is happening on stage with your character.

Look at each moment as a step on a ladder. You can't reach the second rung until you've stepped on the first. With each sure-footed step on the ladder you get closer and closer to your goal: getting to the top. So, with each moment set in place, you move on to the next moment. Each time getting closer to the goal of your character: their objective.

You must keep in mind that the moments that happen to your character, shape their life and ultimately lead them down the path in the script until the play ends. If you approach this "moment-to-moment" process correctly, you will avoid anticipating the end result. This will ensure that your character is "living" on stage and approaching each moment with a fresh look.

Let's examine moment-to-moment with a scene from Neil Simon's *Lost in Yonkers*. Belle is the scattered-brained aunt of Jay, a fifteen-year old boy visiting his grandma. Belle is very high-strung, energetic, and suffers from a very short attention span or ADHD. By the end of the scene, she throws a fit, yells at Jay, and storms out of the room.

When she first enters the room, her first moment consists of removing her coat and talking to Jay about why she locked herself out of the house. As soon as her coat is off, she immediately, runs to Jay, greeting him, and hugging him. As soon as she does that, her next moment becomes looking for her brother, Eddie (Jay's father). When Jay tells her that he is in the other room talking to her mother. She stops and moves to the couch, signaling to Jay to sit with her so they can talk with privacy. Within the first 2 minutes of the play, Belle has already had five different moments she's living through. None of them remotely close to her end result of throwing a tantrum. If she came in already playing the fact that she is mad at Jay for being unreceptive to her, it would not make any sense to the audience or to the other actors.

Additionally, each moment in a scene must be completed or have something stop that moment from continuing before the next one can start. She can't come into the room and immediately start looking for Eddie or be scared that her mother will come out and stop her and Jay from talking. Nothing has been said or insinuated to suggest those moments. Looking for Eddie only happens after she hugs Jay and realizes that if Jay is there then Eddie must be there too. And she doesn't get scared about disturbing her mother until Jay tells Belle that Eddie is in the bedroom talking to her.

By playing each moment for what it is and allowing the intention, tactic, or action to drive the moments in the scene, Belle can seem completely oblivious to what's happening around her and let her ADHD come through with her sporadic mood changes and inability to stay focused.

MOMENT-TO-MOMENT EXERCISE

You are expecting a call from your doctor with test results from your last hospital visit. You come home and check the answering machine. There is no message. You decided to call the doctor's office but you can't remember the number. You try to remember where you put the piece of paper with the number on it. Wherever you look for the paper, it is not there. You know it's in the house, you're sure of it. You decide to make yourself a drink to calm down but still constantly think where the paper could be. You recheck places you've already checked thinking you might have overlooked it. Continue to find other ways of getting the number but not being able to locate it. Finally, when you are at the height of frustration, the phone rings. You answer it and it is the doctor with your results.

EMOTIONAL TONES

Some theories of acting rely on the emotional levels or emotional tones[1] of the character. Every emotion has a level and, by varying it by one or two increments, the emotion changes. Creating a graph or chart for your script will help you to follow the emotional life of your character. Start at the beginning and figure out the emotional state of your character and give it an emotional rating from 1 – 10. Then see where the next level is and write that down. Eventually you will create the emotional graph or chart for your character and the path they take through the entire play. Look at the emotional scale of your character. Where does it begin? Where does it end? Is there a lot of variation?

On the next page is the emotional chart used to map the state of mind for your character. 10 = the highest emotional experience either positive or negative. The higher the number, the more positive/negative your character is feeling emotionally. Use this chart as a starting point and go from there. There are emotions that aren't listed on the chart that you can use: jealousy, envy, love, obsession, and so much more. Decide where you would place that emotion on the chart and adapt accordingly.

Let me be clear that the numbered emotions 1 – 10 on the positive side and 1 – 11 on the negative side represent the emotion your character is feeling, not the level of that emotion. You may find that you start at "cheerful" which is a 6 on the positive chart and the beginning level of your cheerfulness may be set at 8.

During the scene you may keep increasing or decreasing your level of cheerfulness until it is necessary to switch to the next emotional level, either above (excitement) or below (strong interest). You could very well skip over entire emotions on the chart completely, going from cheerful to hostility. Your emotional journey doesn't have to be in

---

[1] Adapted from notes taken from Kjennas, P. (Fall 1992). Acting 3. Pacific Conservatory of the Performing Arts, Allan Hancock College.

consecutive order. It's all relative to the situation your character is in, but it still has to make sense.

Every one of these emotions is contagious. Either you're winning or you're losing. It's your job as an actor to keep fighting. If you're winning, you keep fighting to stay on top. If you're losing, you fight to gain or regain control.

I like to score my monologue or scene with my emotional chart because it helps me keep perspective of where my character is going. Emotions are intangible. We can feel them but we can't touch them or see them. By adding an emotional chart to your scoring, you can make the intangible tangible by seeing where your character is emotionally at all times.

EMOTIONAL CHART

(+) Positive Emotions	(+/-) Emotion	(-) Negative Emotions
1. Indifference	0. Antagonism	-1. Apathy
2. Boredom		-2. Grief
3. Mild Interest		-3. Sympathy
4. Conservative		-4. Numb
5. Strong Interest		-5. Fear/Worry
6. Cheerful		-6. Resentment
7. Excitement		-7. Hate
8. Joy		-8. Anger
9. Enthusiasm		-9. Pain
10. Ecstasy		-10. Hostility

ARCS

Arcs describe the path that a storyline or character makes during the course of the play. Where a character begins at the start of a play is most likely very different from where they end. It is important as you are working on your character to find their main arc. Just like a main objective, the main arc will chronicle the path of the character and refers to their emotional journey.

In conjunction to main and immediate objectives, there are also main and immediate arcs for characters in scenes and monologues. These can be found in the beats of dialogue. However, unlike objectives or tactics, arcs can cover many objectives and tactics within many beats of a scene.

As an actor, you should map out these arcs. I'm not saying to orchestrate and control theses arcs but use them as a guide to where the character is emotionally heading. There can be arcs in monologues and dialogue. There can be one main arc for a scene but that scene may contain many mini-arcs within itself.

I like to measure the arc of a character from the time they enter a scene until the time they leave. This can be anywhere from one page to an entire act. However, when your character leaves the scene, the arc does not end. It continues, unseen by the audience. When they re-enter the scene, the arc either continues where it left off or reflects what might have happened off-stage to the character.

Arcs will either go up or down, depending on what is happening in the monologue. For example, if your character suddenly breaks down after remaining calm throughout your monologue, the emotional state is one of despair. That doesn't mean they wail, moan, and cry loudly. It could be a moment of realization for them.

An arc is created when the emotional level increases or decreases. The top of the arc is the highest level before the energy or emotion begins to drop and the character returns to their normal state of being or status quo. It is not uncommon for a monologue to end at the height of an arc. Finding the arcs in your monologue will give you a better sense of what is happening in the monologue and allow your character to live and experience what is happening around them and to them.

Arcs use a variation of Emotional Tones that I mentioned in the previous section. If you can't seem to find the arc of your monologue or scene, write your levels to the side, see if the numbers correspond to height or depth of emotion your character is experiencing. By seeing this emotional level scored out in your script, you should be able to find the arc and adjust accordingly. I like to mark my script with numbers, putting these numbers next to the lines to visually represent the arc, thus as I said in the previous section, making the intangible tangible.

On the following page is an excerpt of an actual scene from a play I did marked with levels and arcs.

Mapping arcs example:

Page 24   THE WIND IN THE WILLOWS   Act I

RAT. There's not a word of truth to that last part and you
    know it. The Wildwooders don't care for you anymore
    than they care for the rest of us.
TOAD. Well, I don't know what your relations are like,
    old chap, but I happen to get along with them splen-
    didly. Here, I'll show you. *(Shouting.)* Hello, all you
    ferrets! Hello, weasels! It's your old friend, Mr. Toad!
RAT. Toad, stop that this instant.
TOAD. Take back what you said then.
RAT. I will not!
TOAD. Have it your own way. *(Shouting again.)* Yoo-
    hoo! Hello there, stoats! It's your good chum Mr. Toad
    of Toad Hall! I brought along Mr. Rat and Mr. Mole,
    here, to make your acquaintance!
RAT. Toad! Sit down, at once! I promise you, if you do
    not stop this foolish display, I will never again—*(His
    attention is suddenly seized by the sound of an ap-
    proaching motor-car.)* Why, whatever is that?
TOAD. I've no idea. *(The sound gets louder as the ma-
    chine approaches at a terrific speed. The car's horn is
    sounded.)*
RAT. I think it wants us to get out of the way. Toad, get
    us over to the other side, and quickly! *(But TOAD is
    entranced.)*
TOAD. Beautiful…
RAT. Toad?
TOAD. Stirring sight…
RAT. Toad, did you hear what I said?
TOAD. It's a motor-car!
MOLE. Oh my. *(The car is upon them. The horn is
    sounded once again, and then there is a terrible crash.
    The carriage is turned on its side and ALL tumble out*

Using this scene from *The Wind in the Willows* on the previous page, I will break down the marking process. Mister Toad, Rat, and Mole find themselves in the middle of the Wild Wood. I will demonstrate arcs using two beats from this scene. The first one is when Mister Toad is bragging to Rat about his relationships with the weasels and ferrets in the Wild Wood and the second beat is when he sees a motorcar approaching.

Since bragging about himself is status quo for Mister Toad, I marked my script with a 3, when he tries to make his point about how popular he is in the Wild Wood, I marked my script with a 6. I continue this process until the end of the next beat. When he hears a sound but doesn't know what it is, I marked that with a 2, when he recognizes it as a motorcar, I marked that with a 10.

By the end of the two beats of this scene, I have the following numbers marking his emotional journey: 3, 6, 3, 6, 2, 2, 3, 10. As you can see since 10 is the highest number in the graph, it signifies the highest point of the arc of the scene for my character. The two markings of 3 and 6 represent two mini arcs, and the entire sequence starting at 3 and ending in 10 represent the journey of the main arc. You may also notice that I have two 2's in the sequence. The first number 2 represents the emotional tone of confusion, and the second 2 represents the emotional tone of wonder.

In my script, on the left side, I wrote the emotional tone numbers and drew straight lines representing the main arc movement. On the right side, I drew the mini arcs (representing the 3 and the 6) within the main arc.

You will notice, on the left side, that the straight line representing the main arc stops and then starts again. That is okay. I marked my script for my comprehension and know that it is still one arc, even though I have the arcs separated by a few lines of dialogue. As I've said before, you are marking your script to help remind you of the emotional journey for your character. As long as you understand what you mean by what you've written, that's all that matters.

Don't confuse a mathematical arc with an acting arc. A mathematical arc is a single curved line where as with an acting arc there can be a main single line arc with many curved lines beneath it that moves the scene forward. But there should be an arc somewhere in a scene. If you find that there is no numerical change to the emotion of your character in the scene, there are two things to consider:

1. Your character was written that way by the writer (they could be emotionally challenged or emotionally cut-off, devoid of feeling)
2. The character has not been explored enough by your own means of character and script analysis.

Explore all possibilities and chart the arcs your character is experiencing. You will find that your character has as many emotional peaks and valleys as anyone actually living. This concept can take some time to understand.

You may find during the course of rehearsals that the arcs may change and that's perfectly valid as long as you are not changing the arcs to manipulate your acting but to keep your character continuing on in their living and breathing journey.

ENDOWMENT

In the easiest of terms, endowment is the technique of filling an inanimate object with a quality or emotional value. By endowing an object that we interact with on stage, we are able to give it more meaning than just an ordinary object. There are schools of thought that believe an object can also be a person. However, I like to separate the two and use endowment primarily for inanimate objects and substitution primarily for living things. That's my preference but you should choose whatever works best for you. There are always exceptions to the rule but what matters most is that you produce the best results.

This is one of the easier techniques in this chapter to learn. So let's assume that you are doing the Laura/Amanda scene from *The Glass Menagerie* as previously described. You are using wooden figurines instead of glass. As you are doing the scene you find that you are treating the figurines like wood and not like glass so you need to endow it with the quality of glass.

ENDOWMENT EXERCISE

Find something that is glass that closely resembles the texture, weight, and fragility that you want. Now look at this object from all angles. Examine it closely. Look at the way the glass is formed, reflects light, shines, etc. Feel the weight of the object. Is it light? Heavy? How does the object feel? Is it cool? Warm? Rough? Smooth? Use all your senses: sight, sound, taste, touch, and smell. Don't confuse using your senses in this technique as sense memory. You are using them to fully explore your object.

Don't rush this process. Spend 15 – 30 minutes with the object. After you have explored the object, re-create the object in your mind and examine it the same way without actually using it. You are simply imagining it. Everything you did while the object was physically in your presence is now being done without it. Again, be specific, engaging all your senses, and spend about 15 – 30 minutes with the "object."

Once you have finished the exercise and feel you have the qualities of the "object" set in your mind. Go to your wooden figurine and place the value of the glass figurine to the wooden object. While the physical structure of the figurine hasn't changed, you should be able to believably give the wood the quality of glass and treating it as such. Try this with different objects. Find something you like, such as a stuffed animal, a picture, a cup and replace it with the quality of rotten food, a precious secret, a long lost friend, etc., using the same exercise as described.

When using something that is not tangible such as a precious secret, instead of using your senses to explore the intangible object, use your emotions. How does this object make you feel? Does it make you smile? Sad? Does it bring back a memory? Does your breathing change? Does your body move a certain way? You are using your emotions to explore the object; you are not doing an emotional recall.

After exploring this for about 15 – 30 minutes, take the emotion that the object has developed and apply it to another object. If you do this correctly, the object you are using should elicit the same emotional response as the original object.

SUBSTITUTION

This acting tool is a little more advanced than using the magic "if". Unlike the techniques of "if", sense memory, emotional recall, or endowment, substitution is primarily used to mentally take an image or essence of a person and replace that quality for someone or something else on stage. Usually you want to use an appropriate substitution for the scene that will aid in your emotion, tactic, status, etc.

You are not using the substitution directly on yourself but with the actor who is on stage with you. In preparation for this technique you may use your senses to help create that person's image in your mind's eye but when you are using the substitution technique on stage, you are using your brain to trigger or recall that image. If you use your senses to create a physical reaction in your body towards the person on stage you are not using substitution but rather sense memory. This is an entirely different technique. Substitution creates a person's image in your head while sense memory uses your senses to physically react to them.

. . Let's look at the characters Brick and Maggie from *Cat on a Hot Tin Roof.* During rehearsals you find that you have had a hard time creating this relationship on stage. The director has commented that the relationship isn't there and to work on it. At home you decide to use a substitution.

Pick a person who best represents the relationship that you want to create on stage. If you're Maggie, you want to pick someone that you might be close to and get affection from but can't. If you're Brick, you want to pick someone that you can tolerate but don't want to be around and absolutely have no sexual attraction for. It should be a relationship with which you have a strong connection and easily accessible to your memory but not something that might make you feel uncomfortable by bringing up feelings you haven't dealt with or don't want to confront.

When using substitution be as specific as you possibly can. While at home spend at least 15 – 30 minutes exploring the person and setting up the image in your head.

SUBSTITUTION EXERCISE

Start by using the Green Light Exercise from CHAPTER 4 to get yourself in a state of relaxation. Once you are in that state, begin to think about the person you want to use in your substitution. Think of their hair (length, color, smell), eyes (shape, color, spacing, sparkle), shape of their face (round, long, oval, gaunt), body (height, weight, shape, old, young), smell (perfume, cologne, soap, shampoo, sweet, musky), walk (length of gait, shuffles, strides) and talk (fast, slow, melodic, monotone, dialect). How does this person make you feel: happy, sad, angry, mad, jealous, indifferent? Where do you associate with them: work, home, school, park, laundry room? How old are they: baby, child, teen, adult, middle-aged, elderly? The more specific you are, the more successful the substitution will work for you.

Once you have the image or essence of this person firmly in your mind, find something about them to help you trigger their image to you in order to produce the emotion and/or connection that you are trying to re-create for the stage. Usually it will be one of the things you used when creating them in your mind. I find that their face or smell does it for me.

Now that you have your trigger, slowly stand up and go back to your lines, blocking or whatever you were working on. Periodically, use your trigger and see if the substitution works. If it does, then you have a strong connection to your substitution and you can draw on this when you need to, whether on stage or in a scene. If it doesn't, it may not be a strong enough trigger for that person or you may have picked a person that doesn't fit the substitution you need.

Sometimes when the connection isn't strong enough, you may have to do the exercise again, to build that substitution in your mind. If you find that the subject of your substitution still isn't working, change it. Nothing is ever set in stone. This is the beauty of acting...we make the choices and change them according to what we want to achieve on stage.

Sense Memory

Where substitution uses an image of a person, sense memory or affected memory uses one of your senses to trigger a physical state of being. I find using sound, smell, and taste, works best for me but you can also use sight or touch if that works better for you.

Using sense memory is used like substitution except it is your senses that are being activated for the technique and not your thinking. There are so many things in life we remember or feel when we encounter a certain smell, taste, touch, sight or sound. For instance, whenever I first step into a hot bath, I'm instantly teleported back to when I was a child and getting ready for school the night before by taking a bath. I can see the bathtub, the time of night, the day of the week, the feeling of anticipation for the next day of school and the soothing quality of the hot water. The feeling or sense memory only lasts a few seconds after stepping into the tub but I know if I want to create that state of being on stage, all I have to do is use the sense memory of a hot bath.

When using sense memory, pick senses that will create a strong reaction in your body. You are not acting like you are experiencing it but actually allowing your body to physically be affected by the sense memory you are recalling. A couple of strong sense memories that I use include: sandalwood (smell), bleach (smell), fingernails on a chalkboard (sound), jelly bellies (taste) and a puppy (sight). Each sense has an effect on me and each can be used to trigger that emotion if I need it on stage.

Since everyone has their own memories attached to different senses, it is impossible to use another actor's sense memory trigger as your own. You must find your own palette of emotional triggers through sense memory that you can pull out of your bag of tricks and use when you need them. You should have them engrained in your mind so clearly that the mere thought of them will send your mind and body into that emotional or physical state within seconds. This comes from diligent practice to train your brain to respond correctly. Just as with the substitution technique, do not use any sense memory that is hard for you to deal with or will make you feel uncomfortable when you do use it.

SENSE MEMORY EXERCISE #1

Start by using the Green Light Exercise from CHAPTER 4 to get yourself in a state of relaxation. Once you're in that state, you may do one of three things: continue to stay laying down, sit up cross-legged, or sit on your knees on the back of your heels, depending on whatever is comfortable for you. I prefer staying lying down. Keep the breath easy and relaxed. Now we are going to play around with different senses to see which one works best for you for what emotion you're trying to achieve. When you are working on each sensory organ, play around with different triggers and notice how they affect you emotionally. The more you explore, the more triggers you will have at your disposal.

Let's get to work starting with smell. I want you to think of something that makes you cringe when you smell it. Maybe it's bleach, rotten food, a skunk, etc. Imagine that scent, take a big whiff and really allow it to affect you. How does your body react? What does it make you think about? How does it make you feel? Is there an emotion attached to the sense memory? Does it remind you of anyone or a particular time in your life? Once you have experienced that, let it go, clear out your mind and go to the next scent or sense.

Let's try sound. While sitting, imagine a sound that makes you cringe. It may be a baby crying, an automobile crashing, or nails on a chalkboard. Really hear that sound in your head and see how your body reacts. Now find a sound that makes you shudder or react strongly. Ask yourself the same questions as before to get the most out of this sense. Once you have experienced that sense, let it go.

With touch it's a bit different, I want you to stand up and imagine there is a tub filled with nice hot water. Gently get into the tub and sit into it, feeling the hot water cover your skin, warming you up and touching your body. Fully explore the bath: play with the water, lift your legs up as if it is too hot, shampoo your hair – absorb the experience. How does this make you feel? What happens to your breathing? What memories pop up? Emotions? Images? As you are sitting there, I want you to imagine the water suddenly turns ice cold. How does your body react? What changes occur to you when that does happen? After you have completely explored and experienced the cold bath, let the water become hot again to soothe you and then at your own pace and when you are ready gently step out of the "bath" and let it go.

Repeat the same exercise with taste and sight using strong images that will produce a genuine and natural reaction from you. When I'm teaching beginning actors, I always have them sitting down eating a plate of food and describe to them what they are eating. As they get more involved with the exercise, I have them explore different food, eventually throwing in something that most people would not want to eat, i.e., dirt, worms, or maybe have them think of their least favorite food. It's amazing to see how they react and actually believe they are eating something when there is absolutely nothing in front of them.

Keep practicing your sense memory technique and soon you will have a plethora of images in your arsenal of tools to use on stage when you need them.

SENSE MEMORY EXERCISE #2– SUBSTANCE

This is a really fun exercise. Simply find something you would normally not cover yourself in and do just that. Pick something that will create a texture you are not used to having all over your body. Try pancake batter, shampoo, shaving cream, honey, flour, or eggs, the list is endless. Just pick something that texturally will challenge you. As it's going over your body, notice your initial reactions, what gets affected as it is covering your body. What does it feel like? What does it remind you of? How are your senses affected by this strange substance covering your body? Once your body is saturated in the substance that you picked, explore movement, weight, smell, taste, and sounds. Engage <u>ALL</u> your senses. Spend at least 15 – 30 minutes exploring the sensations that this new experience is creating. After you wash it off, notice if your body feels any different.

Emotional Recall

When discussing emotional recall people also use the term "affected memory". This is a technique that should be approached with caution because you can release emotions or memories that have not quite healed and could potentially cause emotional damage. That is why as I'm discussing this technique to remember, it is best to do it with someone who is very familiar with conducting emotional recall exercises and to how intense the session will be. As with any exercise or technique, emotional recall can range from light to heavy.

Now let us get on with the subject at hand. Where substitution replaces a person with an image of another person and sense memory uses the senses to affect our physical or mental state, we use emotional recall when we want to put ourselves into an emotional state that we are not currently in. We do this by choosing an event in our life with a strong emotional tie and recreating it in our mind. We use this emotional memory to trigger an emotional response when we need it on stage and can't get there through natural acting ability. Emotional recall is one of the most potent techniques an actor can use and should be explored judiciously.

Be careful when you are choosing the event that you want to use for your emotional recall. You should use one that is not a recent memory. I've been told to use one that is older than seven years. If you choose one that is fresher in your memory it may not be fully absorbed into your muscle memory to be fully effective or you risk bringing up feelings that you have yet to resolve within yourself and could cause an emotional waterfall. Also, don't use a memory that brings up personally negative feelings for you that you haven't dealt with yet. This could cause emotional repercussions and put you in a state of mind that you don't want to be in.

It is also important to understand that when you use emotional recall, you are actually convincing your mind to produce the emotion that you want to experience. Make sure you are in a safe space so you can experience it without feeling self-conscious that someone is going to walk in on you and your acting coach. Remember, you should not attempt this on your own. Even when you attend and train at an acting school, they usually do this with the class together.

If you do decide to attempt this alone, I've included one exercise (with a variation) on the next few pages to help you achieve your goal of recreating that memory to attain that emotional connection.

EMOTIONAL RECALL EXERCISE # 1

Start by using the Green Light Exercise from CHAPTER 4 to get yourself in a state of relaxation. Once you're in this state, stay lying down and put yourself 15 minutes before the event that you are recreating happened. Be specific. Where are you? What time is it? What is the day like? What season? What do you hear? What do you see? What do you smell? Is there anyone else with you?, etc.

Once you have thoroughly explored what surrounds you, allow yourself to go through the actions that occurred prior to the event (in your head.) As you progress, keep the specifics of your memory clear and focused. Your body should remain relaxed and your breathing nice and easy. As you progress with the exercise, the "time" in your memory should decrease in five-minute increments towards the specific event you are recreating. Each five-minute increment could last as much as ten minutes depending on how specific you are with your exploration. At each increment continue to be specific to the sensory sensations you are remembering. Eventually, you will get to the moment that you are trying to re-create in your mind. When you do, allow the emotion to fill your body, allow your breathing to mirror the emotion that you are feeling, if you need to make a sound as you are bringing back the memory then make it.

Now that you are in the moment of the event, slowly get out of your reclining position, stand up, and allow your body to go through the actions that you did when this event happened. Don't hold back. Let yourself express the emotion openly. Continue to explore the emotion, go beyond the actual "real time" of the event as if that moment has been frozen in time. After you have explored the emotion, and the event has been successfully re-created, both emotionally and physically, bring yourself to a neutral standing position if you're standing or to a neutral lying position if you are on the ground. Allow the memory to gradually recede, use your breath to ground yourself. Take in deep even breaths. This normally should take about 5 – 10 minutes.

With your mind and body relaxed and back to a state of neutrality, slowly stand up and think about what you experienced. What did you feel? What senses were more activated? Try to find one or two senses or images that stood out that you feel could bring back that emotion. Use those moments in your memory/senses as your trigger for this emotional recall memory. If you have the time when you are performing before a show, you can do a shortened version of this exercise to get into that same state of mind. If not, then do the exercise at home and keep the trigger accessible so you can use it to get your mind in that state when you need it.

Take note that, after doing an emotional recall exercise, you may experience emotional residue for the emotion you were experiencing. This is natural, just remember it is only residue and not real. Eventually it will pass. If you continue to feel the emotion, especially if it's a negative emotion you were recreating such as sadness, jealousy, anger, etc., try to do something that you normally do to get yourself out of that particular state of mind.

Also, you may employ the use of an acting coach or fellow actor familiar with emotional recall to lead you through the exercise so you can concentrate completely without the distraction of trying to do it yourself. This is also a very good choice to make so that they can monitor you to make sure that you stay grounded and in control.

Note: If you do use someone to lead you through this, please make sure it is someone you can trust and is very familiar with this exercise since it is a very emotionally opening experience and can place you in an extremely vulnerable state.

Use emotional recall **only** when you are unable as an actor to create the emotion through sense memory, normal ability or talent. It is a tool and should be used as such.

EMOTIONAL RECALL EXERCISE #2 – LOSS/BETRAYAL

Bring back a memory involving loss or betrayal specifically, following the exact instructions as I laid out in the Emotional Recall exercise. Doing this exercise with loss and betrayal is great for opening up and allowing yourself to be vulnerable and truthful.

CHAPTER 5: VOICE

Voice Overview 130

Warming Up the Voice And Exercises 131

Relaxation 132

Posture and Alignment 135

Respiration and Positioning 140

Phonation 143

Support 146

Registration 149

Resonance 151

Articulation 153

Articulation warm-up 158

Your 30-Minute Vocal Warm-Up 161

VOICE OVERVIEW

I've never learned so much or understood the complexities of the voice until I studied with Nova Thomas at Actors Studio Drama School – The New School University. It was here that I finally understood and grasped the concepts behind the voice and what makes a great vocal instrument.

I use the word instrument because it is just that. The voice is the musical instrument of the actor. The breath supports the sound. The sound supports the emotion, objective, and tactic. Together they support the breath of life for your character. As with any musical instrument, you must constantly practice with it: learn how to control the breath, support the sound, energize the last note and sustain the sound without losing the support.

Besides the use of breath, sound is also important. The voice is capable of producing a variety of pitches, tempos, rhythms, and styles. Like singing, the speaking voice is able to achieve staccato, legato, rallentando, glissandos, and other musical expressions associated with singing. Don't be afraid to explore the sound of your voice.

Remember that breath and voice go hand-in-hand. Having control over our breath and sound can help in many situations including nervousness, speaking too fast, forgetting our lines, lack of vocal support, stammering, fumbling over words, and so on. If you find yourself in a situation like that, simply pause for a moment, take a relaxing breath in, and start again. As Nova reminded us so many times, "Redemption is only a breath away."

WARMING UP THE VOICE AND EXERCISES

Warming up the voice is essential before rehearsing or performing. It helps to ease the voice into breathing correctly, creating a strong foundation for support and prepares your lips and tongue for speaking.

The elements of voice[1] consist of Relaxation, Posture and Alignment, Respiration and Positioning, Phonation, Support, Registration, Resonance, and Articulation. You should always perform vocal exercises before a rehearsal, performance, audition, or acting class.

It is very **IMPORTANT** that when you use your voice or warming-up your instrument that you start at the foundation step: relaxation and work in order. Imagine each area as a stepping-stone in a pond. You have to step on the first one before you can proceed further and reach the other side. You could jump to the second or third one but you might slip and fall in the pond. The same can be said for the elements of good vocal production. You can't have good articulation and placement if resonance hasn't been warmed-up, and you can't have a strong hold on resonance if your registration isn't tuned, and so on. So start on relaxation and work in order. I will now introduce you to exercises[2] to help warm up the voice and the order to follow with each vocal area.

---

[1] Notes taken from Thomas, N. (Fall 2006). Voice and Speech III. Actors Studio Drama School, New School University.

[2] Exercise notes taken from Thuman, T. (Fall 1991). Voice I. Pacific Conservatory of the Performing Arts, Allan Hancock College.

RELAXATION

Having a relaxed body is just as important to your voice as is the ease of breath. It is conducive to performing at your best. Remember to always breathe and check in with your body for any unneeded tension. Instead of using your muscles to physically adjust any tenseness in your body, use your breath to release and ease the tension. Always apply tension on the inhale, and release of tension on the exhale. It's never the other way around.

When doing any relaxation exercise lying down, don't drift off and fall asleep. Stay focused at all times. The best way to accomplish this is to do "active breathing". This means the breathing is steady, not too deep and not too shallow. If it's too deep you won't be able to relax and if it's too shallow, you will fall asleep.

LAVA

Lie down flat on the floor. Imagine your body being filled with hot lava. Take nice even breaths in through the nose and exhale through your mouth. Once you have established a relaxed rhythm of breathing, imagine that your body is being filled with lava.

Starting at your toes, imagine it filling your ankles, claves, knees, thighs, buttocks, stomach, back, chest, shoulders, arms, hands, fingers, neck, and head. Go slowly starting at your toes and ending at your head.

As you are imagining your body being filled with the lava, allow your body to sink into the ground. Your breathing should remain steady and unforced. Allow your body to maintain the feeling of this thick liquid filling every space.

Continue breathing and then, starting at your toes and working up in the same order, imagine that the hot lava is cooling down. As it does, it becomes hard and non-pliable. As the lava hardens, imagine your body sinking deeper into the ground.

Once you have maintained the hardened lava in your body, allow it to form back into its original form using the same order of body parts. Once the hardened lava has been transformed back into a hot liquid, allow it to stay in your body and then, starting at your head and working down, replace the hot, heavy lava with a light, airy quality. Your body should still be relaxed and sinking into the ground. Once all the lava has been transformed, continue breathing and then stand up by rolling to your side and gently standing up with your feet firmly planted on the ground, pushing up from the knees, and rolling up the spine.

NEUTRAL POSITION

This is also known as the Center Stance. Stand with your feet parallel to your shoulders. The weight of your body should be evenly distributed to both feet. Your feet should be facing forward, knees slightly bent, pelvis slightly tucked (imagine that a string is attached to your tailbone and it is gently pulling down), spine elongated, shoulders blades slightly touching and dropped, chin forward, head above the spine (imagine that there is a string at the crown of your head and that it is gently pulling up), and the neck free.

DEEP BREATHING

With a nice center stance take a few deep breaths in through your nose and out through your mouth. If you have problems with that, you may breathe in and out through your mouth. Breathe in and out on a relaxed count of 4.

TENSE AND RELEASE

In the neutral position or lying down after doing the "Lava" exercise, tighten and relax all the muscle groups in your body. Starting with the toes and ending with the face, focus on one part of the body at a time and only tighten that part, isolating it from the other parts of your body. Relax that part of the body and move on to the next one.

POSTURE AND ALIGNMENT

The order for tightening and releasing is: feet, calves, thighs, stomach, back, chest, hands, arms, neck, and face. After you have isolated each body part and tightened it, tighten the entire body at once. Hold it for a slow count of 10 and then release on an even, controlled exhalation.

During this exercise always remember to keep breathing and checking in with your body to make sure that you aren't tightening any other

FIRE BREATHING

Sit in a relaxed position, usually in a crossed-leg position. If you are unable to do this then sit on the back of your heels with something under your knees for cushioning. You are going to inhale and exhale six times in total.

For the first two times, inhale/exhale while imagining where you are physically and mentally right now. For the second time, inhale/exhale twice in a neutral state of being. Your mind should be clear. For the third time, inhale/exhale twice, with the idea of being ready to work.

Posture and Alignment

Don't confuse a slouched body with relaxation. When standing, refer to the "Neutral Position" exercise in the Relaxation section for the correct way to stand. In addition, imagine that a string is pulling from the top of your head to the ceiling and a string pulling down from the bottom of your tailbone to the ground. Your body should feel elongated not stretched. There should be no tenseness in your body, only the feeling of ease as your body is occupying space.

NOBLE POSTURE ASSESSMENT

This should be done between exercises to make sure it is in place. This is almost the same as a neutral position except for a few minor differences. Check for the head on top of the spine, neck free, sternum up, shoulder blades slightly touching and down, abs ready to expand.

GARDEN WALK DOWN THE SPINE

Start in a neutral position. On a relaxed exhale, allow your head to drop gently from the neck. Continue to breathe as you roll down the spine, one vertebra at a time, until you are flopped over at the waist with your knees slightly bent and your hands touching the ground.

GARDEN WALK UP THE SPINE

This will be used whenever you are bent over and need to return to an upright position. As you exhale, slowly roll your spine up by placing each vertebra on top of the one before it; your shoulders should remain neutral and not raised. The last thing that is placed is your head on top of your neck. Remember to keep the neck elongated.

MARIONETTE STRETCH

Raise arms up. Stretch them. Imagine reaching for something you want with a string pulling your fingers up. Then drop in order:

135

1. Hands - As you drop the hands the string moves to your wrist, now your wrists are stretching up.
2. Forearms – Drop at the elbows. Now the string has moved to your elbows and you are stretching with them.
3. Upper arms – As you drop your arms, your shoulders should still be raised, the string now pulling your shoulders up.
4. Shoulders – As you drop and release your shoulders, allow an easy, relaxing sigh to exit your mouth.

Remember to keep stretching while dropping and to breathe. Also, keep your neutral position, checking in with your body that everything is in place. Refer to the "Neutral Position" in the Relaxation section if you need a reminder.

SIDE STRETCHES

Raise your left arm and curve it over your head and stretch it to the right. Your right arm should be curved under your chest and pointing to the left. Now gently bend at the waist to the left. Imagine that a string is pulling your hands in the opposite direction. Breathe while you are stretching. Reverse the arm positions and repeat. Use your breath to stretch your ribcage.

RAILROAD CHICKEN

I will admit that this is not my favorite of exercises but some people seem to get something out of it so I am including it in this section.

In a neutral position, look ahead and imagine that a train is approaching. As the train gets closer, increase the rate of your breathing. You should be almost panting by the time the train is on top of you. As it passes through, allow yourself to give a relaxed sigh. Remember, you are directing your energy out as you are breathing and your body is continually in the neutral position. Don't forget to check in with your body.

HEAD ROLLS

With a fluid motion, rotate your neck in a clockwise movement, stretching the neck gently. As you stretch the back of your neck, don't crunch the neck down. This puts pressure on your top vertebrae and can cause damage. Instead, imagine that a string is pulling the neck up and at a slight angle. Once you have completed eight rotations of the neck, reverse the direction. Remember, as you are rotating your head back, think up not down.

ARM LOCK

Put your arms behind your back and clasp your hands. With a gentle stretch, pull your arms up and out, breathing into your ribcage as you do. Your arms should be pointing towards the ceiling, or as close as you can do without hurting yourself. It's about stretching not pain.

SHOULDER ROLLS

Keeping your arms down, imagine there is a pencil attached to the side of the shoulder and draw a circle on the wall that it is facing.

1. Rotate right shoulder backwards in an easy, fluid motion. (8 counts)
2. Rotate it forward. (8 counts)
3. Repeat 1 and 2 with the left shoulder.
4. Rotate the right and left shoulders backwards, alternating between each one.
5. Reverse the direction. (8 counts)
6. Rotate the right and left together
   a. Backwards (8 counts)
   b. Forward (8 counts).

7. Raise your shoulders up and hold (8 counts)
8. Release on a sigh.

ARM SWINGS

Swing your arms in a circle at your sides. Imagine your arms are drawing a giant circle from the ceiling to the floor and that there is a string pulling and stretching your fingers to get the stretch. As your arms are rotating keep stretching and make sure your shoulders are being fully rotated in a fluid motion. Use the same pattern that you did for the shoulders.

NECK STRETCHES

Gently bend your head to the right. Put your right hand on the side of your head and let the weight gently stretch your neck. Stretch for eight counts, allowing the breath to stretch your neck. Let your hand be the weight on your head. Don't strain yourself when you stretch. It should be a gentle stretch. After you perform the stretch to the right, release your hand and let your head and neck return to an elongated position. Repeat this stretch to the left.

NECK STRETCHES WITH ARMS

When you add arms to this stretch, everything is the same, except, as you gently bend your head to the right, raise your left arm so it is out-stretched and parallel to the floor. As you exhale, slowly lower your arm to your side as your hand gently applies its weight to your head. You should feel a stretch in your neck. After you do this to the right, release your hand and let your head and neck return to an elongated position. Repeat this stretch to the left.

RAGDOLL

Bring your arms in and stretch up. As you reach up imagine grabbing for something. Allow that stretch to happen for a count of eight. Drop over at the hips while bending the knees. Allow the body to fold and your arms, neck, head, and shoulders to drop. Feel the stretch in the lower back. Slowly roll back up by doing the "Garden Walk Up the Spine".

TENNIS SWINGS

Start by moving your head slowly, turning it to the right and left. After doing this a few times, allow your shoulders to be included in this movement. This should cause your arms to slowly move back and forth in front of you. Your arms should be relaxed and you should not be controlling them, their movement is a direct result from your head and shoulders alternating from the right to the left. Let your upper torso join in the fun and match the movement of your head and shoulders this should make your arms swing more and start to swing more side to side, your hands slapping gently along your sides. Bend at the knees, and really let your arms swing. Once the whole body is activated, allow yourself to do this a few times, and then going in reverse start to slow down so that your torso comes to a neutral position, then the shoulders, and finally the head, so your body returns to the neutral position.

SIX-SIDED BOX

Imagine your body as a box: Head (top) Chest (front) Abs (bottom), the back (back), Right and Left Shoulders (R and L side of box). Isolate five of the sides and breathe through the non-isolated area. Feel that area that you have isolated expand. Obviously, we can only breathe into our lungs but we want to visualize that the breathe is going to and expanding the isolated area. Repeat until all sides have been done.

Note: For additional Posture and Alignment stretching exercises see the following sections in CHAPTER 7, WARM-UP: BASIC STRUCTURE and ADDITIONAL WARM-UP STRETCHES

RESPIRATION AND POSITIONING

Respiration is another way of saying "breathing." Having control of your breath is very important to the overall production of the sound that comes out. Positioning refers to the placement of the soft palate, which is located at the back of your throat. When you yawn, your soft palate raises up. This is the position your soft palate should be in when you are speaking. Practice making a yawn and opening your soft palate but don't actually yawn. If you do yawn, that's okay though, it means that you are positioning your soft palate correctly. To create proper positioning, keep this checklist in mind: Mouth slightly open, soft palate raised, jaw slightly dropped and relaxed, larynx dropped, and shoulders released.

THE SNAKE

Take in a deep breath and exhale on "sss". Use tiniest opening, allow the "sss" to continue until you are at the point of almost running out of breath and then gently release on a "ah", i.e., "sss – ah".

LUNG VACUUM

Release all air in lungs. Shake out the rest and cover your nose and mouth (this ensures that no breath can get in). Try to take a deep breath and perform the "Chest Expansion" exercise. Really try to take in the breath then release mouth and nose, breathing in deeply.

DO NOT under any circumstances allow yourself to get to the point of light-headedness before releasing the hands and taking in the deep breath. If you find you are getting light-headed, bend your knees and rest your arms on your thighs as you are bending over and looking at the ground. This should help alleviate that feeling.

PICKING GRAPES

Bring arms in and out and up, reach and try to grab grapes. Arms should be stretching and fingers extended. Alternating right and left, stretch your hands up and pick the grapes, taking in breaths as you do, when your lungs are filled up, and can't take any more air into your lungs, release the breath and do a "Ragdoll" followed by the "Garden Walk Up the Spine".

BREATHING ON COUNTS

Take a breath on a four count and release on a four count. Snap your fingers to set the tempo of the count. Increase the counts i.e., inhale on eight, exhale on eight, inhale on twelve, exhale on twelve, inhale on sixteen, exhale on sixteen. This exercise is used to increase your lung capacity for air.

Alternative version – Inhale on a low count and exhale on a higher count. Example: Inhale on one, exhale on four, inhale on two, exhale on eight, inhale on three, exhale on twelve, etc.

GASPS

1. Breathe naturally
2. Breathe slightly faster
3. Breathe a little faster
4. Breathe as fast as you can
5. Breathe irregularly
6. Take a deep breath
7. Gasp deeply
8. Gasp irregularly

How does each of these breaths affect you? How does it make you feel?

RESPIRATION AND POSITIONING

NASAL BREATHING

Plug one nostril and breathe in through other nostril. Hold for a few seconds and exhale through the nostril that was plugged. Reverse order.

ALTOID BREATHING

This is a great exercise to become aware of your open positioning and soft palate. Chew an Altoid and open the soft palate, take a breath, you should feel the cool air on your soft palate.

"KAH"

Keeping your mouth open, take a breath in and exhale the breath, releasing on a "Kah."

PHONATION

Phonation consists of producing sounds. The sound should be clear and relaxed. You should not feel any tension in your throat or any other part of your body when producing sound. Be sure to allow the breath to flow over the soft palate and at the roof of your hard palate as it exits the mouth. If you find you are running out of breath as you are doing these exercises, do not allow yourself to lose the sound. Instead, allow the rest of your breath to be released on a small sigh. The breath should be consistent and controlled. This, in turn, will allow the voiced sound to be the same.

Some people speak in a higher or lower pitch contrary to where their voice should naturally be placed. When warming up with phonation, we want to use the tone where our voice naturally sits. This can also be known as the "Anchor Pitch". You know you have found your correct anchor pitch when you can speak or sing four tones above it and four tones below it and not strain the voice in either direction. It is not uncommon for our "Anchor Pitch" to be a different tone than our speaking voice. Ideally, the "Anchor Pitch" should be our natural speaking voice not the voice we habitually speak in.

Here is an example of finding your anchor pitch. Start with middle C on a piano, move up the scale: D, E, F, G. Now, again starting at middle C, move down the scale: B, A, G, F. If the notes were easily accessible in both directions without strain then middle C is your anchor pitch.

For the purposes of phonation, I like to equate breath and sound with waves and surfing. A surfboard does not ride before the wave, it catches the wave and rides on it. This is the same thing with breath and sound. The breath starts, the voice follows the breath. When sound precedes breath, it will create a glottal or an abrupt sound.

Another example to explain a glottal or abrupt stop is to think of the word "how". In English, we aspirate the "h" in the word. The breath starts, the "h" follows and we get "how. In Cockney, the "h" isn't pronounced so the start of the word becomes glottal. The sound starts before the word, sounding like "ow".

JAW SHAKES

Clasp your hands in front of you, hold them up at chest level and shake them, allow the jaw to be free and move with the shake. Your jaw should move freely. If it is not, then you are holding tension and not allowing it to be released.

JAW SHAKES WITH SOUND

Same as Jaw Shakes, just add a light "Ah" sound as you are shaking your clasped hands.

JAW MASSAGE

Bring thumbs to the top of the jawbone (behind the ears) and slowly massage down to the chin. Allow the jaw to drop and the jaw muscles to be massaged.

Alternate Version - Use the heels of your hands, the side furthest from the thumb and massage down. It should be a firm press starting at the top of the jawline and moving slowly down to the sides of the chin. Don't push too hard. Remember to breathe as you are doing this exercise. If your jaw has tension you will feel some pain. This muscle is usually ignored and doesn't get the same massaging attention like the neck, shoulder and back muscles do. Just breathe through it.

SIGHS

Find a tone that you are comfortable with producing, preferably the "Anchor Pitch". Not too high or too low. Gently inhale and then exhale with a relaxed, unforced sigh of release. The sound should be more on the breathy side with a hint of voiced sound. Once you have done this exercise with your anchor pitch, try using different pitches for your sighs and experiment with falling pitches. The sigh should have more breathy sound to it.

MOANS

Same as the "Sighs" exercise but less breathy with an elongated sound. The moan should have a less breathy sound to it and sound fuller.

SOUND GATHERER

With your lips closed around the teeth, gather a "hmmm" sound in your mouth, filling the cavity with the sound and release on "mah". Do not force the sound out. Let it come out naturally.

SUPPORT

Support comes from your diaphragm, which is situated below your lungs and above your stomach. When you breathe in, your diaphragm expands, pushing your stomach down and, at the same time, causing the lungs and ribcage to expand. As you exhale, the diaphragm, stomach, lungs and ribcage return to their natural position. When you exhale, allow the diaphragm to stay firm until the very end. Again, don't confuse firm with tension. This is the basis of support. Remember this mantra: "Support is the refusal to collapse".

PANTING

Using your diaphragm, allow your diaphragm to move quickly in and out, creating a pant. Start of slowly and then increase the rate which the diaphragm contracts in and out. Keep in mind, that if you get light headed stop and bend at the knees and rest your arms on y our thighs while looking at the ground until the light-headedness goes away.

"HELLO JOE"

Stand 10 – 15' away from a wall. Using a good position with your soft palate, take a relaxed, deep breath and call out "Hello Joe, those old boats won't float." Use a strong, projected, and supported sound with a nice chest voice, keeping it at medium to low tones. It's best to use your anchor pitch. You should practice standing as far away from a wall as you can and still having your voice reach it. Be sure to keep your mouth completely open for the "O" sounds in the phrase. Do not rush through the phrase either. It should have a slight drawn out feel to it as you are saying the phrase.

SUSPENSION

Inhale on a two count, suspend the breath in your chest for four counts then release the breath on a "sss" or "zzz" for eight counts. Try increasing the counts but keep the counts in the same numerical fashion, i.e., inhale on two, suspend for six, exhale on ten. The exhalation is longer than the suspension, which is longer than the inhalation. This pattern will stay the same up to a six-count inhalation. When you reach an eight-count inhalation, the suspension count will lower to avoid getting lightheaded, so if you inhale on an eight count, you may only suspend the breath for a four count and then release on a twelve count.

RIB BREATHING

Inhale with a relaxed breath on a four or eight count and feel the bottom ribs expand, release air on "sss" or "zzz" until almost empty, then end on a sigh. As you exhale, try to keep the bottom ribs expanded. Keep increasing the count. Do this exercise until you feel you have stretched and expanded the ribcage to its fullest.

PAINTING THE ROOM

This is an extension of the "Wall Coloring" exercise in the RESPIRATION section only now you are painting the entire room. Take a nice deep breath on an eight count. As you are breathing in, imagine a color in your mind. This is the color you will be painting the room. As you exhale, create a small opening in your lips like making a whistle and exhale the color through breath and paint the wall opposite of you. As you reach the end of your breath, gently exhale it out. Never under any circumstance should you allow yourself to lose your breath and run out of air. Chose different colors to paint the room. Be specific.

WALL COLORING

This uses the same principle that we used for Painting the Room. Take a nice deep breath on an eight count. As you are breathing in, imagine a color in your mind. This is the color you will be painting on the wall. As you exhale, create a small opening in your lips like you're whistling and exhale the color through breath and paint the wall opposite of you. As you reach the end of your breath, gentle exhale it out. Never under any circumstance should you allow yourself to lose your breath and run out of air. Choose different colors to paint the wall.

SPELLING NAME

The process is exactly the same as the Wall Coloring exercise except when you exhale you will spell your name on the wall.

UMBRELLA

Imagine you are opening up like an umbrella. Put your hands under your armpits like a. chicken. As you take a deep breath in, lift your elbows up, and imagine your breath is opening them up like an umbrella.

MOVE OBJECT

Find an object in the room. Imagine how it would feel to pick up and move that object using your breath. Take a nice, relaxed, deep breath and while looking at the object, expel the air with the force that would move it. Pick different objects. Each object should require a different amount of breath to be moved.

REGISTRATION

The voice has the capability to reach high and low pitches. Registration refers to these vocal qualities. Chest voice usually refers to the lower pitches while head voice refers to the higher pitches. However, when warming up the voice for speaking and singing, try to incorporate aspects of chest in your head voice and head in your chest voice. The idea is that both are connected not separated.

"HOO"

Take a relaxed, deep breath. On the exhalation, use a head voice texture (not too high), and allow a "Hoo" to come out. You should sound like an owl.

"ZAH"

Take a relaxed, deep breath. On the exhalation, use a chest voice texture (not too low), and allow a "Zah" to come out easily and relaxed.

SIREN

Starting with a relaxed breath, release on a "Zah", go up the scale starting with your chest voice and open to your head voice on a "Ooh" sound and then back down to your chest voice on a "Zah." Try to blend the two registers together. This is good for helping to smooth over the break in the two registers and creating a fuller sound.

YODELS

Same as the siren only you are going at a quicker pace and you do it about 4 or five times.

PIANO EXERCISES

If you can play piano, run basic scale exercises. Alternate between "Zah" and "Hoo". Stretch your high and low range but don't strain the voice. It's about warming the vocal chords and range, not about over-doing it.

RESONANCE

Sound bounces off our skull and the roof of our mouth (the hard palate). This creates resonance and adds a nice vocal quality to the sound we produce. When you are warming up with humming, you should feel a buzzing on your lips. If you are very observant, you can feel the resonance in your skull when you allow the sound to leave the exit route (your mouth).

HUM ON "M"

With an open position, take a breath and then hum through your lips with the sound of "mmm". You should feel the resonance in the mask and a slight tickling sensation in your lips and nose.

CHEW AND HUM ON "M"

This is the same as the previous exercise only you are adding a "chew". With an open position, chew and hum through it with the sound of "mmm". As you are chewing move your jaw up and down and all around as if you are grotesquely chewing. You should not feel a tickling sensation.

HUM INTO CUP

Starting in the neutral position with your feet slightly wider apart, bend over at the waist, put the back of your hand into the palm of the other, creating something that looks like a cup (when you drink water with your hands), hum into the center of your hand as you slowly do a "Garden Walk Up the Spine". Halfway up, open arms out to your sides as hands open, release "ah" sound, slowly bringing arms to your side. Your arms should reach your sides as you are finishing the sound. Don't let yourself run out of breath, which will tighten your throat. As you near the end of breath and sound, let it end on a gentle decrescendo.

PUMMEL AND RIB HUG

Slightly pummel your back as you are rolling down, find bottom ribs, place thumbs 1" from spine, breathe into hands, release on "Zah". Feel the resonance in the chest.

A, E, I, O, U

This exercise uses the long vowel sounds "AY", "EE", "EYE", "OH', and "OOH'. Start by taking a nice, relaxed breath in. As the breath is released say the vowels but keep them connected, use a "yuh" sound to connect the vowels if needed. There should not be a separation between the sounds. The breath starts the sound. There should be an awareness of resonance. This exercise works on range as well.

FACE STRETCH (JACK O'LANTERN)

With a nice "Ah" sound, stretch your face as wide as you can then tighten it, imagining that you are squishing your face into your nose as you are saying "Ooh". Repeat this stretch, going quicker and quicker. This works on tone.

ARTICULATION

No matter how much you warm-up your instrument, if you speak quietly, mumble your words, or speak too fast the audience won't understand you. Your tongue and lips are just as important to producing sound as anything else. Do not over enunciate the consonant sounds. They should be crisp and clean.

PINKY PRESS
Stick your tongue out and press the tip against your pinky. Release and continue. This will help strengthen your tongue and tighten the tip of it so you can produce the sounds that require it especially T's, D's, S's and Z's.

LICKING ICE CREAM
Imagine you are holding an ice cream cone and licking it, starting with the flat of your tongue and ending at the tip. This stretches tongue and helps flatten tongue.

TONGUE SIGHS
Stretch your tongue out of your mouth and release a relaxed sigh. This exercise stretches the back of the tongue.

TONGUE SNAPS
Snap your tongue at the edge of your hard palate just above and behind your front teeth. This strengthens tongue.

LIP AND TONGUE FLUTTERS
Flutter your lips on a hum. Keep the breath moving. If you find your lips stalling out on you it's because you are not getting enough air out. Add tongue flutters to this drill by trilling it behind your teeth while you flutter your lips.

B'S, P'S, D'S, T'S, G'S, K'S, V'S, F'S – AH

Say each consonant sound with an "Ah" sound attached: bah, pah, dah, etc. This loosens the articulators and helps you use your lips and tongue more.

VOICED AND UNVOICED CONSONANTS

Take a nice, easy inhale in and exhale out as you do each consonant in the set. The consonants that you will use are:

Buh - Puh, Duh -Tuh, Guh - Kuh, Vuh - Fuh, and Zuh - Suh.

The pattern goes like this:
Buh, Buh, Buh, Buh/
Buh-buh-buh-buh-buh-buh-buh-buh-buh-buh/
Buh-buh-buh-buh-buh-buh-buh-buh-buh-buh/
Buh-buh-buh-buh-buh-buh-buh-buh-buh-buh/
Buh-buh-buh-buh-buh-buh-buh-buh-buh-buh/

Puh, Puh, Puh, Puh/
Puh-puh-puh-puh-puh-puh-puh-puh-puh-puh/
Puh-puh-puh-puh-puh-puh-puh-puh-puh-puh/
Puh-puh-puh-puh-puh-puh-puh-puh-puh-puh/
Puh-puh-puh-puh-puh-puh-puh-puh-puh-puh/

Repeat with each set of the voiced and unvoiced pairs. Below is the rhythmic pattern written out musically.

TONGUE TEASERS

Use your favorite tongue teasers to work on diction, speed and clarity. Here are a few to get you started:

1. "Will you walk a little faster?" said the whiting to the snail,
    "There's a porpoise close behind us and he's treading on our tail."
    "See how eagerly the lobsters and the turtles all advance?"
    "Will you, won't you, will you, won't you, will you join the dance?"
    "Won't you, will you, won't you, will you, won't you join the dance?"
    Will you, won't you, will you, won't you, will you join the dance?"

2. You need New York
    Unique New York
    You know you need unique New York.

3. Whether the weather be cold.
    Or whether the weather be hot.
    We'll be together, whatever the weather
    Whether we like it or not.

4. What a to-do to die today at a minute or two 'til two
    A thing distinctly hard to say but harder still to do
    For they'll beat a tattoo at a twenty to two
    With a rat-a-tat, tat-a-tat, tat-a-tat-too
    And the dragon will come when he hears the drum
    At a minute or two 'til two today, at a minute or two 'til two.

5. Amidst the mists and coldest frosts
    With stoutest wrists and loudest boasts
    He thrusts his fists against the posts
    And still insists he sees the ghosts.

6. She clasps the asps and wisps of wasps,
    She risks the thefts of all the masks,
    She sifts the rifts in all the gifts,
    But asks that lisps be not her tasks.

7. Peter Piper picked a peck of pickled peppers
    A peck of pickled peppers Peter Piper picked
    If Peter Piper picked a peck of pickled peppers
    How many pecks of pickled peppers did Peter Piper pick?

8. To sit in solemn silence in a dull, dark dock,
    In a pestilential prison, with a life-long lock,
    Awaiting the sensation of a short, sharp shock,
    From a cheap and chippy chopper on a big black block!

9. They giggled and scribbled and gurgled and squabbled and
    burbled and battled then judged it and loathed it, so moved it and
    changed it – enlarged it and clothed it and dubbed it and loved it
    all.

10. Betty Botta bought some butter
    "But", she said, "this butter's bitter.
    If I put it in my batter
    It will make my batter bitter.
    But a bit of better butter
    Will make my bitter batter better."
    So she bought a bit of butter
    Better than the bitter butter

And it made her bitter batter better.
So 'twas better Betty Botta bought
A bit of better butter.

11. Give me the gift of a grip-top sock
    A clip drape ship shape tip-top sock
    Not your spiv-slick slapstick slip shod stock
    But a plastic elastic grip-top sock
    None of your fantastic slack swop slop
    From a slap dash flash cash haberdash shop
    Not a kick-knack knit lock knock-kneed knickerbocker sock
    With a mock shot blob-mottled trick ticker-top clock
    Not a rucked up puckered up flop top sock
    Not a super sheer seersucker rucksack sock
    Not a spot-speckled frog-freckled cheap sheik's sock
    Off a hodge-podge moss-blotched Scotch-botched block
    Nothing slipshod drip drop flip flop or glip glop
    Tip me to a tip-top grip-top sock.

12. She sells seashells down by the seashore.

13. Mommala Poppala

14. Culligan and Calla-Lily

15. Rubber baby buggy bumpers

16. Red leather, yellow leather

17. Round the rugged rocks the ragged rascals ran

18. When tweedle beetles battle with paddles in a puddle
    They call it a tweedle beetle puddle paddle battle.

19. The lips, the teeth, the tip of the tongue, The tip of the tongue,
    the teeth, the lips.

ARTICULATION WARM-UP

Prepare the body with facial isolations, stretches, shakeouts, and lip blowing.

1. THE LIPS
    Cover the lips with each other; "shoot staples," replace breath between each "buh."
    a. Buh-Buh-Buh-Buh (repeat several times)
    b. Buhbuhbuh-buhbuhbuh-buhbuhbuh-buh (repeat)
    c. Bibble-bi, bibble-bi, bibble-bi-bi
    d. Repeat the whole series on a whisper, substituting "P" for "B."

2. TONGUE TIP
    No jaw movement; tongue tip is on upper gum ridge just behind where the teeth and gums meet.
    a. Duh-Duh-Duh-Duh (repeat several times)
    b. Duhduhduh-duhduhduh-duhduhduh-duh (repeat
    c. Diddle-di, diddle-di diddle-di-di (repeat)
    d. Repeat the whole series on a whisper, substituting "T" for "D."

3. BACK OF TONGUE AND SOFT PALATE
    No jaw movement; tongue tip is anchored behind the bottom teeth; work for increasing speed with precision; this is often our most unlimbered area.
    a. Guh-guh-guh-guh (repeat several times)
    b. Guhguhguh-guhguhguh-guhguhguh-guh (repeat)
    c. Giggle-gi, giggle-gi giggle-gi-gi (repeat)
    d. Repeat the whole series on a whisper, substituting "K" for "G."

4. TONGUE TIP
   Light, strong hammer taps:
   a. Yellow lily - yellow lily - yellow lily (repeat and increase speed)
   b. Yellow lily dales (repeat)
   c. Twelve cold miles of yellow lily dales (repeat)
   d. Twelve cold miles of brilliant yellow lily dales (repeat)

5. LIPS
   Create a bounce with the lips on "W"
   a. Woo-wee-way, woo-wee-way, woo-wee-way (repeat)
   b. William, will you wait (repeat)
   c. Will you wait for Willy (repeat)

6. LIPS WITH NASAL RESONANCE
   a. Remember my mother, remember my mother, remember my mother, remember.
   b. Pumpkin marrow and cucumber narrow have grown through the spangled June hours.

7. TONGUE TIP WITH NASAL RESONANCE
   a. Alone, alone, all alone.
   b. Bronzed and blackened thickened chickens.

8. SOME TONGUE TEASERS
   a. "AMIDST THE MISTS" (*See* Tongue Teasers, pg. 148)
   b. "SHE CLASPS THE ASPS" (*See* Tongue Teasers, pg. 148.
   c. "THEY GIGGLED" (*See* Tongue Teasers, pg. 148.
   d. "GRIP-TOP SOCK" (*See* Tongue Teasers, pg. 149) for agility and speed.

  e. Many fifths, many sixths, and many twelfths make up many hundredths.

  f. The sex ceaseth and it sufficeth us.

Keep volume light, but demand ultimate firmness of the specific muscles involved. Keep the breath flowing from the center and bite the consonants with the lips and tongue tip.

YOUR 30-MINUTE VOCAL WARM-UP

Use this page to create your own personal 30-minute vocal warm-up.

CHAPTER 6: SPEECH

Speech Overview 164

Honing Speech Through Listening Skills 165

Rhythm And Tempo 166

Utilizing Patterns of Speech 169

Freeing the Voice Through Singing 173

Pitch Exercises and Drills 174

Musical Terms in Sheet Music 176

Theatre/Acting/Music Terms 183

International Phonetic Alphabet 211

Vowel Placement 215

Regional, Neutral, & Standard American 217

Removing A Regional Dialect 219

Quick Dialect Reference Guide 220

SPEECH OVERVIEW

In the previous chapter on voice, you learned how to warm up your vocal instrument and ready it to produce sound correctly. Using the same principles as I stated in that chapter, you must have all the elements of the vocal structure in place when producing sound and speaking: beginning with relaxation and ending with articulation. With the voice properly warmed up to speak, now it's time to add other qualities to the voice.

When we speak, we are giving information to the audience. The audience listens but our ears also tune into patterns, rhythms, and tempo. If you don't vary the way you speak the audience will tune out and not hear everything you say. Analyze what you are saying and how you are saying it to avoid this deadly trap. The way you speak should reflect the objectives and tactics that you've chosen for your character.

Listen to people as they are telling a story. Their cadence, rhythm, tempo, and pitch changes as their story progresses and they get more invested into the retelling of their story. Listen for the passion in their voice and notice when their objective changes within the story. On the other side, try to notice when you inadvertently stopped paying attention or if you missed something they said.

When you are acting you should use the same vocal qualities and intonations that you use when you speak in normal life but pay close attention to your vocal patterns. Make sure you are utilizing all the areas of the voice that we use to tell a story: pitch, cadence, rhythm, tempo, and volume. Do this and you will always keep the audience members' ears engaged.

HONING SPEECH THROUGH LISTENING SKILLS

In CHAPTER 2 I spoke about listening as a skill needed by actors. One way to hone your speech is to listen to others. Listening to others in this way will help you understand how they are using inflection naturally in their own speech to express what they mean. Identify what happens to a person's use of inflection in emotional situations when the words alone can't describe what they are feeling or fulfill what they need.

Compare how someone who is speaking extemporarily ("off the top of their head") uses his or her voice versus someone who is reading a scripted piece aloud.

Always remember that inflection work often describes how people naturally use their voices. When we actors pick up a script, we work to rediscover and experience the initial impulses behind the words that lead us to real, human communication. Unfortunately, that sounds easier to do than it is. Exploring different inflections and how they affect one's impulses can clarify how an action affects the voice.

A practice that I like to do is when I'm watching a play, movie, or TV show if hear something an actor says that catches my ear. I repeat it back the way I heard it. Yes, with this practice you are mimicking them but it is only for you to hear how it sounds with your voice. This is a great way to explore range and variety through listening.

Listen to yourself only while drilling exercises; then let your acting impulses carry your voice. Do not use these exercises to monitor yourself. These are not line readings.

Rhythm And Tempo

The dictionary defines rhythm as "the systematic arrangement of musical sounds, principally according to duration and periodic rests." and tempo as "the speed of which a passage of music is played." Keeping this in mind, the way we speak on stage should also include rhythm and tempo. If the rhythm and tempo of your speech remain the same every time you speak, you will sound monotonous, lifeless, and emotionless, losing the ear of the audience. In addition, you will also lose the flow of text, intention, tactic, relationship, and status, basically everything that brings life to your character: a very deadly state for an actor to be in on stage.

The principles behind speaking on stage use the same principles as singing. Rhythm is the pattern of your speech and tempo is the speed at which you speak. Without getting too much into music theory, I will explain rhythm and tempo using a 4/4 time signature. This means that there are 4 beats to a measure.

In basic music theory when using a 4/4 time signature, you have an eighth note (1/2 a beat), quarter note (1 beat), half note (2 beats) and a whole note (4 beats.). Clap your hands in a slow but constant rate. The rate of speed at which you are clapping is the tempo. Now to explain rhythm, on the 1st clap say one, 2nd clap say two, 3rd clap say three, and 4th clap say four. This represents a quarter note because each number being said represents one clap (or beat.) The rhythm established is one sound on every clap.

Now clap again at the same speed and this time say the word "one" for the duration of the first two claps and the word "two" for the duration of the second two claps. This represents a half note since each word is taking two claps (or beats) instead of one. Now, clapping at the same speed as last time, I want you to say the word "one" for the duration of the four claps. This represents a whole note since you are saying one word on four claps (or beats.) Finally, clap again at the same rate of speed as you previously did. On the first clap, say "one, two", on the second clap say "three, four", third clap, five, six, and on the fourth clap "seven, eight". The clapping should not stop as you are saying the two numbers in the space of one clap. This represents an eighth note since you are saying two words in the space of one clap (or beat.) These are the basic principles of rhythm and tempo.

When we speak we have our own rhythm and tempos of speech. Sometimes we speak fast, other times slow. We may elongate certain words and say others with alacrity. To help free our speech and allow rhythm and tempo to be explored, here are a few exercises I learned while at school.

SPEECH EXERCISES #1 – RHYTHM

LEGATO (CONNECTED)

Say your lines with a legato feel to them, smooth and connected. The words should be connected. If you say each word with a sharp, distinct separation between them, you are speaking with a staccato feel, which is not the quality we are trying to achieve. Be observant that you don't speed up as you do this exercise. This works best if you use a monologue from your script. If you don't have a monologue in your script to use for this exercise then say a group of lines that are connected by the same objective or tactic.

STACCATO (DISCONNECTED)

Say each word separately or with a staccato effect. The thought is connected but a breath or a very short silence will separate the words. You will say your lines slowly but using the staccato accent.

167

SPEECH EXERCISES #2 - TEMPO

ALLEGRO (FAST)

Say your lines as fast as you can, keeping the fluidity of the words as you speak. Don't rush the words to the point that you can't understand what you're saying. Just as in the first exercise, use a monologue or a series of lines.

LENTO (SLOW)

Say your lines as slowly as you can, keeping the fluidity of the words as you speak. Don't overly pronounce the words. Allow the vowels to come out. Just as in the first exercise, use a monologue or a series of lines.

COMBINATION

Combine the rhythm and tempo exercises together. Alternate the lines between "slow and legato", "fast and legato", "slow and staccato" and "fast and staccato." This is not about sounding believable; it's about freeing the flow of your speech and breaking any habits that prevent you from freeing the rhythm and tempo of your regular habitual speaking patterns. This may also help you make discoveries for your character's intention or tactic.

In addition, mix and match the different styles so that you are creating different rhythmic patterns and tempos within the sentences of the monologue.

Utilizing Patterns of Speech

This is something that I talk about in my scene study class. Patterns of speech happen all the time. There are numerous ways we use our patterns of speech that we aren't aware of because they are habitual to us. There are many terms that I use to describe patterns of speech and I'm not aware of any acting or voice books that use the terms I'm about to describe.

While each pattern of speech has its own unique style, it is equally important that each one is reflected truthfully through the character's voice. No two characters would speak the same way. Let the character's voice reflect the pattern of speech being used without compromising who they are. Below you will find a list of speech patterns. These are the basic rules, but as I've stated before, rules can be broken, adjust accordingly.

MATTER OF FACT

This is used when you are stating a fact or giving an opinion that you stand behind. The tones are more even with only a slight adjustment in tones.

Example: *"You are an intolerable bore and you know it."*

TELLING A STORY

This is used when you are recounting something to someone. Your voice tends to be more expressive with this pattern and your thoughts are connected. There is more use of varying tones, depending on how you feel about what you are saying.

Example: *"Don't you remember? I went downstairs to get the newspaper and found that old shoebox with pictures…"*

EXAMPLE

This is in the same family as "Telling a Story" only while the thoughts are connected, we tend to have a beat interspersed between the thoughts in order to make your point. Usually an "example" sentence will contain a "qualifier".

Example: "*The point I'm making is this, suppose...*"

LISTS

These can be included with many other styles of speech. Lists are unique and how you say them depends on what you are saying in the list. A list is when you have three or more ideas connected in one thought, or objective within a sentence or paragraph. You can have slight beats or no beats when saying a list. Each thing that you say in your list should have different varying pitches depending on what you are saying and how strongly related it is to the point you are trying to make. But they should never be monotone or said with little or no pitch variation.

Example: "I don't want to see you ever...*here, there, across the street, near my car, at the store, nowhere.*

STEPPING STONES

These are used when you are setting up a story, list or idea with examples. This is a slight variation of "Making a Point".

Example: "*I don't want to see you ever...*here, there, across the street, near my car, at the store, nowhere.

ANTHESIS

This pattern of speech is usually used when two or more words are used in contrast within the same line or separated by other dialogue. I call it Yin and Yang because the two words you are comparing should have a change in pitch so that you are highlighting the differences.

Example: "No, no, I'm a *good man*. Just a *bad wizard*."

JUXTAPOSITION

This is like Anthesis except this pattern of speech uses complete sentences that play off each other through their opposition within lines of dialogue.

Example: "*Of course you're happy, you have everything*. Anything you want you get. *Why should I be happy? I don't have that.*

QUALIFIERS

These are in the same family as Yin and Yang and Juxtaposition. Qualifiers are used when a conjunction such as "but", "or", "if", "however", etc., expresses a reason that is going against what the first part of the sentence implies, such as: "That's a very good story *however* I beg to differ." You can also use a qualifier when the conjunction supports the first part of the sentence or thought in order to make a point.

Actor 1: "He doesn't listen to me"

Actor 2: "Well, most bosses don't listen to their employees"

Actor 1: "<u>But</u> you can see the problem."

MAKING A POINT

This usually summarizes a train of thought with a strong emphasis. It can follow any of the previous patterns of speech depending on the situation and what point is being made.

Example: "*Messing with me. I wouldn't advise it.*"

Note: Not every sentence will end with this pattern of speech. Used only when summarizing a thought.

On the next page is a line from *The Wind in the Willows* marked with the different patterns of speech.

UTILIZING PATTERNS OF SPEECH

[**Matter of Fact/Example**] Here's the real life for you, Ratty, embodied in this little cart. [**List**] The open road, the dusty highway, the heath, the commons, the hedgerows, the rolling downs! [**List**] Travel, change, interest, adventure! [**Matter of Fact**] And mind, this is the very finest carriage of its sort that was ever built, [**Qualifier**] without exception. [**Making a Point**] You'll see exactly what I mean when we make our start this afternoon."

Look for these patterns of speech in your lines. I believe that these will help to bring out the most when you act. But remember: **use patterns of speech to support your objective or tactic. They aren't used to choreograph how to speak.**

FREEING THE VOICE THROUGH SINGING

The techniques of singing are an excellent way to free up the voice and learn to use your voice in new and exciting ways when speaking. Stanislavsky says, "Singing is speaking on pitch." There is no reason why the way we speak on stage shouldn't reflect the same musical qualities that a song contains: pitch, tone, rhythm, tempo, glissandos, decrescendos, rallentandos, etc. It doesn't matter if you can sing or not. This is not about how beautiful you can sound; it's about freeing your voice with a song-like quality.

SINGING EXERCISE

With your script, pick a line and sing the line with the objective that you have chosen. The "song" should have varying pitches and tones. Try mixing rhythm and tempo while you are singing your lines. Sing your lines like a rock song, opera, country, Broadway, pop, etc.

There is no wrong way to do this exercise as long as you are incorporating the qualities of song. There is a glossary in this chapter with a huge list of musical terms that you can refer to and help you as you explore this exercise.

Do not allow yourself to become self-conscious about the way you sound. If you are worried about being on pitch or voice breaking, you are not doing the exercise correctly. If you are having a hard time, try singing your lines to a song you already know but it works better if you make up your own song because then you are free to explore your vocal range without a predetermined rhythm, tempo, pitch or style.

Pitch Exercises and Drills

INFLECTION EXERCISES AND DRILLS

Rising   Falling   Level   Circumflex

Practice the following list of words using each inflection pattern. Also practice higher and lower pitch ranges.

you   me   law   I   oh   now   doom   no   long

PRACTICE SENTENCES

Read each sentence aloud as many times as there are words. Emphasize a different word each time, using pitch, and analyze how the objective changes for each statement.

I leave tonight.	The time is now.	This will do.
I've had enough.	I'm hungry.	I'm glad I'm done.
The sun is setting.	Harry came alone.	You've heard the truth.
That's a lie!	That will be all!	Give him the book.
I know the way.	I don't want to go.	Call me at eight.
I guess that's so.	Can you come?	Is the pie good?

PITCH EXERCISES AND DRILLS

FINDING YOUR WORKING PITCH RANGE

Say the numbers one through five just changing the pitch up and down and discover what happens to the intensity and meaning. Work with this pitch range until you are comfortable with the impulses and the vocal range.

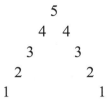

Now try to match the pitch of your voice to the words of this poem:

Let your tone hum down evenly smooth as a sigh,
Then evenly up and ever so high.
Hold your tone level and high today,
Then level and low tomorrow, I say
Let your no glide up, let no glide down.
Let no glide half down, then up to town.
Let your tone run from mountain to valley;
Let it run up and down in the alley.
Let tones glide high, and slide down low.
Learn to say no and no and no.

                                        Margaret D. DeWitt

MUSICAL TERMS IN SHEET MUSIC

Here is a glossary of musical terms[1] that you will find in sheet music. This is a great source if you don't know what a particular phrase means when you are learning your music.

A - to, at, in

A `Cappella - Singing without any form of instrumental accompaniment.

A deux *(a 2)* - to be played by both instruments

Accelerando *(accel.)* - growing faster

Accent - emphasis placed on a note or chord

Ad libitum *(ad lib.)* - *freely;* not in strict time

Adagio - slowly

Affettuoso - with feeling and emotion

Agitato - agitated, restless, hurried

Al fine - to the end

Alla - in the style of

Alla breve (¢) - cut time; two beats to the measure; one beat to each half note

Allargando *(allarg.)* - *growing* slower and louder

Allegretto - a bright tempo; faster than moderato but slower than allegro

Allegro - fast

Amoroso - affectionately

Andante - a moderately slow but flowing tempo

Andantino - a little faster than andante

Animato - animated; with spirit

Apiacere - at pleasure; equivalent of *ad libitum*

Appassionato - with passionate emotion

---

[1] Handout from Carroll, B. (Spring 1992). Musical Theatre II, P.C.P.A., Allan Hancock College

MUSICAL TERMS IN SHEET MUSIC

Appoggiatura - a grace note which takes the accent and part of the time value of the following principal note; often called long grace note

Arpeggio - notes of a chord played consecutively; a broken chord

Assai - very

Atempo - in the original tempo

Attacca - begin the next portion of the music without pausing

Bassa - low. 8va bassa means play the notes an octave lower than written

Bel Canto - Singing that focuses on beautiful sound. An Italian phrase literally meaning "beautiful singing." A traditional Italian style of singing that emphasizes tone, phrasing, coloratura passages and technique. Also refers to opera written in this style.

Ben - well

Bis - twice; repeat the passage

Bravura - boldness

Brillante - brilliant

Brio - vigor, spirit

Cadenza - an elaborate solo passage, frequently unaccompanied, used as an embellishment

Calando - gradually softer and slower cantabile - in a singing style

Capriccioso - in a fanciful and capricious style

Chromatic - proceeding by semitones (half steps)

Chromatic Scale - A musical scale that includes all the notes within an octave, including sharps and flats. Total of 12 distinct notes within a chromatic scale.

Coda - a closing passage

Con, col - with

Con anima - with animation and boldness

Con brio - with vigor and brilliancy

Con espressione - with expression

Con fuoco - with fire and passion

MUSICAL TERMS IN SHEET MUSIC

Con moto - with motion

Con spirito - with spirit and energy

Crescendo (cresc.) - increasing the volume or loudness of the tone

Da, dal - from

Da capo (*d.c.*) - from the beginning

D.C. al fine - from the beginning to the word fine (the finish or end)

dal segno (*d.s.*) - from the sign, 𝄋

D.S. al fine - from the sign to the word fine

Decrescendo *(decresc.)* - decreasing the volume of the tone

Diminuendo *(dim.)* - gradually softer

Divisi (*div.*) - divided; each part to be played by a separate instrument

Dolce - sweetly

Dolcissimo - very sweetly

Dolore - sorrow, sadness

Doloroso - sadly

Dynamics - expression produced by the different degrees of volume of the tone

E - and

Elegante - elegant, graceful

Energico - energetic, vigorous

Enharmonic - alike in pitch but different in notation

Espressivo - expressively

fermata (⌒) - a pause or hold

Finale - the concluding movement

Fine - the end

Forte *(f)* - loud

Forte-piano *(fp)* - accent strongly, diminishing immediately to piano

Fortissimo *(ff)* - very loud

Forza - force, power, strength

Forzando *(fz)* – the note or chord strongly accented

Fuoco - fire, energy

Furioso - furious

MUSICAL TERMS IN SHEET MUSIC

Giocoso - humorous

Giojoso - joyous

Giusto - exact; in strict time

Glissando - slurred smoothly in a gliding manner

Grace notes - small notes added for an ornamental or embellishing effect

Grandioso - in a grand manner

Grave - solemnly and very slowly

Grazioso - gracefully

Gruppetto - a group of grace notes; a turn

Il - the

Impetuoso - impetuous

Key note - the tonic or first note in a scale

Lamentoso - lamenting, sad

Largamentto - in a full, broad style

Larghetto - slowly, but not as slowly as largo

Largo - a slow, broad tempo

Ledger lines - short lines added above or below the staff for notes too high or too low to appear on or within the staff

Legato - in a smooth, connected manner, indicated by the slur

Leggiero - lightly

Lento - slow

L'istesso tempo - at the same tempo as the previous passage or movement

Loco - as written; generally used after a passage marked 8va

Ma - but

Ma non troppo - but not too much so

Maestoso - majestic, dignified

Maggiore - the major key

Marcato - in a marked and emphatic style

Marcia - march

Marziale - in a martial style

MUSICAL TERMS IN SHEET MUSIC

Meno - less

Meno mosso - less motion; slower

Mezzo - half

Mezzo forte (*mf*) - moderately loud

Mezzo piano *(mp*) - moderately soft

Minore - the minor key

Misterioso - mysteriously

Moderato - moderately

Moho - much, very

Molto vivace - Very lively, or at a very quick speed.

Mordent - an embellishment of two or more notes that make up a very short trill

Morendo - dying away; softer and softer

Mosso – movement

Motto - motion

Non - not

Non tanto - not too much

Notation - the art of representing music by written or printed characters (*notes, rests, etc.*)

Obbligato - a counter-melody which complements the main theme and which constitutes an indispensable part of the composition

Octave - an interval of eight diatonic sounds; notes an octave apart have the same letter name, but one of them is higher than the other

Opus - a work or composition

Ossia - otherwise; or else: indicating another way of playing a passage

Ottava *(8va.)* - to be played an octave higher

Passionato - passionate

Patetico - pathetic

Pause - a pause, also called hold or fermata

Perdendosi - gradually softer and slower; dying away

Pianissimo *(pp)* - very softly

Piano *(p*) - softly

MUSICAL TERMS IN SHEET MUSIC

Piu - more, as piu forte, piu lento, etc.

Piu mosso - more movement; faster

Poco - a little

Poco a poco - little by little

Pomposo - pompous, grand

Prestissimo - as fast as possible

Presto - very fast; faster than allegro

Primo (1 *mo*) - the first, as tempo primo

Quasi - like; in the style of

Rallentando (*rall.*) - gradually slower

Recitativo *(recit.)* - *a* style of performance intended to sound like a dramatic recitation in natural speech.

Replica - repetition

Rinforzando (*rfz.*) - reinforced; played with added strength and emphasis.

Risoluto - in a resolute and bold manner

Ritardando (*rit.*) - retarding; gradually slowing the tempo

Ritenuto *(riten.)* - in a slower tempo; held back

Rubato - robbing or taking from the notes their strict time value by alternately hurrying and retarding for the purpose of expression

Scherzando - playfully

Segue - follows on; continue

Semplice - in a simple, unaffected manner

Sempre - always; continually

Sempre piu - Always more.

Senza - without

Sforzando *(sfz.)* - with sudden force or emphasis

Simile - similarly; in like manner

Smorzando *(smorz.)* - extinguished; suddenly dying away

Solo - a composition or passage for a single voice or instrument

Sordino - a mute, such as used for a violin, a trumpet

So tenuto - sustained

MUSICAL TERMS IN SHEET MUSIC

Sotto voce - in a quiet, subdued tone

Spirito – spirit; energy

Staccato - detached; cut short

Stringendo *(string.)* **-** pressing; accelerating the tempo

Subito - immediately, suddenly

Syncopation - a type of time structure in which an accented note occurs on an ordinarily weak beat and is prolonged through an ordinarily strong beat

Tacit - be silent; do not play

Tempo - rate of speed

Tenuto *(ten.)* **-** held for the full time value

Tranquillo - quietly, calmly

Tremolo - repetition of a note or chord with great rapidity producing a tremulous sound

Trill - a rapid alternation between the printed note and the next note above it

Triplet - a group of three notes played in the time usually given to two notes of the same value

Troppo - too much

turn (∽) - an embellishment consisting of four rapidly played notes that wind around the printed note

Tutti - all together

Un - a, one, an

Vivace - lively, briskly

Vivo - animated, quick

Volti subito *(v.s.)* **-** turn the page immediately

THEATRE/ACTING/MUSIC TERMS

Absolute Pitch - Ability to determine the exact pitch of a note as played on a musical instrument just by listening to it.

Accessible - Music that is easy to listen to and understand.

Accidentals - Any of various signs that indicate the alteration of a note by one or two semitones or the cancellation of a previous sign.

Accompaniment - Music that is played as background to a solo singer or lead instrumentalist

Accompanist - A pianist who plays music beneath the singing.

Act - A portion of an opera or musical designated by the composer, which has a dramatic structure of its own.

Adam's Apple - Common term used to describe the part of the larynx (voice box) which protrudes from the front of the neck. More noticeable in men than women.

Adducted - The term for vocal cords getting pulled together when you sing high up in your vocal range.

Alto -   Lowest female voice part in a choir group

Aria - A solo piece written for a main character, which focuses on the character's emotion.

Art Song - In classical music, a song not from an opera, but sung in classical style. Art songs were created primarily for concerts.

Articulation - The formation of clear and distinct sounds in speech.

Artist Manager - An agent who represents artists by publicizing their talents, finding roles for them, negotiating their contracts and handling other business matters for them.

Atonal - Music that is written and performed without regard to any specific key.

Attack - Describes the process of a singer first hitting a note, as in "his attack on that high C was too harsh," or "her attack at the beginning of the song was very gentle."

Ballad - A slow tempo, sentimental or romantic song.

Back phrasing - A stylistic technique where the singer is either ahead or behind the beat, on purpose. Jazz singers typically use this technique, as do some pop singers.

Banda - A small group of instrumentalists who play either on the stage or backstage, not in the pit, often as part of a crowd or military scene.

Bar - A specific number of musical sounds that are organized within a measure, and that are contained within two solid lines called bar lines.

Baritone - The male mid-range singing voice between bass and tenor, with a range that extends from the second G below middle C to the first G above middle C.

Baroque - Time period in music history ranging from the middle of the 16th to the middle of the 17th centuries. Characterized by emotional, flowery music; written in strict form.

Bass - The lowest of the male singing voice, with a range of the second E below middle C to the first E above middle. In serious or dramatic opera, low voices usually suggest age and wisdom; in comic opera, they are generally used for old characters.

Bass Clef - A symbol placed on the fourth line of a staff to indicate that the fourth line of the staff corresponds to the F next below middle C; F clef.

Baton - A short stick that the conductor uses to lead the orchestra or choir.

Beat - Regular pattern of musical rhythm within a bar or measure.

Belting - Originally a term applied to female voices only - "This is a loud, driving sound that is produced by pushing the natural chest register beyond its normal limits. Although the original terminology didn't include men, male singers can also belt.

Blend - In solo singing, the smooth transition between the head and chest voice.

THEATRE/ACTING/MUSIC TERMS

Blending - A term used in choirs in order to make a group of singers sound like one voice, as opposed to lots of individual voices. This is done by encouraging singers to listen to each other and modify their voice accordingly to sound like what is being produced by everyone else.

Break - The sudden change in tone between the head and chest voice, caused by vocal tension. When a singer hits his or her break, there may be a "popping" sound, or some other sound that is jarring and ugly. This can be avoided with good vocal technique.

Breath Support - Efficient use of the singer's stream of breath, controlled primarily by the diaphragm.

Bravo - Literally, a form of applause when shouted by members of the audience at the end of an especially pleasing performance. Strictly speaking, "bravo" is for a single man,"brava" for a woman, and "bravi" for a group of performers.

Bridge - A transitional passage that connects 2 sections of a composition or song. Usually placed after the chorus of a song. The term bridge is also used to describe moving from one voice register to another. eg chest voice into head voice.

Broken Chord - A chord in which the notes are not played simultaneously at once, but in some consistent sequence. Notes are played either consecutively one after another, or 2 notes by 2 notes in a specific order.

Buffo - From the Italian for "buffoon." A singer of comic roles (basso-buffo) or a comic opera (opera-buffa).

Cabaletta - Second part of a two-part aria, always in a faster tempo than the first part.

Cadence - A musical term referring to a chord sequence that brings an end to a musical phrase either in the middle or the end of a composition.

Canon - Musical form where a melody or phrase is imitated by individual instrument or voice parts at various intervals of the song. The melody or phrase may be repeated backwards, inverted, or even at various tempos.

Cantabile - A style of singing which is characterized by the easy and flowing tone of the composition.

Cantata - Music written for chorus and orchestra. Most often religious in nature.

Canzone - (Canzonetta) A folk-like song commonly used in opera buffa.

Capo - Head; the beginning

Capriccio - A quick, improvisational, spirited piece of music.

Carol - A song or hymn celebrating Christmas.

Castrato - Male singers who were castrated to preserve their alto and soprano vocal range.

Catch Breath - A quick, short, unobtrusive breath.

Cavatina - A short and simple melody performed by a soloist that is part of a larger piece. It now usually refers to the opening, slow section of a two-part aria.

Cave - The round shape at the back of the mouth.

Centered - Everything balanced, working as one. Getting the greatest amount of power from your voice, using the least amount of effort.

Chamber music - Written for 2 to 10 solo parts featuring one instrument to a part. Each part bears the same importance.

Chant - Singing in unison, texts in a free rhythm. Similar to the rhythm of speech.

Chest Voice - The lower notes of a singer's range; in the same general range as the speaking voice. When singing in the chest voice, the vocal cords become naturally thick, and the resulting sound is generally associated with deep, warm tones. Also known as chest register.

Chest Resonance - The resonance sounds it comes from the chest area.

Chiaroscuro - The voice-pedagogy term that is used universally to refer to the balancing of the light or clear (chiaro) and dark (oscuro)

186

aspects of timbre, or balancing tonal brilliance and depth of the resonance.

Choir - A group of singers in a chorus with 3 or 4 notes sung simultaneously in specific harmony.

Chorale - A hymn sung by the choir and congregation. Originally refers to a German Protestant hymn tune. In composition, it typically means a choral composition for voices or instruments, such as a Bach chorale. The word "Chorale" is also sometimes used as the name of a choir or chorus.

Chord - When two or more notes or pitches are sounded simultaneously a chord is created.

Chord Progression - A series of chords played in succession.

Chorus - A group of singers, singing together, who sometimes portray servants, party guests or other unnamed characters; also the music written for them.

Chorus Master - The one in charge of choosing chorus members and rehearsing them for performance. If there is a backstage chorus, it is usually conducted by the chorus master who is in communication with the conductor of the orchestra

Claque - A group of people hired to sit in the audience and either applaud enthusiastically to ensure success or whistle and boo to create a disaster. In past years, leading singers were sometimes blackmailed to pay a claque to insure that claqueurs would not create a disturbance. Even now, a claque is sometimes used but rarely acknowledged.

Classical - The period of music history which dates from the mid 1700's to mid 1800's. The music was spare and emotionally reserved, especially when compared to Romantic and Boroque music.

Classicism - The period of music history which dates from the mid 1800's and lasted about sixty years. There was a strong regard for order and balance.

Clavier - The keyboard of a stringed instrument.

Clef - In sheet music, a symbol at the beginning of the staff defining the pitch of the notes found in that particular staff. Most common clefs are the treble and bass clef.

Coda - Closing section of a movement.

Coda Tail - Closing section appended to a movement or song.

Coloratura - Elaborate ornamentation of vocal music written using many fast notes and trills. Can also refer to a Soprano voice suited for such colouration or ornamentation.

Commedia dell-arte - A type of comic opera popular in Italy in the 16th to 18th centuries that involved improvisation using stock characters and gestures. The characters were often masked to represent certain archetypes.

Common Time - The time signature of 4/4; four beats per measure, each beat a quarter note (a crotchet) in length. 4/4 is often written on the musical staff as 'C'.

Composer - A person who writes music.

Compound Time - Metrical time such that 3 beats are counted as one; each beat is divisible by 3

Comprimario - A secondary or supporting role or a person singing such a role.

Concertato - A large ensemble of soloists and chorus generally found in the second movement of a central finale, to which it forms the lyrical climax.

Concerto - A composition written for a solo instrument. The soloist plays the melody while the orchestra plays the accompaniment.

Conductor - The leader who directs a group of performers. An accomplished musician with a strong sense of rhythm and an in-depth understanding of the voice and instrument,The conductor indicates the tempo, phrasing, dynamics, and style by gestures and facial expressions. Sometimes called Maestro

Consonance - Groups of tones that are harmonious when sounded together as in a chord.

Consonant - A speech sound produced as the result of a temporary partial or complete constriction of airflow (b d f g l etc)

Contralto - Lowest female classical singing voice part. Often known simply as "alto."with a range extending from the F below middle C to the second G above middle C.

Counterpoint - Two or three melodic lines played at the same time.

Countertenor - Highest male classical singing voice part with an elevated range. With training and practice this higher range, similar to that of a woman's alto, becomes the natural voice.

Cover - The name given to an understudy in opera; someone who replaces a singer in case of illness or other misfortune.

Covering - A term used mostly in opera to describe a darker tone.

Crotchet - Quarter-note; 1 beat in duration.

Cue - A signal to a singer or orchestra member to begin singing or playing.

Curtain Call - At the end of a performance, all of the members of the cast and the conductor take bows. Sometimes this is done in front of the main curtain, hence the name curtain call. Often, however, the bows are taken on the full stage with the curtain open.

Cut - To omit some of the original material from the score.

Deceptive Cadence - A chord progression that seems to lead to resolving itself on the final chord; but it does not.

Demi-semiquaver - One out of 32 parts of a Whole Note; 1/16th of a beat in duration

Diaphragm - The dome shaped muscle attached to the bottom of the lungs that separates your chest and stomach cavities. Its main function is to initiate inhalation.

Diction - The clear pronunciation of words. This requires attention to both consonants and vowels. Different types of music may require more or less diction; for example, in musical theatre, it's essential that the audience understand the lyrics, but in jazz or blues, the singer may occasionally slur words on purpose in order to achieve a desired sound. Good diction helps produce good sound, however, so all singers should pay attention to it.

Diphthong - Two vowel sounds occurring in the same syllable. Also known as gliding vowels.

Director - One who prepares an opera or play for production by arranging the details of the stage settings and stage effects, and by instructing the performers in the interpretation of their roles.

Dissonance - Harsh, discordant, and lack of harmony. Also a chord that sounds incomplete until it resolves itself on a harmonious chord.

Diva - Literally "goddess," it refers to an important female opera star. The masculine form is divo.

Dominant - 5th note of a musical scale

Double Aria - An aria which consists of two parts. The first part, or cavatina, is usually slow and the second, or cabaletta is faster. There is often recitative between the two sections.

Downbeat - The first beat in a measure as conducted by the leader of an ensemble is called the downbeat.

Dramatic - As in a "dramatic soprano," "dramatic tenor," etc. A type of singing that is heavier than "lyric," often accompanied by more focus on acting than on making a "pretty" sound.

Dress Rehearsal - A final rehearsal that uses all of the costumes, lights, etc. While sometimes it is necessary to stop for corrections, an attempt is made to make it as much like a final performance as possible.

Drone - Dull, monotonous tone such as a humming or buzzing sound. Also a bass note held under a melody.

Duet - Piece of music written for two vocalists or instrumentalists. They may or may not sing simultaneously or on the same musical line.

Dynamic - The variations of softness and loudness in music.

Eighth - An interval of a distance of 8 notes.

Elegy - An instrumental lament with praise for the dead.

Encore - Additional song(s) played at the end of a recital responding to the audiences enthusiastic reaction to the performance, shown by continuous applause after the last song of a concert or performance.

Energico - A symbol in sheet music a direction to play energetically.

Ensemble - The performance of either all instruments of an orchestra or voices in a chorus.

Enunciation - The act of pronouncing words clearly.

Epiglottis - The leaf-like cartilage that separates the functioning of your oesophagus (channel to stomach) from the functioning of your trachea (channel to the lungs).

Etude - A musical composition written solely to improve technique. Often performed for artistic interest.

Exercise - In singing, a device (a note or sequence of notes sung in a certain manner) used to condition and/or strengthen your vocal muscles to work with the proper airflow.

Exposition - The first section of a movement written in sonata form, introducing the melodies and themes.

Expressionism - Atonal and violent style used as a means of evoking heightened emotions and states of mind.

Falsetto - It means False Singing. In male singers, a high register (actually, sung in the female range) similar to the head voice. It has a Minnie Mouse Sound about it. However, unlike the head voice, falsetto cannot blend with the chest voice. Female's can also sing in a falsetto range.

Fifth - An interval of a distance of 5 notes between two notes.

Finale - The last musical number that concludes the end of a musical composition.

Flat - A symbol indicating that the note is to be diminished by one semitone. For example, if we have the note D and we add a flat to it the note now becomes D-flat or D♭.

Flat (Singing) - When your pitch is too low. To be under the correct pitch, not quite in tune.

Forced - Singing that is forced may sound strained, and is accompanied by unnecessary tension in the throat.

Form - Musical term referring to the shape and structure of a piece of music.

Fourth - An interval of a distance of 4 notes between two notes.

Fugue - A composition written for three to six voices. Beginning with the exposition, each voice enters at different times, creating counterpoint with one another.

Full Voice - As loud as a person can sing without creating imbalance between airflow and vocal cord tension. Also refers to a tone that has a balanced resonance quality.

Gregorian Chant - Singing or chanting in unison without strict rhythm. Collected during the Reign of Pope Gregory VIII for psalms and other other parts of the church service.

Half-step - A musical interval of a semitone eg C to C#

Hard Palate - The hard area of the roof of your mouth, just behind your teeth.

Harmony - A pleasing combination of two or three tones played together to create a pleasant sound or musical effect in the background while a melody is being played. Harmony also refers to the study of chord progressions.

Head Resonance - The vibration of a soundwave which is bounced around the structures of your head such as sinuses, nasal cavities and mouth to create a better sounding note. Head voice is usually associated with lighter, brighter and higher notes.

Head Voice - The higher part of the vocal register, which resonates around the structures of your head such as sinuses, nasal cavities and mouth. Head voice is usually associated with lighter, brighter and higher notes. Falsetto is also resonated in head voice.

Homophony - Music written to be sung or played in unison.

House Manager - For performances, the person who is responsible for the audience and all that happens from the entry to the theatre, to the box office, to the seating and audience behaviour in the hall.

Hymn - A song of praise and glorification. Most often to honour God.

Imagery - The situations, people, or emotions a singer pictures in his or her head while they sing, in order to achieve emotion and a good level of acting in their songs. Imagery may also be used to help a singer achieve better vocal technique.

Interlude - Instrumental music played between scenes in an opera, musical or play. Can also refer to the music break in a song when the singer does not sing.

Intermezzo - Short movement or interlude connecting the main parts of the composition.

Intermission - A break, usually of about 20 minutes, between the acts of an opera, musical or show, during which the audience is free to move around.

Interpretation - The expression the performer brings when performing.

Interval - The distance in pitch between two notes.

Intonation - The rise and fall of the voice in speaking or singing.

Introduction - The opening section of a piece of music or movement.

Inversion - A chord that is not played with the root note at the bottom, but with the other notes of the chord taking the bass position

Karaoke - Musical entertainment where the singer sings along to a pre-recorded track and follows the lyrics on a video screen.

Key - A combination of sharps and flats to indicate the pitch of a piece of music.

Key signature - A group flats and sharps at the beginning of a piece of music, indicating the key or pitch of music the piece is to be played.

Larynx - The structure at the top of your trachea (windpipe) made up of cartilages, ligaments and muscles. Inside, attached from front to back are your vocal cords. Outside of the larynx sits your thyroid gland. Certain muscles of your larynx affect the tension of your vocal cords as they work with air from your lungs in producing vocal sound.

Leading note - The seventh note of a scale where there is a strong desire to resolve on the tonic (the first note of the scale).

Legato - Word to indicate that the movement or entire composition is to be sung or played smoothly as though all the notes were tied together.

Libretto - A book of text containing the words of an opera.

Licks - This is a very short solo that is performed to a complicated and fast melody during a little break in the song. During the battle rounds, it was basically when one singer would break off from the song and do a proper fancy technical bit and then return to the normal song.

Ligature - Curved line connecting notes to be sung or played as a phrase.

Lighting Designer -

One who designs and coordinates the light changes that help create a show's overall effect. Much of this is now computerized.

Lyrics - The words of a song.

Madrigal - A secular vocal music composition of the Renaissance and early Baroque eras. Traditionally, madrigal were unaccompanied. The number of voices varies from two to eight, and most frequently from three to six.

Maestro - Refers to any great composer, conductor, or teacher of music.

Magic Opera - An opera in which there are many magical effects and often animals appearing on stage. Often the plot of a magic opera involves the rescue of one of the major characters.

Major - One of 2 modes of the tonal system. Music that is written using the major key has a positive or happy character.

THEATRE/ACTING/MUSIC TERMS

Major Scale - A diatonic scale with notes separated by whole tones except for the 3rd, 4th, 7th and 8th.

Marking - When a singer chooses to sing half-voice for a rehearsal, A full-length opera is very hard on a singer's voice so many mark during rehearsals.

Mask - The area around and including the eyes which is often used to create head resonance.

Measure - A measurement of time in music that contain a specific number of pulses within a bar as defined by a time signature eg, in 4/4 time, a measure has 4 crotchet beats to a bar.

Mediant - 3rd note of a musical scale.

Medley - Musical term referring to using passages from the various songs of a composition, that are performed one after another forming one complete song of its own. It is often used in overtures.

Melisma - The singing of a single syllable of text whilst moving to several different notes in succession.

Melodrama - In a technique which originated with the French; short passages of music alternating with spoken words.

Melody - A sequence of notes producing an identifiable sound or tune.

Metronome - A mechanical or electrical instrument that makes repeated clicking sound at an adjustable pace. Used for marking rhythm in practicing music.

Mezzo Soprano - The second highest female classical singing voice part, just below the Soprano voice, extending from the A below middle C to the second A above middle C.

Middle Voice - Middle voice is where we mix the elements of head and chest voice to create a better sound. Think of it as adjusting the balance of treble and bass on your sound system and is achieved by resonance and voice placement.

Minim - Half-note value; 2 beats in duration

Minor - One of 2 modes of the tonal system. Music that is written using the minor key has a negative or sad character and can be identified by the dark, melancholic mood.

Minor Scale - A diatonic scale with notes separated by whole tones except for the 2nd, 3rd, 5th & 6th.

Minuet - Slow and stately dance music written in triple time.

Mix - A mix between head and chest voice. Also known as middle voice. It is where we mix the elements of head and chest voice to create a better sound. Think of it as adjusting the balance of treble and bass on your sound system and is achieved by resonance and voice placement.

Modes - The way notes of a scale are arranged within the character of the mode. The two main modes in modern music are **major** or **minor**. The other modes used in music theory are - Ionian, Dorian, Phrygian, Lydian, Mixolydian, Aeolian, Locrian.

Modulation - To transition to another key.

Monotone - Repetition of a single tone.

Motif - An identifiable succession of musical sounds, but shorter than a complete melody.

Movement - A large unit within a symphony or concerto. It usually is comprised of many themes or musical ideas.

Musicology - The study of forms, history, science, and methods of music.

Nasal - When the voice is focused purely around the nose and nasal area.

Natural - A symbol in sheet music that returns a note to its original pitch after it has been augmented or diminished.

Neoclassical - Movement in music where the characteristics are crisp and direct.

Nocturne - A musical composition that has a romantic or dreamy character with nocturnal associations

Nodules - A type of polyp on the vocal cords that prohibits good singing. When vocal cords get irritated (from fatigue, poor technique, an infection, etc.), they swell. Singing repeatedly with swollen vocal cords causes nodes. The only way to know if you have or are developing nodes is to go to a throat specialist (ENT). If you have frequent hoarseness or a constant sore throat, see one immediately. Treatment is usually rest, although surgery may be required in severe cases. Also known as **Nodes**

Nonet - A composition written for nine instruments.

Notation - First developed in the 8th century, methods of writing music.

Notes - Symbols to represent sounds or pitches and duration of those sounds.

Number Opera - An opera composed of individual numbers, such as recitative, arias, duets, ensembles, etc. Between the numbers there is often a chance for applause. Most of the operas of Mozart, Rossini and Bellini can be called number operas.

Octet - A composition written for eight instruments.

Opera - A drama where the words are sung instead of spoken. In opera, singing is the way characters express feeling; as it often takes longer to say something in music than it would in speech, the action may seem delayed or even interrupted. Like a play, an opera is acted out on a stage with performers in costumes, wigs and makeup; virtually all operatic characters sing their lines, although there are exceptions for a role that is spoken or performed in pantomime.

Operetta - A short light, sometimes comical musical drama, some of which is spoken but with many musical numbers.

Opus - Convenient method of numbering a composer's works where a number follows the word "opus". For example, Opus 28, No. 4. Often the opus numbers are assigned in order of composition, but at times the numbers are assigned by order of publication.

Oratorio - An extended cantata on a sacred subject.

Orchestra - A large group of instrumentalists playing together, led by the conductor, accompany the singers.

Orchestration - The art of applying orchestral colour to written music by assigning various instruments different parts of the music. This requires a complete knowledge of instrumentals and their timbre, range, etc.

Ornaments - Tones used to embellish the principal melodic tone.

Ostinato - A repeated phrase.

Over breathing - Taking a huge breath in and then constricting the lungs, making it difficult to sustain a note.

Overtone singing - Harmonic singing from the throat, in which the singer manipulates the resonances created as air travels from the lungs through the vocal cords and out of the lips to produce a melody.

Overture - An orchestral introduction to an opera, musical or other large musical work.

Operetta - A style of theatre in-between opera and musical theatre. Generally, it's a comedy with both music and script. It contains classically-inspired music, sung in a legitimate style.

Parlando Singing - A style where the rhythm–and often the pitch–of the tune are usually observed, but the "singing" sounds more like the speaking voice than the singing voice. Notes are often shortened, and the ends of phrases often have a downward inflection, simulating natural English speech. Rex Harrison was a master of this technique and used it in his role in *My Fair Lady*, among other musicals.

Patter - A "patter song" is one with many lyrics sung rapidly. Patter also refers to the brief periods in-between songs where a singer talks to the audience.

Part - A line in a contrapuntal work performed by an individual voice or instrument.

Partial - A harmonic given off by a note when it is played.

Passaggio - The parts of a singing voice where register transitions occur.

Pause - To suspend or stop momentarily.

Pentatonic Scale - A musical term referring to a musical scale consisting of only 5 basic tones.For example - the five black keys of a keyboard make up a pentatonic scale. Often used in Oriental or Chinese music.

Phrase - A single line of music played or sung. A musical sentence.

Phrasing (Song) - Essential in singing to give life and expression to your sound, instead of it sounding monotonous or robotic. Phrases are formed through different inflections extremely similar to natural speech, however these may vary slightly depending on the genre or style of music being sung.

Phrasing (Breath) - Refers to the breaths or "stops" in between notes. Natural phrasing will include "stops" after all periods, commas, semicolons, or colons. Additional phrasing may be necessary for the singer to take catch breaths or to achieve a certain style. It's an excellent idea for singers to sit down with sheet music in hand and mark their phrasing before they begin to sing. This helps prevent unexpected losses of breath and awkward phrasing that draws attention to itself.

Piano - An instruction in sheet music to play softly. Abbreviated by a "p".

Pit - A sunken area in front of the stage where the members of the orchestra play.

Pitch - The frequency of a note determining how high or low it sounds. It can also refer to being "on" or "off" pitch. This means the singer is either singing in tune or is off by being singing too sharp or flat.

Pitch - The sound of a particular note. When pitch is referred to, it's usually in reference to being "on" or "off" pitch. "On pitch" means the singer is singing in tune. "Off pitch" means the singer is either flat or sharp.

Placement - A singing technique that uses the sensation of vibrations in the head to achieve healthy sound that resonates and carries well. Most healthy singing is done in what is often referred to as "forward placement" (or "the mask"), with vibrations behind the teeth/lips, on the cheekbones, and sometimes the forehead and/or nose. The resulting sound is full, not nasally or thin.

Projection - Generally, the ability to be heard by the audience. Sometimes also refers to the ability to communicate emotion to the audience, as in "she projects great sadness."

PV - Abbreviation for Piano Vocal Score. It is a sheet music of a song which comprises of a vocal line and the treble and bass lines for piano accompaniment.

PVG - Abbreviation for Piano Vocal Guitar Score. It is a sheet music of a song which comprises of a vocal line and the treble and bass lines for piano accompaniment and also the guitar chords or tablature.

Polyphony - Combining a number of individual but harmonizing melodies. Also known as counterpoint.

Polytonality - Combination of two or more keys being played at the same time.

Portamento - A mild glissando (sliding from one pitch to another) between two notes for an expressive effect.

Pre Chorus - The section of a song between the verse and the chorus.

Prelude - A short introduction that leads into an act without a break. However not lengthy enough to be considered an overture.

Prima Donna - Literally "first lady;" the leading woman singer in an opera. Because of the way some have behaved in the past, it often refers to someone who acts in a superior and demanding fashion. The term for the leading man is primo uomo.

Principle - A major singing role, or the singer who performs such a role.

THEATRE/ACTING/MUSIC TERMS

Production Manager - The administrator responsible for coordinating the sets, costumes, rehearsal facilities and all physical aspects of a production. Often, the person who negotiates with the various unions representing stage hands, musicians, etc.

Production - The combination of sets, costumes, props, lights, music, etc to put on a show

Progression - The movement of chords in succession.

Projection - The strength of singing whereby the voice is used loudly and clearly so it can be heard by the audience. It commands respect and attention. Also refers to the ability to communicate emotion to the audience, eg. she projects great sadness.

Prompt - To help a singer remember lines, some opera houses will place a person (prompter) in a box below and at the very front of the stage.

Pronunciation - The result of producing sounds of speech and the accepted standard of the sound and syllable.

Props - Small items carried or used by performers on stage.

Pure Note - A clear, sustained note with a controlled breath and without vibrato. To create a true pure note, everything needs to be in balance. Placement of the note and vowel, diaphragmatic control and vocal cords energized yet relaxed.

Quadruple Time - Measure consisting of 4 beats or pulses, with accents on the 1st and 3rd beats

Quartet - A group of four musicians performing a piece of music written for four parts.

Quaver - One-eighth of a Whole Note; ½ a beat in duration.

Quintet - A group of five musicians performing a piece of music written for five parts.

Range - Refers to the notes that a given performer can sing comfortably.

Recapitulation - A reprise.

Recital - A solo concert with or without accompaniment.

Recitative - Words sung in a conversational style.

Refrain - A repeating phrase that is played at the end of each verse in the song.

Register - A range of tones produced in the human voice by the vibrations of the vocal folds. Includes chest voice, head voice and falsetto.

Relative - Major and Minor keys that share the same notes in that key. For example - A minor shares the same note as C major.

Relative pitch - Ability to determine the pitch of a note as it relates to the notes that precede and follow it.

Renaissance - A period in history dating from the 14th to 16th centuries. This period signified the rebirth of music, art, and literature.

Repeat - To play/sing a certain section again

Repertoire - The songs a singer knows well and can perform.

Repetiteur - A member of the music staff who plays the piano for rehearsals and, if necessary, the piano or harpsichord during performances. They frequently coach singers in their roles and assist with orchestra rehearsals.

Reprise - To repeat a previous part of a composition generally after other music has been played.

Requiem - A hymn, or musical service for the repose of the dead.

Resolution - A group of chords can create harmonic tension. When this tension is released with a calm chord, or a chord without tension, it is "resolved" and is thus called a resolution.

Resonance - The amplification of the vibrations that create tone through and within your mouth, throat, sinuses and nasal passages. Large, full resonant tones are desirable in some styles of music but inappropriate in other styles. In musical terms this is known as timbre.

Rest - To stop playing or singing for the specific note duration.

Reverb - A termed used by musicians, and sound engineers for reverberation. Usually created by a machine, or mixing desk, it gives the voice more colour, tone and presence. Usually used in studio's and live performances.

Rhythm - The element of music pertaining to time, played as a grouping of notes into accented and unaccented beats.

Rococo - A musical style characterized as excessive, ornamental, and trivial.

Romantic - A period in history during the 18th and early 19th centuries where the focus shifted from the neoclassical style to an emotional, expressive, and imaginative style.

Rondo - A musical form where the principal theme is repeated several times. The rondo was often used for the final movements of classical sonata form works.

Root - Principal note of a triad.

Run - When a singer starts off at a very high note and drops quickly through the scale down to a very low note in the space of a second or two. Also known as Roulade.

Round - A tune where the melody is sung in two or more voices. After the first voice begins, the next voice starts singing after a couple of measures are played in the preceding voice. All parts repeat continuously.

Scale - Musical term referring to successive notes of a key or mode that are either ascending or descending in a specific defined pattern.

Scat   - Using the voice as an instrument. A jazz term referring to a technique where singers use wordless sounds and improvised notes, often imitating jazz instruments. Cleo Laine "doo-be-doo-be-do" is an example of scatting.

Scoop - Beginning a note beneath it's pitch, then sliding up to the correct pitch. Scooping was the prominent feature of "crooners" in the 1920s-50s; Bing Crosby, Frank Sinatra, and Perry Como were among the singers famous for this style.

Scena - Literally "a scene;" a dramatic episode which consists of a variety of numbers with a common theme. A typical scena might consist of a recitative, a cavatina and a cabaletta.

Scherzo - Pertaining to the sonata form, a fast movement in triple time.

Scordatura - The retuning of a stringed instrument in order to play notes below the ordinary range of the instrument or to produce an usual tone color.

Score - The written music of an opera or other musical work.

Second - An interval of a distance of 2 notes

Semiquaver - One-sixteenth of a Whole Note; 1/8 of a beat in duration.

Semitone - Half of a tone; the basic pitch unit of the classical music system.

Septet - A set of seven musicians who perform a composition written for seven parts.

Sequence - A successive transposition and repetition of a phrase at different pitches.

Serenade - A piece of music honoring someone or something.

Seventh - An interval of a distance of 7 notes.

Sextet - A set of six musicians who perform a composition written for six parts.

Sharp - A symbol indicating the pitch of the specific note by 1 semitone

Sharp - To be above the note When your pitch is too high. (often the result of oversinging) when you can't hear yourself properly, so you are not in tune.

Sight Singing - The ability to look at sheet music and read sing it with near-perfection. Very few singers have this ability. Most professional singers can read music and sight read with at least some accuracy.

Simple Time - Rhythm characterized by 2 or 3 beats or pulses to a measure.

Siren Sound - Making a sound like an old-fashioned war siren. A vocal technique used to create one voice within the registers, it is used to smooth out breaks, flips and cracks within the voice.

Sixth - An interval of a distance of 6 notes.

Slide - A glissando or portamento. Also refers to the moving part of a trombone.

Slur - A curve over notes to indicate that a phrase is to be played legato.

Soft Palate - The fleshy part at the back of the roof of your mouth.

Solar Plexus - Located at the centre and base of the ribs, the soft part just above the stomach. The centre of diaphragmatic power.

Solo - To perform or sing alone.

Song cycle - A sequence of songs, perhaps on a single theme, or with texts by one poet, or having continous narrative.

Soprano - The highest female voice with a range extending from middle C to the C two octaves above it.

Spinto - A type of soprano or tenor. Translated, the word literally means "pushed," and describes a more dramatic, dark sound, and usually a heavier voice.

Staff - Made up of five horizontal parallel lines and the spaces between them on which musical notation is written, indicating their pitch or key

Stage Areas - The various sections of the stage. Left and right are as seen by those on stage, not in the audience. Since many stages are raked, that is higher in back than in front, upstage is at the back and downstage at the front. If an actor stays upstage, all the others have to turn their backs to the audience when speaking to him. This is the origin of the phrase "to upstage someone."

Stage Director - The one responsible for deciding the interpretation of each character, the movements of the singers on stage, and other things affecting the singers. Is in charge at rehearsals.

Stage Manager - The person in charge of the technical aspects of the entire opera, including light changes, sound effects, entrances (even of the conductor) and everything else that happens.

Stagehand - One who works behind-the-scenes setting up lighting, props, rigging, scenery and special effects for a production.

Staggered Breathing - Staggered breathing is a technique used in choirs where there is an extremely long phrase in a piece of music. If it is deemed impossible for each individual singer to get through the phrase without running out of breath, staggered breathing comes into play. This is where singers in the same part take short breaths at different times to their neighbour, to create the illusion that the overall sound created by the choir is one single unbroken line.

Stave - Also means Staff. Made up of five horizontal parallel lines and the spaces between them on which musical notation is written.indicating their pitch or key.

Step - A musical interval between pitches (such as C–D or C–B♭) comprising two semitones or two half steps.

Stretto - Pertaining to the fugue, the overlapping of the same theme or motif by two or more voices a few beats apart.

Strophic - Describes an aria in which the same music repeats for all stanzas of a text.

Subdominant - 4th note of a musical scale.

Submediant - 6th note of a musical scale.

Suite - A loose collection of instrumental compositions.

Supertitles - Translations of the words being sung, or the actual words if the libretto is in the native language, that are projected on a screen above the stage.

Supertonic - 2nd note of a musical scale.

Sustain - To sing or play a specific note for the specified duration.

Sustaining - Sustaining is a breathing technique, which allows a vocalist's sound to stay consistent throughout a phrase. It involves tensing the abdominal muscles around the diaphragm and controlling the air flow as the sound is produced. It is often overlooked outside of classical music, however it is an extremely important technique in any genre if you want your overall tone to sound consistent.

Swallowing the Note - Pushing down too far on the larynx, strangling the vocal cords.

Synopsis - A written description of an opera's or musical's plot.

System - A combination of two or more staves on which all the notes are vertically aligned and performed simultaneously in differing registers and instruments.

Tab - Tablature – A system of notation for stringed instruments. The notes are indicated by the finger positions.

Tempo - Indicating speed of a piece of music or a song.

Tenor - Highest male voice with a range from one octave below middle C to the A immediately above middle C.

Tessitura - It means texture and defines the average pitch level that most frequently occurs within a given piece. Eg, the song may start low, but if most of the notes are in a higher range, so the song would be described as a high tessitura.

Theme - The most important melody at any specific time in a musical work. There can be one main theme in a work, or many themes.

Third - An interval of a distance of 3 notes.

Tie - A musical term referring to a curved line over 2 notes that indicates that the note is to be held for the duration specified.

Timbre - Tone colour and quality of sound that distinguishes an instrument or singer from another.

Time Signature - A numerical symbol at the start of a song or music score, indicating the number of beats to a measure or bar.

Tone - The quality of your voice that results from the resonance reinforcement of the tone initially produced in your larynx. Every voice has a specific color, which can be described as warm, dark, light or heavy . Two singers singing exactly the same notes will sound completely different to each other.

Tonal - Pertains to tone or tones.

Tonality - The sound quality of a note. Can also refer to the quality which affect the mood, expression or feelings.

Toneless - Unmusical, without tone.

Tonic - The first note of a musical scale, also called the keynote

Transpose - To change the key of a song; to lower or raise the notes of a song or a portion of a song.

Trill - An operatic technique used mostly, by sopranos. A trill consists of a rapid alternation between two notes, usually a half step or a step apart.

Treble - Highest part in harmonized music. Or, highest pitch or range.

Treble Clef - A sign that indicates the G above middle C, placed on the second line of the staff; Also known as the G clef.

Triad - Three note chords consisting of a root, third, and fifth.

Trio - A composition written for three voices or instruments.

Triple Time - Time signature with three beats to the measure.

Triplet - Three notes played in the same amount of time as 1 or 2 beats.

Tritone - A chord comprised of three whole tones resulting in an augmented fourth or diminished fifth.

Tune - A rhythmic succession of musical notes, a melody for instruments or voices

Tuning - The raising and lowering a pitch of an instrument to produce the correct tone of a note.

Twang - A nasally vocal technique used to achieve a powerful, crisp breathless head voice and to help create one voice. When singing from your head voice and moving into your chest voice.

Twelve-tone - Music composed such that each note is used the same number of times.

Unison - Two or more voices or instruments playing the same note simultaneously.

THEATRE/ACTING/MUSIC TERMS

Upbeat - The preparatory sign given prior to the first beat in a bar.

Verse - Section of a song usually at the start, leading to the chorus or pre chorus

Vibrato - A natural wavering pulsating change of pitch to accent expression in a piece while singing a note. It is usually inadvertent as opposed to a trill. The voice is alternating subtly and very quickly between two different pitches that are very close together. The larynx and diaphragm both play a part in contributing to the vibrations. The best singers have full control over their vibrato and use it to accent certain words or phrases for dramatic or emotional effect.

Virtuoso - A person with notable technical skill in the performance of music.

Vocal Coloring - Painting the tones of your voice with emotion including bright and dark tone.

Vocal Cords - Also known as **vocal folds**. Elastic bands of muscles found inside the larynx (or voice box), which sits within the windpipe. They are fixed at one end and open and close due to adjustments in tension. As air passes through, it causes them to vibrate producing sound. The change of closure and vibrating length affects the pitch and intensity of your tone.

Vocal Fry - A low creaky vibration caused by fluttering vocal chords or informally known as the 'Husky Voice'.

Voce - Italian for voice

Voice - One of 2 or more parts in polyphonic music. Voice refers to instrument parts as well as singing voice parts. Voices can sound distinguishable, even when singing the same pitches. This is down to timbre. You may have a very resonant and deep sounding voice, or a crystal clear and bright voice. Different types of timbres are suitable for different genres of music. While all singers have a different natural timbre, creating new timbres with the help of different registers help give a much bigger variety to a singer's sound.

Vowel - A specific resonance structure through which a tone is sustained. Produced primarily by altering the size and shape of the mouth cavity and changing the position of the tongue, which determines how the resonance cavities will reinforce certain frequencies of the initial cord tone. The result of each alteration is a recognizable sound – Ah, Aye, Oh Eh Ee Oo.

Warm Up - Anything that helps the singer prepare for a rehearsal or performance. Typically, a warm up consists of vocal exercises, such as running scales. It may also include warming up the body with stretches to relieve tension and help wake the sense, with special emphasis on the jaw, tongue, and lips. The latter may include tongue twisters.

Whole note - A whole note is equal to 2 half notes, 4 quarter notes, 8 eighth notes,

Whole Tone - A musical term referring to a musical scale that consists of only whole-tone notes. This scale only has 6 basic notes.

Yodeling - A form of singing that involves repeated and rapid changes of pitch and alternation between the normal voice and falsetto.

INTERNATIONAL PHONETIC ALPHABET

Before I talk about The International Phonetic Alphabet or I.P.A., I want to emphasize that this section should in no way replace learning I.P.A. or dialect through classes, acting coaches or dialect coaches. This is only to give you the basic idea and get you started to help you understand how it works. To get a more in-depth understanding of I.P.A. and how it works you should check out *Speak with Distinction* by Edith Skinner focusing on Standard American and *Classically Speaking* by Patricia Fletcher focusing on Neutral American.

I.P.A. uses symbols to represent every sound that we make in the English Language. The wonderful thing about I.P.A. is that the symbols for each sound don't change. Some symbols look like the letters in our alphabet but might not make the same sound that you are expecting to pronounce.

Once you have learned the I.P.A. symbols and sounds, you can use it to learn dialects and accents easier since all you have to do is replace one I.P.A. symbol with another. It is probably one of the most useful tools an actor can have in their toolbox. Continue to practice until you know and understand all the I.P.A. symbols and sounds without having to think about it. This will greatly improve your learning rate for neutralizing and learning dialects.

On the next page you will find a list of the symbols and the sounds they represent. It will take some time to get used to the symbols but do not get discouraged when trying to learn I.P.A. It is just like learning a new language and you are training your brain to understand this new concept.

INTERNATIONAL PHONETIC ALPHABET

International Phonetic Alphabet (I.P.A.)
* = Used in Standard American and British Dialects.
: = Elongation of sound

INTERNATIONAL PHONETIC ALPHABET

Vowels

1. a = **a**sk*
2. ɑ = f**a**ther, ɑɚ = car
3. ɒ = h**o**nest*
4. æ = **a**nswer
5. ʌ = c**u**p
6. ə = **a**bout
7. ɚ = wat**er**
8. ɛːr = st**ir**
9. o = **o**mit
10. ɔ = law, ɔɚ = oar
11. ɪ = w**i**ll, ɪɚ = ear
12. iː = f**ee**l
13. ʊ = p**u**t, ʊɚ = sure
14. uː = cre**w**

1. aɪ = h**i**de, aɪɚ = ire
2. eɪ = l**a**te, eɪɚ = air
3. oʊ = g**o**
4. aʊ = h**ow**, aʊɚ = our
5. ɑʊ = h**ow***

INTERNATIONAL PHONETIC ALPHABET

Voiced Consonants

1. b = **b**ad
2. d = **d**ad
3. g = **g**ag
4. v = **v**est
5. z = **z**oo
6. ð = **th**e (voiced)
7. ʒ = lei**s**ure
8. dʒ = **ju**dge
9. w = **w**ent
10. j = **y**ou
11. r = **r**ed
12. m = **m**om
13. n = **n**o
14. ŋ = si**ng**
15. l = **l**ittle

Unvoiced Consonants

1. p = **p**assion
2. t = **t**ick
3. k = **c**ap
4. f = **f**eet
5. s = **s**ome
6. θ = **th**ink
7. ʃ = **sh**ip
8. ʧ = wat**ch**
9. hw = **wh**y*
10. h = **h**e

VOWEL PLACEMENT

The beginning of learning to speak properly, and by properly, I mean the standard that is most acceptable on stage and screen, begins with understanding vowels. In fact, vowels are important for every dialect since they are the most distinguishable characteristic. Consonants are also important and some dialects do have consonant replacements but not as often as vowels.

Before I continue, let me expound something I said in the previous paragraph. I'm not saying that if you have a dialect you shouldn't use it. There are many actors out there who speak with a dialect. But if you don't know how to neutralize it for roles that may not require your personal dialect, you could hurt yourself in the long run.

A few actors that you may not have known actually have a dialect but when appearing on TV or movies seem to have an American or Neutral sound include Hugh Laurie, Christian Bale, Ryan Kwanten, Naomi Watts, Guy Pearce and many others. I was actually surprised when I heard them speak outside of their TV show and heard their accent. This proves that being able to adapt your sound will open the door of opportunity to get more work.

The sounds that comprise any sort of dialect for the most part are the vowels. In fact, it is the vowel that carries the emotion while the consonant carries the intention. Vowel sounds are made from a combination of different areas of your mouth: the front, mid, and back of the mouth combined with the high (hard palette), low (the tongue) and mid (between the palette and tongue). Besides the placement of sound in the mouth, the tongue also reshapes itself to produce these vowels. It is very important that you are aware of the correct placement of tongue for all vowels and which area it is coming from in the mouth.

If you have a dialect, your sounds might not be as pure as the sounds we use for Neutral American. This is the standard to which all vowel and consonant sounds contain no affectation due to regional or foreign influence. It is best to hire a voice coach or acting coach who specializes in voice to help with neutralizing your dialect or in learning a new one.

Below is a chart that shows you where vowel sounds are produced in the mouth. For the "Front" and "Mid" mouth sounds, the lips are neutral and the jaw is most open. For the "Back" mouth sounds, the lips are rounded except for the vowel sound used to make the word "father." The lower jaw is still most open.

Using a mirror, pronounce these words that are found on the chart and pay bring awareness to were the sound is coming from with each one. Once you have done that with all the words, repeat them again, this time watching your tongue and seeing how it is placed in your mouth when making those vowels sounds.

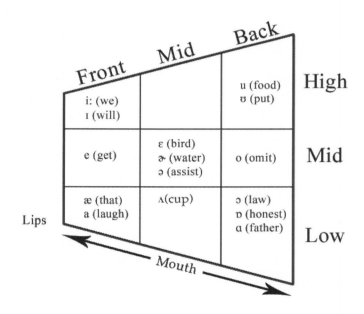

REGIONAL, NEUTRAL, & STANDARD AMERICAN

There are three variations of the American dialect that Americans use: Regional, Neutral and Standard. Most of us speak with a regional dialect. Most actors who study in school usually will speak with a neutral dialect.

REGIONAL AMERICAN

Regional American (a term which I like to use) refers to the section of the U.S. where you live. It usually reflects where you grew up and were raised. West Coast, Midwest, Southern, and East Coast are the most common regional dialects. Within those dialects are even more distinct versions of those sounds. Because of the increase in migratory patterns, Americans often move from one place to another. If you move to an area that has a different regional dialect, depending on how old you are and still adaptable to speech patterns, you may end up picking up that region's dialect and add it to the current one you have.

This can create a dialect that is specifically native only to you. You may have noticed when you talk to someone they may say, "I can't seem to place where you're from." This may be due to the fact that you have lived in different regions and picked up pieces of speech patterns from each place you have lived. So, you can see why most of us speak with some sort of regional dialect.

NEUTRAL AMERICAN

Neutral American is the preferred "dialect" for acting and the preferred dialect to work off of when learning a non-neutral dialect. By having a Neutral American sound, your regionalism is removed and it would be hard for someone to detect where you are from originally. It will open you up to roles because you won't be easily categorized by your speech. Most schools teach Neutral American within their Voice and Speech programs. If you have a strong regional dialect I would

REGIONAL, NEUTRAL & STANDARD AMERICAN

suggest taking a class on I.P.A. and Neutral American if it is offered in your area or find an acting/dialect coach to help remove it from your instrument.

You will always retain your original dialect and, if needed, you can draw on it if an audition or character requires it. You want Neutral American to be your habitual way of speaking while the regional becomes a vocal choice, not your standard way of speaking.

STANDARD AMERICAN

Standard American is primarily used by the upper class in the U.S., usually found on the West or East coasts. Its primary base is Neutral American with additional vowel changes particularly in the "ask", "honest", and "how" vowels and the "why" consonant. Because of these tiny shifts in these vowel sounds, it can take on a slightly British sound.

The Standard American dialect is used on stage when performing plays earlier than the 1960s that take place on the East coast or Classical pieces by Shakespeare, Moliere, Wilde, and others from that stylized era usually between the 15th and 19th centuries. It can also indicate an upper class status.

These days Standard American isn't used as frequently on stage as Neutral American or Regional American but it is used, so you should be familiar with it when the need arrives for you to use it on stage.

REMOVING A REGIONAL DIALECT

If you have a regional dialect and wish to neutralize it, the best way to do this is study with someone who understands I.P.A. and the process of neutralization. You can try to use books and do it on your own but it can be difficult to do since we cannot hear our own dialect and therefore aren't able to distinguish when we are pronouncing our vowels correctly.

The easiest way to neutralize your dialect without a coach or taking a class is to write down in I.P.A. all the vowel sounds that you create when you speak and then, next to the vowel sound write the neutral vowel that should be replaced by it. Or, even easier, would be to look at the I.P.A. alphabet chart that I provided in the I.P.A. section and write down the vowel/consonant sound you make next to Neutral American symbol. Practice speaking in your "dialect" and then, in the neutral way. Pay attention to the difference in the sounds. Listen for any single syllable sounds transposed into diphthongs, triphthongs, or vice versa. Also, observe your consonant sounds. Are they pure? Do you dentalize the t's (sounds like d's), drop the l's, (found in Cockney) or invert plosive/non-plosive (p/b) and fricative/non-fricative sounds? (v/f)

You must practice daily since removing the regional dialect is exactly like learning any other dialect and you are training your mouth, lips and tongue to produce new sounds that they aren't used to shaping and forming. Also use a recording device so you can try and hear the difference in the sounds you are making.

Whether on your own or with a coach, you must diligently work at it. You cannot teach yourself if you don't put the work and daily practice into the process of neutralization. Most actors who have gone to school have studied I.P.A. for 2 years or more and you will require the same amount of dedication and hard work.

QUICK DIALECT REFERENCE GUIDE

I have included a quick reference chart for British, Cockney and General Southern on the following page. This is to get you started and to also show you how I.P.A. can improve your ability to master a dialect by vowel and consonant substitutions. This quick reference guide should not in any way substitute studying with a dialect coach to properly learn the dialect you wish to achieve.

QUICK DIALECT REFERENCE GUIDE

Vowel	Neutral	Standard	British	Cockney	General Southern
father	ɑ		ɑ:	ɑ::	ɑ
honest (ɒ)	-	ɒ		ɔ::	-
ask (a)	-	a		ɑ:	-
answer	æ		a	e	æə/æjə
cup	ʌ				
bed	e				ɪ/ɪə/eə
about	ə				
water	ɚ		ə		
bird	ɛ:r		ə	ɛ:ɪ/ʌ	ʊ
omit	o				ə (unstressed endings)
will	ɪ				ɪə
feed	i:			ɪi:/əi:	ɪ ("y" endings only)
put	ʊ				
food	u			ʌu/ɪu	u:
law	ɔ			ɔ::	ɑo/ɑwə/ɑ:
hide	aɪ			ɔɪ/əɪ/ɑɪ	ɑ: (can get length)
made	eɪ			ʌɪ/əɪ/æɪ/aɪ	ei:
go	oʊ			æou/ʌu/əu	eou
how	aʊ			æu	æu
boy	ɔɪ			ɒɪ	oɪ/owɪ
forest	ɔr	ɒr		ɔ:r	ɑr
dear	ɪɚ		ɪə		
care	eɚ		eə	æə	eə
poor	ʊɚ		ʊə	ɔ:	oə
sort	ɔɚ		ɔə	ɔ:	ɔə
car	ɑɚ		ɑə	ɑ:	ɑə
fire	aɪɚ		aɪə	ɑ:ɪə	aɪə
hour	aʊɚ	aʊɚ	ɑʊə	ɑʊə	ɑʊə

QUICK DIALECT REFERENCE GUIDE

Voiced	Neutral	Standard	British	Cockney	General Southern
bad			b		
dad			d		
duke	d	dj		dʒ	d
gag			g		
vest			v		
zoo			z		
long			l		
old		l		l or u	u
bill		l		u:/o	(dropped at ends of syllables after vowels)
them		ð		v	ð
leisure			ʒ		
judge			dʒ		
went			w		
you			j		
red		r			(dropped unless at beginning of syllable)
mom			m		
no			n		
sing		ŋ		ŋ/nk	ŋ
doing		ŋ		ɪn/nk	ɪn

Unvoiced

	Neutral	Standard	British	Cockney	General Southern
home		h		omit	h
passion			p		
tick			t		
bottle		tt		glottal (lɪ'əl)	d
cap			k		
feet			f		
some			s		
think		θ		ð/f	θ
ship		ʃ			
watch		tʃ			
why	-	hw		w	

CHAPTER 7: MOVEMENT

Movement Overview 224

Leading 225

Weight...227

Laban 231

Warm-Up: Basic Structure....................................233

Warm-Up Exercise #1 - Relaxation 235

Warm-Up Exercise #2 - Stretching 241

Warm-Up Exercise #3 – Relaxation and Voice........245

Warm-Up Exercise #4 - Thirty-Minute Warm-Up 249

Additional Warm-Up Stretches...............................252

Massages 254

Movement Overview

If voice and speech carry the objective, tactic and emotion to the ears then movement carries those same principles to the eyes. The body is always the key element to informing us through sight what the actor is truly feeling or doing. An actor's body must match what he is feeling. Like Shakespeare wrote in *Hamlet*, "Suit the action to the word, the word to the action." But movement goes beyond that principle; it's also used to create our character on the stage. Movement defines how our characters walk, gesture, pick up things, use body language, etc.

We use our body to move through space physically and kinesthetically. We move with different speeds and weights. We explore this space both vertically and horizontally. Our body is our physical tool for expression. Just as a dancer uses their body to express their emotion through music or lyrical movement so should an actor use their bodies in the same fashion.

In order to achieve this, we must make sure our body is warmed up and ready for action. Many of the beginning voice exercises, use physical warm-ups for the body, refer to CHAPTER 5 for those exercises.

I've also included in this chapter some physical warm-ups for the body. If you keep your body warmed up and relaxed like a well-oiled machine, you will be able to produce any movement, character based or otherwise with clarity, ease, and full expression.

LEADING

Leading refers to the part of our body that is in front when we walk or move. You may think that everyone leads from the same place but we do not. Some people walk with their head down indicating that they lead with their head. Some walk with a slight slouch, which could indicate leading with their chin. Someone who is trying to be seductive might lead with their hips or possibly their shoulders.

As actors we must be aware of our body and how it moves in space so we can make choices for our characters and give them their own unique way of life on stage, including how they move through space and where their movement initiates from their body.

Being aware of leading can help us delve deeper into our character, making creative choices through discovery not habitual patterns. Leading isn't used only for our character's walk. We can use it to create a limp, an age, a gender, a station in life, or the illusion of intoxication to name a few.

Leading can also indicate to us where we have tension in our body when we move. And as I've stated before, unnecessary tension in our body is detrimental to our acting ability on stage.

LEADING EXERCISE

Start in a neutral position or center stance. Then start walking around the space you are in. As you are walking, focus on the part of your body that is foremost in front. Don't try to adjust yourself, just take note of the body part. It may take some time to figure it out since you are not used to using this type of self-awareness.

Once you have established where it is in your body that you lead from, change it to another part of your body. Let's assume that you lead from your hips. Now try leading with your shoulders. How does this inform you? Try to imagine what kind of person would walk like this? Justify the reason for leading with your shoulders. After you have fully explored leading with that body part, change it to your feet. Again, imagine what kind of person or character would walk like that.

Continue to explore leading with different parts of your body: the head, right shoulder, knees, hips, arm, hands etc. Each time, justifying the movement. Try using different levels, crouching, crawling, on all fours, don't restrict yourself to only standing.

By understanding the principles of leading you will no doubt uncover aspects of yourself and your character. I encourage you to explore this technique with every role you undertake. You will no doubt bring an aspect of your character to the surface and undoubtedly bring more of your character to life.

WEIGHT

This is a deceptive term. Weight does not refer to your actual weight but rather the pace or speed of your body as it moves through space. By assigning a weight value to one part of your body or all of it, you can affect the speed in which your body moves, whether quick, slow, slouched, elongated, etc.

To understand this process, I like to use an exercise that I learned while attending my Shakespeare class at P.C.P.A. in Santa Maria, CA. Gale Fury-Childs taught that class and was the single reason why I fell in love with Shakespearean text.

WEIGHT EXERCISE: "THE MUD EXERCISE"

Start out by walking around the room in your everyday fashion. Notice how your body moves in the space. Notice the gait in your walk, your arms' natural swing, how your head sits above your neck. Check in to see if any unnecessary tension is in your body when you are walking.

With your natural, unaffected movement through space established, assign yourself a "0" as your starting weight of your body in space. As you progress, you will add a +1 to heaviness or a +1 to lightness, depending on the weight value you want to achieve. Now I want you to apply a +1 heaviness to your feet. Imagine that the ground has a slight coating of mud covering it. The mud is a thick mud so your feet should "stick" slightly to it as you raise them to walk. How does this added "weight" affect the rest of your body? Is there any change in where you lead from? Is there newly added tension in your body? Don't purposely try to make your body move differently, let it happen naturally. You are only checking in with your body to see if there is a change.

After thoroughly exploring this weight value, I want you to increase the value another +1, this should bring your heavy weight to +2. As you increase this value imagine that the mud has risen to your ankles.

You must now lift your feet up higher through this thick mud to take a step. Do you feel the mud surrounding your feet? Can you feel the resistance slightly building and making you have to work a tad bit more to get your feet out of the mud to take a step? Explore this the same way you explored the previous "weight".

Continue to explore your walk and then increase the weight once again another +1 or +3 for the total weight value. The mud has now risen above your ankles to your mid-calf. Since the mud never loses its thickness or mass, you should feel a stronger resistance as you move through it. How do the other parts of your body react when your feet and calves have those values added to them? Do you find that you have to lead with a different part of your body to move? Does your breathing increase? Do you find you are adding tension to create this feeling of moving through mud?

After exploring this weight value, continue to add one more +1 value as the mud rises, covering more of your body. The mud should rise to below your knee, then above your knee, mid-thigh, upper thigh, pelvis, lower abs, upper abs, ribcage, neck, and finally the head. The weight value should be around +12. Notice how your body moves through space. It should be slow, controlled but still have fluidity to its movement. There should be resistance as you make your way through this thick substance.

Pay attention to your body at all times, be aware of your breathing. What does it feel like to explore this weight value? Try to use different levels as you move through the mud. Keep exploring the mud for about 15 – 20 minutes then slowly decrease the weight values by -1 as the mud recedes back into the floor. You should notice that as you do, you can feel a lightness returning to the parts of your body that aren't affected by the mud.

Once the mud has disappeared and you are now in your "0"weight value, write in your journal your experience. You can also use different weight values for different liquid masses. Try using the consistency of honey, thick cement, water, or pudding. How does your body react differently moving in these liquids?

You can also go the opposite direction by starting at your "0" value and adding a +1 to your lightness. Imagine that your body is becoming lighter and easier to move. You may find yourself walking faster, possibly even running. You should increase your +1 weight value as your body continues to fill with air. Maybe your body reacts differently when it is filled with air, or anything that is lighter than air. See how your body moves differently. Pay attention to this. After exploring the positive light values of weight, allow your body to return to its natural weight value of "0", decreasing by -1 slowly just as you did in the mud exercise.

How did your body move differently when it was light/heavy? How was your breathing affected? What parts of your body had to be used to move? Where did you lead from? By exploring the weight values in this manner, you can open yourself up to many character possibilities.

Now that you explored your entire body with weight, it's time to isolate certain body parts and give them their own weight values. Try making these different parts of your body affected by different weight values.

1. Shoulders
2. Arms
3. Torso
4. Chest
5. Legs

As an alternative, instead of applying a weight value to both shoulders at the same time, try isolating only one shoulder. Did you notice anything different? Do this with the arms and legs as well. Explore as many body parts as you can, not just the ones that I have listed above. Now go even further, give one body part a heavy weight and another body part a light weight. What can you decipher about a character from the way your body is affected?

Use weight values to re-create these characters:

1. A baby walking
2. A toddler running
3. An intoxicated/drugged person
4. An old person
5. An injured person
6. An energetic person

By exploring these characters with weight values applied to different parts of your body, you will see that weight is a vital tool for an actor to use when creating a character on stage and utilizing every aspect of their body.

LABAN

Laban is a system developed by Rudolph Laban for keeping track and writing out the various movements of the body. This is a wonderful way to see how different actions of the body can be recorded and preserved for future references. There are many levels to Laban work. This section will only cover the way one is able to identify and record the way we carry out a physical action.

This area of Laban focuses on observations of effort used in a specific movement. It focuses on the manner in which a motion is performed. Similar gestures performed by two people of widely different temperaments will have different expressions because the inner motivation behind the gestures is different; just as a simple work pattern may be performed with different effort patterns depending on the mood of the individual at that moment.

Behind each motion lies the inner originating impulse to which we give the named effort. Every action, from a tiny shiver to jumping out of the way of an oncoming car, originates in some effort made by the individual.

Effort is analyzed in the following terms: space, timing, exertion and sometimes, flow.

SPACE can be direct or flexible.
TIMING can be quick or slow.
EXERTION can be strong or light.
FLOW can be bound or free.

THE EIGHT BASIC EFFORTS

By combining the basic elements described above, we find that there are eight basic efforts. For identification, each basic effort is given the name of a common movement with which it is closely associated. They are:

Space	Timing	Exertion	=	Resultant Effort Name
Direct	Quick	Strong	=	Punch
Direct	Slow	Strong	=	Press
Direct	Quick	Light	=	Dab
Direct	Slow	Light	=	Glide
Flexible	Quick	Strong	=	Slash
Flexible	Slow	Strong	=	Wring
Flexible	Quick	Light	=	Flick
Flexible	Slow	Light	=	Float

Note: Each of these efforts can be made using free flow or bound flow.

WARM-UP: BASIC STRUCTURE

The exercises used in the basic structure can be adjusted to what you want to use as long as you hit each of the three areas. I picked these exercises because I use them when I need a quick warm-up and don't have a full 20 minutes. Basic Structure exercises that are **UPPERCASED AND BOLDED** means it is a new exercise being introduced.

You must warm-up each area within the basic structure: Physical Centering, Stretching & Limbering, and Breath. This is the minimum requirement needed when warming up. Please do not skip any of these areas even when doing a quick 5 – 10 minute warm-up.

PHYSICAL CENTERING (*See* CHAPTER 5)
   1. Deep Breathing – For exercising diaphragm & increasing breath and stamina. Aligns body and mind. (Relaxation)
   2. Railroad Chicken – Centers body and mind. (Posture and Alignment)
   3. Suzuki Basic Stomp – Grounds feet and the core. (*See* CHAPTER 13)

STRETCHING/LIMBERING (*See* CHAPTER 5)
   1. Side stretches – Increases side stretch and rib stretch. (Posture and Alignment)
   2. Garden Walk Down/Up the Spine - Loosens lower back. (Posture and Alignment)
   3. Picking Grapes – Increases stretch in the calves, ribcage, shoulders, arms, and fingers. Helps increase your breath intake. (Respiration and Positioning)
   4. **PELVIC CLOCK** – Imagine you are in the center of a clock. Isolate your hips and move them with a staccato feel towards the numbers in this order: 12, 9, 6, 3, or front, left, back, right.

233

Do this pattern 4 times. Then move your hips in a fluid motion around the entire clock 4 times. Reverse direction (12, 3, 6, 9 or front, right, back, left) and repeat isolations and fluidity. Loosens pelvic area.

5. **CHEST ISOLATIONS** – Same as the Pelvic Clock only it is your chest that is isolated and moving to hit the numbers. Loosens chest muscles, stretches the intercostals, allows chest to open and take more breath. Helps stretch the lumbar area.

6. The Cobra (*See* CHAPTER 7) — Stretches the lower lumbar area. (Additional Warm-Up Stretches)

BREATH

1. **BLOWDARTS** – With quick, even breaths, imagine blowing a dart through a blow dart gun. Be specific where you are aiming the dart and how far the target is away from you. Activates diaphragm.

2. Inhale/Exhale on Count - Increases breath. (Respiration and Positioning)

3. **BACON SIZZLES** – Lying on your back, breathe into the sides and lower back. Increase the inhale and exhale on a "sss". Allow your body to flop like sizzling bacon, eventually going into a sideways fetal position, like crisped up bacon. This is also good for stretching the lower back.

You may use any exercise that you feel fits your needs within the basic structure. The ones listed are only a suggestion and not meant to be the definitive choices. In the next section you will find five different warm-up exercises to help with movement. While some of them consist of similar elements, they are still different and may have a different effect for you when you have completed them.

WARM-UP EXERCISE #1 - RELAXATION

WARM-UP EXERCISE #1 - RELAXATION[1]

1. Take off your shoes, loosen your belt (if you're wearing one), and lie down on the floor with your knees up.
2. Relax your arms at your sides with your palms facing up.
3. Close your eyes and let your legs slide down.

Be aware of which parts of the body are in contact with the floor. Is the contact the same on each side? Be aware of the floor touching the tailbone, between the shoulder blades, elbow, fingers, upper arms, back of the head, calves, buttocks, and shoulders. Look down at yourself from above the whole body.

4. Picture the bones of the toe. Imagine they could drop off the feet.
5. Release the feet from the ankles as if they were not attached. Think of them being an immense distance from the torso.
6. Let them warm up and melt.
7. Put your attention in the calves of the legs. Let the mind massage the muscles of the calves so they melt and the shinbones seem to fall on the floor.
8. Imagine a space where the knee joints are and with the mind, melt the joints of the thighs and let the knee joints drop to the floor.
9. Put your attention in the thighs. Let the mind massage the muscles of the thighs so they melt and fall on the floor.
10. Imagine a space where the hip sockets are and let the legs travel away from the body. Put your awareness in the buttock

---

[1] Barbour, K. (1991-92). Movement I. Pacific Conservatory for the Performing Arts, Allan Hancock College

muscles and let them melt.

11. Relax the lower stomach muscles.
12. Imagine the pelvic girdle to be wider than it is so it flows out toward the hands on either side. Imagine it really wide with great spaces that the breath inhabits.
13. Let the breath move down into the lower spaces.
14. Soften the diaphragm and imagine melting the bones of the ribcage so it doesn't feel rigid, but can be moved by the breath that exists inside the ribcage.
15. Imagine the shoulder girdle to be wider than it is.
16. Let your arms move out across the floor from the shoulder sockets.
17. Get an image of space in the wrist sockets.
18. Get an image of the hands miles away from the shoulders.
19. Send attention back up the arms to the neck.
20. Feel the throat melt.
21. Feel the back of the neck give into the floor.

Let there be a large space between the shoulders and the skull so the head is very far from the torso.

22. Melt the jaw muscles so the jawbone drops toward the floor.
23. Let the face muscles melt so you can feel the skin lying on the bone. Feel the weight of the eyelids on the eyes.
24. Relax the scalp muscles.
25. Relax the tongue inside the mouth.
26. Feel the spaces behind the nose.
27. Feel the space behind the cheeks.
28. Feel the space under the eyeballs.
29. Feel the weight of the head on the floor.
30. Take in a nice, long deep breath of positive energy and exhale any negative energy you may have.

Be aware of the whole weight of the body lying abandoned on the floor.

In the middle of your wide and spacious body, there is an inevitable movement as the BREATH enters and leaves.

31. Picture the breath as energy that radiates throughout the body and out through the arms and legs unifying the whole body by breath.
32. Picture the breath coming out through the mouth, fingers, and toes.
33. Now let there be a conscious willing of breath up through the center and out through the lip and turn the breath to vibration.
34. "Huh hummmuh"(speak from your center).
35. Blow lips...mmm...ah" (up the scale and back down).
36. "Huh hummmuh" (speak from your center).
37. Alternate "Huh hummmuh" and Blow lips ...mmm...ah" up and down scale while moving.
38. Raise head, clasping it at base of skull to lengthen the neck.
39. AND: Clasp one knee at a time up to chest
40. AND: Roll head up off floor to clasped knees
41. AND: Rock knees from side to side
42. AND: Do pelvic clock
43. AND: Turn over onto stomach
44. AND: Move into Cobra
45. AND: Move into egg position.
46. "Huh hummmuh"(speak from your center).
47. "Hee-a-hee-a-hee-a" (tongue loosening up & down scale).
48. Repeat on all fours.
49. Sit on heels and roll head on hum.
50. Back to home on "Huh-huh-huh".
51. Breathe in and out on "Kah" several times.

52. "Hi-yi-yi-yi" (rolling tongue).

53. "Kah" (breathing in) "Hi yi-yi-yi-yi-yi-yi" (up and down on an arpeggio). Do this five times up the scale and down the scale ON ALL FOURS.

54. "Ng-ai-ai-ai-ai-" (standing and stretching hands to ceiling).

55. "Hey" Shimmy whole body.

56. "Hey" Undulate vigorously.

57. The Colossus
    a.   Head back
    b.   Throat open
    c.   Finding breath beneath the feet.

58. "Haa-haa-haa" to the ceiling on a low pitch gently beat out vibrations to the ceiling from the chest with loose fists.

59. "Huh-huh-huh" to the wall straight ahead, raise the pitch and feel the vibrations forward on the roof of the mouth.

60. "Hee-hee-hee" to the floor by the feet, raise the pitch even higher and feel the vibrations on the back of the upper front teeth.

61. "Hey" using the range of the voice, feeling the vibrations in each of the above places.

62. Big sigh of release.

63. Vacuum the lungs.

64. "Hi-yi-yi-yi" calling out over long distance several times (if the jaw is coming forward, the soft palate is not going up).

65. "Hey" while shaking the jaw loose.

66. "Hey" while shaking the tongue loose.

67. "Hey" while bouncing shoulders up and down.

68. Sit on heels with the body absolutely loose.

69. Press the whole of the lips together so that they cover each other...exaggerated for the exercise.

70. Feel the pressure a moment and then say: "Pah" - "PPP-PPP-PPP-pah" several times

71. Press the lips together again, feel the pressure a moment so you place it in your mind, then: "Bah" - "BBB-BBB-BBB-Bah several times.

72. Find about 1/8 inch of the flat of the tongue to be pressed against the gum ridge and send it down quickly to get a clean "t".

73. "Tah" - "TTT-TTT-TTT-Tah" several times

74. "Dah" - "DDD-DDD-DDD-Dah" several times

75. Press the back of the tongue up against the soft palate, which lowers to meet it.

76. "Kah" - "KKK-KKK-KKK-Kah" several times.

If you press the tongue too far up, there will be tension and if too far back, the sound will be throaty.

77. "Gah" - "GGG-GGG-GGG-Gah" several times.

78. "TK" - kt-tk-kt-tk

Feel the front and back of the tongue; feel real connection with middle of body and breath fluttering.

79. "PuhTuh-PuhTuh-PuhTuh-PuhTuh"

80. "TuhPuh-TuhPuh-TuhPuh-TuhPuh"

81. "GuhDuh-GuhDuh-GuhDuh-GuhDuh"

82. "DuhGuh-DuhGuh-DuhGuh-DuhGuh"

83. "BuhDuh-BuhDuh-BuhDuh-BuhDuh"

84. "DuhBuh-DuhBuh-DuhBuh-DuhBuh"

85. Precede each of the series with a little sigh of relief (Huh) to be sure the breath flows out and is not held.

86. Return to the "GuhDuh/DuhGuh" and "BuhDuh/DuhBuh" section and do them in all forms, directions, inflections, speeds, intensities and volumes. Ask questions, argue, and

make love with them.

Do this every day as a drill to strengthen the lips, tongue, and muscles of the mouth so as to be able to handle words of high voltage and great volume.

Note: Keep the mind and energy in the sound to the very last drop to establish the pattern of going through to the end of a sentence.

Don't get cut off from your middle and your breath. It's easy to do.

Think of the lips and the tongue shaping and testing the feelings from the middle. Remember ...the jaw is on vacation...no work at all.

87. Stand, stretch and yawn on "HEY".
88. Go into side swing of arms as you flop over at the waist with a line of text on each swing.

And now, your motor should be running.

WARM-UP EXERCISE #2 - STRETCHING

1. DEEP BREATHING
2. HEAD ROLL (8, 4, 2)
   a. Forward and Back
3. SHOULDER ROLLS (8, 4, 2)
   a. Forward and Back
   b. Together and Syncopated
4. DEEP BREATHING (into)
5. PICKING GRAPES
   a. Stretch for 8
   b. Drop and Rebuild for 8
   c. Repeat 4 times
6. ARM CIRCLES
   a. Right Arm – Back 8
   b. Left Arm – Back 8
   c. Right Arm – Back 4
   d. Left Arm – Back 4
   e. Right Arm – Back 2
   f. Left Arm – Back 2
7. ALTERNATE ARMS for 8 Counts
   a. Backwards and Forwards (Alternating arms)
   b. Arms back together for 8 counts
   c. Arms forward together for 8 counts
8. HUG YOURSELF
   a. Arms crossed around chest
   b. Hold for 8 counts
   c. Reverse Arms
   d. Hold for 8 counts
9. TWISTED VINES
   a. Right leg over left leg
   b. Arms stretched up

      c. Balance on toes

      d. Lean Right, hold and focus as you stretch

      e. Reverse legs and repeat on other side

10. SHAKE OUT ARMS

11. CHEST ISOLATIONS – Each rotation counts as 1 count

      a. Move your chest - Forward, Right, Back, Left

      b. First count of 8 – clockwise direction – Isolated

      c. Second count of 8 – clockwise direction - smooth

      d. Third count of 8 – counter clockwise direction – Isolated

      e. Fourth count of 8 – counter clockwise – Smooth

12. FLAT BACK STRETCHES

      a. Bend at waist

      b. Allow the back to flatten

      c. Imagine a string is pulling the top of your head forward

      d. Go to the right, drop your torso at the waist, and circle around back to center

13. Go to left, drop your torso at the waist, and circle back to center

14. Center, drop your torso at the waist, then "Garden Walk Up the Spine"

15. SIDE STRETCHES

      a. Left arm over head – Right arm under chest

      b. Reach to the right

      c. Reverse arms and stretch to the left

      d. Repeat 2x

          i. Return to center, stretch up, drop at the waist, and slowly "Garden Walk Up the Spine".

16. PELVIC CLOCK – Same as Chest Isolations except with pelvic bone.

      a. Move your pelvis - Forward, Right, Back, Left

      b. First count of 8 – clockwise direction – Isolated

    c. Second count of 8 – clockwise direction - smooth

    d. Third count of 8 – counter clockwise direction – Isolated

    e. Fourth count of 8 – counter clockwise – Smooth

17. PELVIC PENDULUM

    a. Move your pelvis to the right and left – 2 counts of 8

18. PELVIC THRUST

    a. Move your pelvis forward and back – 2 counts of 8

19. HIP ROTATIONS

    a. Lift right leg and rotate it to the right in a circle to your side. Imagine drawing a circle with your knee. 1 count of 8. Bring back to center. Reverse direction.

    b. Lift left leg and rotate it to the left in a circle to your side. Imagine drawing a circle with your knee. 1 count of 8. Bring back to center. Reverse direction.

    c. Bend down at the waist; grab the ankles and gently stretch the thighs/quads by bending and straightening your knees then "Garden Walk Up the Spine". Remember to breathe.

20. ANKLE CIRCLES

    a. Lift right ankle off ground and rotate clockwise – 1 count of 8.

    b. Rotate counter clockwise – 1 count of 8

    c. Return to center

    d. Lift left ankle off ground and rotate clockwise – 1 count of 8

    e. Rotate counter clockwise – 1 count of 8

    f. Return to center

21. LUNGES

    a. Side (Quad Stretches)

    b. With a wide stance, bend at knee and lunge to the right, keeping knee over feet

DO NOT BRING THE KNEES PAST THE FOOT
  i.
  ii. Stretch for 8 counts. Reverse sides.
 c. Forward (Calf Stretches)
  i. Right foot forward, with knee bent over foot
  ii. Left leg extended back. Nice stretch with just a slight bounce. Reverse legs.

22. BACK STRETCHES
 a. Lean forward and with hands on ground, slowly bring yourself down to the floor, legs and pelvis pressed into the floor, press arms and elbows into the floor and raise your torso up and out (like a cobra) elongating the lower back.
 b. Slowly get into a hunkered position from the cobra, and make your way to the floor on your back.
 c. Bring your knees into your chest and pull them in. Feel the stretch.
 d. Keep right leg pressed to chest and stretch out the left leg.
 e. Bring left leg back to chest and hug your knees to your chest.
 f. Keep left knee to chest and stretch out the right leg.
 g. Bring right knee back to chest and hug your knees.
23. Alternate right and left leg stretches - 4 counts of 8
24. Then bring both knees to chest and hug them
25. Slowly roll to your side and return to a hunkered position. Put your feet on the ground and do a slow "Garden Walk Up the Spine".
 a. Take a deep relaxing breath. Exhale.

You are ready to work.

WARM-UP EXERCISE #3 – RELAXATION AND VOICE

This is another warm-up[1] that I learned in school. This is the same warm-up that they use at Southern Methodist University before doing Stage Combat..

The entirety of this warm-up is executed in counts of eight. Count out loud. Use your voice; it is the only way to ensure that you are using breath. Choose a pitch slightly higher than your speaking voice and you will warm your voice more quickly.

This warm-up should not be an aerobic workout, nor should it be a singularly muscular experience. Send your thought and energy to the task of releasing structural tensions and opening up your skeletal support system. Be gentle yet thorough with this warm-up. You will be amazed at the little amount of energy it takes to ready and limber your body; but the energy must be careful and clear.

1. Feet shoulder-distance apart; arms swing forward, up and over, while going up onto the toes and then feet return to the floor; then reverse, arms swing back, up and over, while going up onto the toes and then feet return to the floor (2 sets of 8).
2. Right arm over left side, stretch to the left, reaching up and out with the right hand (8 counts), then repeat on the right side (8 counts). Do two sets of this (twice on each side).
3. After the last right of the last exercise, come forward and roll up the spine; head and neck are the last things up.
4. Bend at the waist and the knees as arms reach down to the floor and then swing forward (1 set of 8).

---

[1] Handout from Coffin, G. (1992) Weekly Warm-up, P.C.P.A., Allan Hancock College

5. Bend only at the waist (straight legs) as if reaching over a fence; arms reach down and then back at waist (1 set of 8).

6. Legs take a wider base. Arms out in "the form" as if holding a large beach ball. Bend at the waist, hands touch toes, return to standing (2 sets of 8).

7. Bend in the knees, arms come down and into your sides, then shoot out in front of you as legs straighten, torso bends at the waist and arms go through your legs; return to standing (2 sets of 8).

8. While down after the last count of previous exercise, swing torso to the left, then standing, then right, then front; reverse directions (2 sets of 8 each direction).

9. After last "front" in previous exercise, roll up the spine; head and neck are the last to arrive.

10. Roll shoulders back then front (2 sets of 8).

11. Single shoulder rolls back (1 set of 8).

12. Single shoulder rolls forward (1 set of 8).

13. Chin to the chest, center, then head lifted and back, center; do not shorten the back of the neck (2 sets of 8).

14. Left ear to left shoulder, center, then right ear to right shoulder, center (2 sets of 8).

15. Nod your head up and down. Nod your head side to side. Wide base, left foot points left, right foot points front, swinging lunges with left knee over left foot (1 set of 8); then repeat on right side, right foot points right, left foot points front (1 set of 8).

16. Do this twice.

17. Deeper lunges. Bend right knee, left leg straightens, drop to the right, handclap brings you up and over to the left (2 sets of 8).

18. Feet together, bend at waist and knees, hands on knees. Knees articulate a circle to the left, then to the right (2 sets of 8).

19. Turn right hand palm-out with left hand; reach up through centerline of body and back down, shake out; repeat on left, shake out. Repeat and roll ankles in a circle; shake all over.

20. Down to the floor, one knee bent at a time. Sit up on sit bones, legs out straight in front.

21. Arms reach up and gently take torso over legs (2 sets of 8).

22. Hands hold onto lower leg, elbows bend to the sides for a deeper stretch (2 sets of 8).

23. Roll up to sitting straight, arms up and over one last time, grab hold of lower leg, breathe, reach deeper, breathe, reach deeper. Roll up to sitting.

24. Legs apart, still up on sit bones. Arms swing forward and up while rolling pelvis (2 sets of 8).

25. Arms cross then open out straight to the sides while doing the same pelvic movement, switch top arm after 8 counts (2 sets of 8).

26. Arms up and over, hang to the left for 8 counts, DO NOT BOUNCE, then pass through front and hang to the right for 8 counts (2 sets, each side)

27. After last set on right, pass to center and hang there, arms on the floor in front of you, breathe and reach further, breathe and reach further. Roll up to sitting on sit bones and straight back.

28. Draw feet up off the floor. Alternate kicks out while staying on sit bones (2 sets of 8). Draw knees in. Do not return feet to floor.

29. Straight kicks out, both legs at once (2 sets of 8). Draw knees in. Do not return feet to floor.

30. Arms reach up and over to the left while knees bend to the right.
31. Reverse. Arms up and over to the right while knees bend to the left (2 sets of 8).

WARM-UP EXERCISE #4 - THIRTY-MINUTE WARM-UP

A THIRTY-MINUTE WARM-UP by Kristin Linklater[1]

1. PHYSICAL AWARENESS WITH NO SOUND (5 minutes)
    a. Stretch and drop down the spine.
    b. Build up ("Garden Walk Up the Spine").
    c. Roll the head and neck.
    d. With your hands loosen your jaw.
    e. Stretch and relax the tongue
    f. Limber the soft palate.
    g. Yawn and stretch all over.
    h. Roll the neck.
    i. Drop down the spine again.
    j. Build up (Garden Walk)
2. BREATHING (4 minutes)
    a. Stand with awareness of alignment and balance.
    b. Close your eyes and be aware of the skeleton.
    c. Turn your attention inward and be aware of your everyday rhythm of breathing.
    d. Allow the breath to release on small "fff"'s.
    e. Repeat several times until involuntary rhythm takes over.
3. TOUCH OF SOUND (2 minute)
    a. Central awareness of vibrations on "huh-huh".

---

[1]Freeing the Natural Voice handout from Barbour, K. (Fall 1991) Movement 1 Class, P.C.P.A., Allan Hancock College

4. VIBRATIONS (4 minutes)
    a. Lip vibrations on "hummmuh".
    b. Move lips around on vibrations.
    c. Blow out through lips.
    d. Do facial stretch exercises. Sneers, top lip up and down, diagonal stretches, bottom lip up and down, snarl, right and left smile, eyebrows, prune face, jack-o-lantern stretches, etc.
    e. Stretch lips with fingers. Let them go.
    f. Blowout through your lips on sound.
    g. Repeat several times going down one tone at a time.
    h. Repeat "hummmuh" on descending pitches.
    i. Roll your head on a hum.
    j. Alternate directions, changing pitches 6 or 7 times.
    k. Drop down your spine on a hum.
    l. Come up and release sound at the top.
    m. Repeat several times on descending and ascending pitches.
    n. Speak "hummmuh".
5. TONGUE (2 minutes)
    a. Sigh out from center while loosening the tongue (hi-yuh-yuh-yuh).
    b. Repeat on ascending and descending pitches.
    c. Repeat it hanging head down and building up the spine to relax the breathing muscles.
6. SOFT PALATE (2 minutes)
    a. Breathe in and out on whispered "kah", stretching the soft palate into a yawn stretch.
    b. Sigh out from center over stretched soft palate in ascending and descending pitches on "hii-yi-yi-yi" loosening the back of the tongue and releasing it.
    c. Call out on "hi" through the mouth in the back of the

neck.

7. THROAT (1 minute)

    a. Drop head back to free throat and find connection with the center on "Haa". Sigh as if drawing "water out of a well."

8. RESONATORS (5 minutes)

    a. Experience chest vibrations with head dropped back on "Haa-haa-haa".
    b. Mouth vibrations with neck straight, head up "huh-huh".
    c. Front teeth vibrations with head dropped forward on "Hee-hee-hee".
    d. Reverse the process, and then alternate it, front to back and vice versa.
    e. Repeat with colors and/or imagined scenes.

9. FREEING (5 minutes)

    a. Call to free yourself "he-e-e-ey"
    b. Shake the "hey" out, bouncing the shoulders, the knees, the whole body. Jumping on sound. Undulate the sound.
    c. Roll your head around calling on "he-e-ey".
    d. Drop down your spine calling on "he-e-ey".
    e. Do a nursery rhyme on all of the above.

ADDITIONAL WARM-UP STRETCHES

THE SUNDOG SALUTATION
1. Inhale
2. Clasp hands, stretch up to the ceiling and bend slightly backwards.

DO NOT PUT PRESSURE ON LOWER BACK

3. Make sure hips are tucked in.
4. Exhale
5. Inhale, bring hands to floor and stretch calves and lower back.
6. Exhale.
7. Bring right leg back. (Inhale) Stretch hip.
8. Bring left leg back. (Exhale)
9. Bend knees. (Inhale) bring head between hands (as if going under a fence) into cobra position. (Exhale)
10. Return to the downward dog position. (Exhale)
11. Roll up spine and bring arms back. (Inhale)
12. Clasp hands in front of chest. (Exhale)
13. Repeat. Reverse leg positions.

PSOAS MUSCLE STRETCH

The psoas muscles, pronounced "so us", is a pair of large muscles that run from the lumbar region of the spine to the groin area on either side and assist in flexing the hip. Remember to breathe.

1. Lie on table with legs dangling over the ledge.
2. Bring right knee into chest.
3. Push left leg down from upper thigh.
4. Repeat three times.

5. Switch legs.
PSOAS MUSCLE STRETCH (cont.)

ALTERNATE VERSION

1. Lie on stomach.
2. Bring right leg over.
3. Lift leg in air.
4. Have someone push leg as you push against it.
5. Repeat three times, switching legs.
6. Walk around

THE COBRA

1. Lay on your stomach
2. Bring your arms up so you are resting on your elbows, arms out in front of you with the palms down on the floor.
3. Keeping the palms, forearms, and elbows on the ground, gently push up from them to stretch the lower back in an arch.
4. The pelvis and legs should also remain on the ground so only the lumbar region is being stretched.
5. Think out and up as you do this stretch.

I also like to use this stretch for posture and alignment even though it doesn't require standing.

MASSAGES

One of my favorite parts of movement class was learning massages. Because of the stress of classes, rehearsals, and performances, our teachers wanted us to be as relaxed as possible. We learned these massages to help each other during times of stress and to help with staying relaxed and focused.

Obviously, you need two people to perform a massage, one getting and one receiving, so if you find yourself with a partner, here are two massages that you use.

IRONING OUT THE BACK

1. With flat part of fist, start directly behind right ear and apply body weight pressure to the trapezius through to the shoulder. The head should remain up. Repeat three times.
2. Three knuckles with pointers allowing space for the back. Starting at neck, apply pressure; let the head start to fall. With your legs in a lunge position, continue to bring hands down applying more pressure to the rhomboids and bring knee to floor continue through lower back. Repeat three times.
3. Face person, rest head on knee. With pointer and index finger, start at top of neck and continue through to the rhomboid, following the curve of the scapula.
4. After the massage, take a few deep breaths before standing up.

Be aware of knots in muscles. Repeat if knot is persistent. If it hurts, slow down and apply more pressure. Remember to breathe through the pain.

POLARITY MASSAGE

Before starting, have the person who is receiving the massage lie on his/her back. They should be wearing shorts and a loose fitting tee-shirt; their shoes and socks removed. If they feel comfortable, no shirt is best. Make sure they are relaxed and in their natural state of breathing. Be aware of their breathing at all time. Remind them to breathe if necessary.

1. Sit cross-legged. Cradle the head, focusing energy through the hands to the head. Do this until they are completely relaxed. Move the head back and forth to make sure there is no tension in the neck. They should feel completely safe with you and give no resistance.

2. Gently place head on ground and move to their torso (counter clockwise). Put left hand over forehead and right hand over stomach (about 1 or 2 inches away). Focus energy from you to your partner and receive energy from the recipient to yourself. In other words, energy should be flowing between both of you in a continuous circle.

3. Place both hands on stomach and gently rock them back and forth.

4. Move to the feet. Brush off the left foot, beginning at the knee and going through the toes. This should be down in a light sweeping motion.

5. Place the heel of the foot in your right hand and the ball of the foot with the left hand. Push ball towards head. This is a strong stretch. It should be pushed firmly but gently.

6. Pull foot towards you. This is a gentler stretch. This is also firm but gentle.

7. "The Inside Heel Press" - Press fingers around the heel area. Gently pressing and massaging any sore spots. Be aware of your partner's reactions.

8. Rotate the heels in a clockwise circle. Reverse circle.

9. Pull the toes.

10. Rub the sole of the foot with the first three knuckles, again massaging the sore spots.

11. Flex the foot towards the head. Press tendon with thumb. (Tendon is usually located in the middle of the sole area.

12. Repeat steps 4 - 11 on the right foot.

13. Move back to the head and repeat step 1, adding Occipital pull (holding head firmly in your hands, gently pull head towards you and place on ground gently).

14. Move to hand, massaging web between thumb and pointer, massage the forearm near elbow, alternating between forearm and webbing.

15. Repeat step 14 on the other hand.

16. Place left hand on shoulder and right hand on opposite hip. Apply slight pressure. Imagine pulling apart.

17. Repeat on the other side.

18. Chest and pelvic cradles. Put hands on each side of pelvic area. Focus energy into that area. Gently rock. Put hands on each side of chest cavity. Gently rock.

19. Repeat step 2.

20. Brush hands over entire body three or four times, switching to the smooth side of your nails halfway through.

21. Gently sit this person up and brush off their body.

22. Brush front, starting at sides of face, bring to chest, brush to the sides of the shoulder, down sides of torso through opposite hip.

23. Have partner remain still and continue breathing until ready to stand.

CHAPTER 8: CREATING A CHARACTER

Character Analysis Overview 258

Research...259

Character Analysis – From a Play............................261

Character Analysis – Not from A Play.....................263

The Nine Questions 265

Observations..267

Slice of Life..270

Animal Work..272

Meet Your Ancestor 277

Portrait Exercise 279

Private Moments...281

Loss and Betrayal 283

Character Analysis Sheet..284

CHARACTER ANALYSIS OVERVIEW

One of the challenging aspects about acting is creating a character. The best way to prepare yourself for Character Analysis is by using the exercises and techniques I described in the previous chapters. Creating a character does not happen in the blink of an eye. It takes more than just saying, "The character should be like this." You need to explore, discover, and investigate all possibilities.

Stanislavsky's *Building a Character* expounds deeply into this topic. He uses a fictional classroom setting to give examples on how to create a character. I definitely recommend reading it if you need a more thorough explanation into this process.

It's important that when you are creating a character that you don't have a preset notion for him or her. It's all right to have a general idea about your character. When you start to do your character analysis that's when your character will begin to come to life and develop into a full, living person not a caricature of what you want to represent.

The exercises I describe in the following sections help with character analysis and development. I put them in order of execution from easiest to hardest.

RESEARCH

Whether you are working on a monologue, scene or entire script, it's time to research your role. With the internet so readily available it should be easy to find information to help you build your character. If your character is based off of a real person, find as much information as possible online, at the library, or local bookstore and read up on them. Take notes on everything. Research can also be used when auditioning, especially for film when they request that you have a certain skill.

Use reliable sources when doing research. The last thing you want to do is garner information that is incorrect and apply it your work. It's not a bad idea to double check and cross-reference information to be sure that it is correct.

When doing research, always look up anything that is pertinent to the play: location, year, character's occupation, relationships, etc. This will help you flesh out ideas for your character including moving and speaking. For instance, if you are doing research and learn that it is very hot where the play takes place, you make choose to slow down the speech a bit to indicate how hot it is.

If the character has a special skill or is doing something in the play that you do not know how to accomplish, do your best to learn the basics so you can actually do it on stage or at least look like you know what you're doing. Some skills or characteristics that I had to do on stage or for a film audition and either knew or had to research were knitting, cooking in a restaurant, dressing in drag, mental illness, animal-work, drug use, being a man-servant, being shot, and working a cash register just to name a few.

Names of non-fictional people are every important in a script as well, if you don't a particular person that you are playing or referencing to or the meaning of certain words, look them up. You must know what you're saying throughout the entire script. If you don't know, then your character won't know. This is especially important when you are working on Shakespeare since the language is very foreign to us and many words he uses have several meanings.

When I was doing research for the role of Fagin in Oliver Twist, I researched London from 1838 – 1849, (this is the time periods that the play takes place), the life of Charles Dickens, and the original story of Oliver Twist. I discovered that Fagin was based off a real person, so I looked up information on him as well. With my first round of research finished, I had over 38 pages of material to work from. You never know what information you will glean from your research and what you will use to enrich your character work.

The Portable Acting Coach

CHAPTER 8: ACTING
CREATING A CHARACTER
CHARACTER ANALYSIS – FROM A PLAY

CHARACTER ANALYSIS – FROM A PLAY

Whether creating a character from a play or for an exercise you must ask yourself important questions to flesh out the exploration process and make it easier for you to act.

There are three types of characters:

1. A character from a play or scene.
2. A character based on a real person.
3. An original character for an exercise. This would include any re-creations of a person not specifically from a play and would also include yourself.

Let's look at creating a character from a play first. In order to start the process of building a character you must first read the play. Once you have read the play, read the play again – marking down on a list:

6. The things you say about your character.
7. The things other characters in the play say about you (your character).
8. The way the character's lines are written.
9. Any side notes or descriptions that the playwright might have included in the script referring to you (your character).

Make note of anything that is pertinent to your character: They are married, have a limp, written without any pauses in their speech, young, old, shy, outgoing, etc. Add this to the list you are creating about your character. Nothing is too minute when it comes to the description of your character.

After you have done this, look over the list and see what words you have written down. You will be amazed at how much you can discover from this beginning process. As you start to discover who your character is from this initial detective work, begin with one area of your character and begin to flesh it out.

You should be exploring objective, obstacle, tactics, etc. from CHAPTER 2 finding the voice of your character with CHAPTERS 5 and 6, discovering how your character moves with CHAPTER 7, and using techniques to help put you in the emotional state of your character with CHAPTER 4.

There are many exercises to explore character. I've included a few of them in the next sections to get you started. At the end of this chapter you will find a character analysis sheet that I find helpful to explore my character even further. I also use this as a tool for my actors to help them hone in on their characters during the rehearsal process and with my students when working on character development in the classroom.

CHARACTER ANALYSIS – NOT FROM A PLAY

Now let's look at creating a character not from a play. If your character is based on a real person, then you must do research and learn everything you can about that person. Watch videos if they are available, listen to them speak, watch how they walk, move, interact with other people. Write down anything you notice as if you were doing an observation exercise.

If you are creating a character from scratch, you will not have previous information to research or any help from a playwright. The information you gather about your character comes from any observation notes you may have taken, the situation they are in and the circumstances surrounding them. You have to take into account everything you know about them. You may not have much information to start with at the beginning but over time you will be able to bring more into the character from the exercises described later on in this chapter.

Things you need to consider when creating a character based on a real person or from scratch can include but are not limited to:

1. Age
2. Height
3. Weight
4. Location
5. Occupation
6. Status
7. Objective
8. Obstacle
9. Movement
10. Voice (pitch, breath, tone, vocal quality)
11. Speech (tempo, rhythm, enunciation, patterns, etc.)

Since this is your own creation you have unlimited potential for the character. They can be anyone you want. Live wherever you want them to live. To help develop your character look at Leading and Weight from CHAPTER 7, Voice and Speech from CHAPTERS 4 & 5 and from this chapter: Observations, Slice of Life, and Animal Work. Once you have your character more fully developed you can try Character Private Moments.

Starting from scratch and building a character that is not in a play can be a little difficult at first since there is no point of reference but as you start to fit the pieces of the puzzle together the character will grow.

THE NINE QUESTIONS

Whether creating a character from a play or for an exercise you must ask yourself important questions to flesh out the exploration process and make it easier for you to act. Uta Hagen's first book *Respect for Acting* has a list of nine questions that I feel are essential to further development and will inform you more about your character. These questions are:

1. Who am I?
2. What time is it?
3. Where am I?
4. What surrounds me?
5. What are the given circumstances?
6. What is my relationship?
7. What do I want?
8. What's in my way?
9. What do I do to get what I want?

Answer these questions with as much specificity as you can. The more you know about your character the more you will be able to act and portray them truthfully. Let's examine what each question is asking and what it pertains to in the context of your character.

1. Who am I? – This is your character, either original or from a play. Be descriptive and specific.
2. What time is it? – This refers to all matters with time: day, date, month, year, century, etc.?
3. Where am I? – This is the location of your character: country, state, city, the neighborhood, living area, room, etc.
4. What surrounds me? – Refers to everything around your character: people and objects.

5. What are the given circumstances? – This is everything that you know already including the past, present, future, events that have happened or scheduled to happen, weather, etc.
6. What is my relationship? – All relationships that you have including: to yourself, other characters, objects, etc.
7. What do I want? – The objective.
8. What's in my way? – The obstacle.
9. What do I do to get what I want? – The tactic.

With these questions fully answered, you should be able to dig deeper into your character and discover more about them: giving you an in-depth and more substantial way to understanding your character.

OBSERVATIONS

This is a great character development exercise because it's one of the few acting exercises that you can do outside of the house. You will need your journal, a pen, and about an hour to devote to this character development exercise.

Take your journal and go to a public place (park, museum, mall, zoo, etc.), anywhere that has a lot of people around and hopefully where you can sit and observe. The best part about this exercise is that all you do is watch people and notate their characteristics. This particular exercise will help to develop your observation skills in your daily life. Every time you do an observation, push yourself to be specific and detailed.

In an inconspicuous position, watch the crowd until you spot someone that draws your attention. Write down everything that you notice about this person. Nothing is too specific for this exercise. Ask yourself these questions as you observe them.

1. How are they dressed?
2. How tall are they?
3. How much do they weigh?
4. How do they interact with other people?
   a. Eye contact
   b. Leaning in or out
5. How is their posture?
   a. Are they elongated?
   b. Are they slouched?
   c. Do they look relaxed?
   d. Do they look stressed?

6. How do they walk?
   a. With which part of the body do they lead?
   b. What is the weight for their body parts?
      i. Arms?
      ii. Legs?
      iii. Head?
7. What is their breathing like?
   a. Quick?
   b. Slow?
   c. Uneven?
   d. Deep?
   e. Strained?
8. How do they speak?
   a. Head voice?
   b. Chest voice?
   c. Legato?
   d. Staccato?
   e. Fast?
   f. Slow?
9. Do they have any quirks?
   a. Tics
   b. Stutters
   c. Limps
   d. Awkward movements?
10. Look at the rhythm of their movements?
    a. Is there a connection?
    b. Does their body move as one part?
    c. Do they move other parts of their body when they don't have to?

11. If they are with someone can you determine the relationship?
    a. Parent?
    b. Son/Daughter/Grandchild?
    c. Friend?
    d. Caretaker?
12. What is their status?
    a. Rich?
    b. Poor?
    c. High?
    d. Low?

Analyze everything about that person. Ask yourself questions to glean as much information from watching them as you can. Once you have done this, find two other people to observe.

Once you have analyzed three people, go home and start to build a character from the profiles you have developed. From your notes, re-create these people. Do not mimic what you saw but try to become these people. Embody their physicality and personality. Assign them an occupation. Let them speak from what develops. Become the person you observed. Give them a name and then write down in your journal a description of yourself (as this character).

Do this for all three observations. Once you have done that, you now have character profiles that you can pull from to use when you need to build a character for a play, scene, monologue, etc.

The wonderful thing about this exercise is that it can be done anywhere, anytime, anyplace as long as you have your journal and something to write the information down. You will notice, as you continue these observations, that people may appear to be all the same, but everyone is different. They have their own ways of life and in their own right, a character all unto themselves.

SLICE OF LIFE

This is a tamed version of the Private Moment exercise described later on in this section. It can be done for exploration work at home and in a classroom setting. It is perfect for demonstrating that any action can be interesting to watch and engaging no matter how mundane if the principles of objective, obstacle and tactic are observed. When doing this exercise, just as with everything else I've discussed in this book, be specific. The more details you create, the more you will gain from it and, in turn, be more engaging for the audience.

The basic principle of the exercise is to re-create 5 – 10 minutes of your day. Other people can be "present" in your "scene" but you will not speak their lines. You will only talk to them or respond to them as you did when it was happening. There are three versions of this exercise: entering, leaving and action. Let's go over how each version will work.

ENTERING

This involves you recreating 5 - 10 minutes of entering into a space. It could be your home, a friend's house, your work, a store, the gym, anywhere. Re-enact the moment. Be as specific as you possibly can. Look at the Nine Questions.

LEAVING

This version of Slice of Life involves re-creating 5-10 minutes before you leave a space. The space doesn't have to be the same one that you used for entering. Use the Nine Questions.

ACTION

This 5 - 10 minute re-creation doesn't involve entering or leaving but deals with you doing an action that day (washing a car, cleaning house, writing a paper, organizing files, etc.) Again, ask yourself the Nine Questions to flesh out the specifics.

ADDING THE URGENCY

Using one of the three events that you re-created, it's time to add a sense of urgency. Pick something that puts you in a different state of mind while accomplishing the event (running late, have company coming over in 10 minutes, heard some bad news, lost something you need, coming or going into bad weather). You still must complete the entering, leaving or action event. How does this effect the actions that you are performing? Did anything change? Did you reprioritize to finish quicker? What happened to your body? Your breathing?

Try this for all three versions using different senses of urgency and see what you discover in the process.

ANIMAL WORK

This exploration exercise uses the traits of an animal and transfers them to your character to add an extra level of depth to them. There are many ways to explore character through animal work.

Note: The first exercise in this section will be the basis for which all other animal exercises and variations of it come from, so be familiar with it.

ANIMAL EXERCISE: EXPLORING AN ANIMAL

1. Pick an animal. Do research on the animal like you would for your character. Try to watch as many videos about the animal and study it. Learn about its habitat, study its movement, how does it walk, run, stretch? Is it a pack animal? Is it a loner? How does it defend itself? Is it aggressive, passive? Study the way it makes sound. Is it loud? Quiet? Is it an elongated or short sound? Is it legato or staccato? Don't look at a video for 5 minutes and think you have the animal. Spend as much time as you can studying it before moving on to the next part of the exercise.

2. Once you have studied the animal it's time to explore. Start by using the Green Light Exercise from CHAPTER 4. Once you're in a state of relaxation, picture the animal in your head. Allow the animal to sink into your mind and slowly inhabit your body. Do not move yet. Simply let the essence of the animal permeate your body. After 15 minutes of this, I want you to slowly roll to your side and position yourself in a hunkered position: sitting on your knees, your chest to your thighs and your arms to your sides on the ground. Continue to think about your animal.

3. When you are ready, allow the animal inside you to emerge. Imagine that it is waking up from a sleep. Picture your surroundings. Eventually move around so the animal is exploring its surroundings. Is it hungry? Is it curious? Keep exploring the animal and allow time to pass at a slightly faster pace so that you can explore the animal at all times of the day. Use its voice to communicate with others of its species. Be specific in what it is saying through its animal sound.

4. Allow the day to continue until it is time for the animal to go back to sleep. Once you have gone back to sleep, allow yourself to roll onto your back in the relaxed position and let the animal drift away back into your mind. Keep breathing and eventually allow your animal to fade into your subconscious and come into focus as yourself. Allow yourself to stand up and take a few breaths. Now write in your journal about your experience.

ANIMAL EXERCISE, VARIATION #1: SENSE OF LOSS AND BETRAYAL

1. Repeat steps 1 – 3 from the exercise: Exploring the Animal.
2. Once you have awakened the animal and explored its surroundings, allow it to experience one of the following:
   a. Sense of loss
   b. Sense of betrayal
   c. Sense of being lost
   d. Sense of being abandoned
3. Explore what happens to your animal in this state of mind. How is it different? Does it move differently? Are the sounds different? Be specific in the situation. Continue to explore the emotion for at least 20 – 30 minutes then go to step 4 from the exercise: Exploring the Animal.

ANIMAL EXERCISE, VARIATION #2: ANIMAL TO HUMAN

1. Repeat steps 1 - 3 from the exercise: Exploring the Animal.
2. Slowly allow your animal to transfer into a human. Don't rush. Let one quality be infused and then add another. Keep doing this until the animal is fully integrated into a human. How do the animal movements and thoughts transfer into a human? Justify these with human characteristics. Explore your newly created character. Give them a voice. What kind of surroundings would this person be in? Where would they live? What kind of person would they be? What is their personality? How do they relate to other people?
3. Keep exploring this character for 20 – 30 minutes then allow the character to transform back into an animal.
4. Repeat step 4 from the exercise: Exploring the Animal

ANIMAL EXERCISE, VARIATION #3: CHARACTER'S ANIMAL

1. Think of your character. Imagine what kind of animal they would be. With the animal you have chosen, repeat steps 1 - 4 from the exercise: Exploring the Animal.

ANIMAL EXERCISE, VARIATION #4: CHARACTER'S ANIMAL: SENSE OF LOSS AND BETRAYAL

1. Repeat the same exercise from Variation #1: Sense of Loss and Betrayal except have your character's animal in mind

ANIMAL EXERCISE, VARIATION #5: ANIMAL TO CHARACTER

Repeat steps 1 - 3 from the exercise: Exploring the Animal.

1. Slowly allow your animal to transfer into your character. Again, don't rush it. Let one quality be infused and then add another. Keep doing this until the animal is fully integrated in your character. How do the animal movements and thoughts transfer into your character? Explore your character with the animal traits.
2. Keep exploring this character for 20 – 30 minutes then allow the character to transform back into an animal.
3. Repeat step 4 from the exercise: Exploring the Animal

ANIMAL EXERCISE, VARIATION #6: CHARACTER TO ANIMAL

1. Walk around the room as your character. Allow your body to become adjusted to your character and then slowly allow them to transform into the animal.

2. Explore the animal for 15 – 20 minutes as described in step 3 from the exercise: Exploring the Animal,

3. Repeat step 2 from Variation #2: Animal to Human. This time, allowing the animal to transform back into your character. How did this affect the way your character moves? Were there any differences? What did you notice?

Doing animal work is a great way to explore and gain more information about your character and create a more interesting and developed character for the stage.

MEET YOUR ANCESTOR

Before beginning this exercise, set up two chairs facing each other about two feet apart. Begin the exercise by using the Green Light Exercise (4: BEYOND THE BASICS). Once you're in a state of relaxation, allow yourself or your character, (whoever is meeting their ancestor), to stand up and sit in one of the chairs.

Imagine that you are looking into a mirror and, through your mind's eye, see your face in the mirror. Examine it thoroughly. Look at the shape of the face, your skin, the eyes, the shape of your lips, the hair, everything. Spend 10 – 15 minutes doing this.

After you have done that, allow the image in the mirror to change and become an ancestor of yours. How is their face different? Explore their face the same way as you explored yours. Again allow 10 – 15 minutes for this exploration.

Next, slowly stand up and sit in the other chair. Now you are your ancestor. Look at the "person" sitting across from you and examine that face from your perspective. How is their face like yours and how is it different? Be specific. Examine their face. What do their eyes tell you? After you have explored your "descendant's" face, reach over to them through the "mirror" and hand them something. It can be anything that can fit in a hand.

Stand back up and sit in the other chair once more. Now, you are yourself again and receiving the object from your ancestor. What is the object that they have given you? Take the object and look at it. Examine it and be specific in what you see. How does this object make you feel?

Again, return to the other chair and watch your "descendent" take the object. How does that make you feel? Look into their eyes and tell them something that you think they need to hear.

After you have spoken to them and told them what you wanted to say, stand up and return to the other chair. Look at your ancestor and into their face and receive the message they are telling you. How does it make you feel? Let their words sink into your body. Keep looking at them and build that connection.

With their object in your possession and their words imparted to you, it is time to say good-bye. Say anything you want to say to them and watch as their face slowly fades away and is replaced once again by your reflection in the mirror. Allow yourself some time to let sink in what has happened. Take the object they have given you and place it safely away.

Close your eyes, and use your breath to bring yourself to the present surroundings. Write in your journal what you experienced.

PORTRAIT EXERCISE

This is a great way to put your character development exercises to the test using everything we have learned in the previous chapters. You begin by finding a picture that has at least one person in it. Someone in the picture who you think would be an interesting character. Try to find a picture that could have a story behind it. It can be from a magazine, a work of art, or the cover of a book, anything but an everyday photograph.

With your picture chosen, choose the person from the picture that you want to use. Now you will re-create the background of the picture filling in everything but leaving the person you chose out. So, you will fill in that space with what that picture would have if that person wasn't there.

You can use anything as the canvas as long as it's tall enough to be completely behind you and you can be in front of the canvas without being taller than it. You can also use whatever drawing media you choose: crayons, pens, paint, watercolors, etc.

To the best of your ability re-create the background. Depending on your skill level this could take 1 day up to 3 weeks. Once you have the background completed, think about the character that you took out of the picture and imagine everything about them using the Observation exercise from this chapter. These observations will be strictly from your own imagination.

After completing your observation, think of the situation they would be in, in this picture. Create a story for them. There should be a beginning, middle, and an end. Once you have a story for them, you will act it out, using your own dialogue. You can be talking to other people in this story but you will not use any actual people in this scene. This is a solo exercise. During this story that you are acting out, find a point where this character assumes the position in front of the background

279

when the photo was taken and then continue on with the story until its conclusion.

You will learn from this exercise that not only can you develop a full living character with a background story but that a character is more than just what you see when they are on stage (or in a picture). They all have stories that start before and continue after they appear.

PRIVATE MOMENTS

Private moments are one of the most difficult exercises to do. Not simply because of the level of execution but from the vulnerability that we put ourselves in. We expose ourselves openly and truthfully without anything to hide behind, revealing our soul and spirit in the process. To get the most out of doing a private moment with our character we must first do one for ourselves.

Here is how a private moment works. You set up the private moment by recreating a place where you would be alone but with the potential of someone walking into the room at any time. Then you allow yourself for 30 minutes to do something, that if someone were to walk in, you would immediately stop. It's common for us to think of something along the sexual nature but that isn't always the case.

There are many things that we do alone that we wouldn't want other people knowing, such as revealing our inner personal struggles, our weaknesses, our secret triumphs, our need for acceptance. We often talk to ourselves truthfully, admitting things that no one else should know. We laugh, we cry, we get angry, we jump up and down out of joy, we sit, and we contemplate, the list goes on and on.

When you truly perform a private moment, you open up your soul and let the true you out because no one else can see you and see how you really feel. The hard part comes when you perform this in front of people and let them see the private moment for themselves. You are not performing for them; you are inviting them to take in your secret, innermost feelings, and thoughts. The exercise is not about entertaining them; it's about sharing with them.

After you have done the private moment for yourself, I challenge you to invite someone that you know to your place to re-create it for them. If you find yourself hesitant because you would feel susceptible, defenseless, completely open, and vulnerable, then the private moment you picked is the right choice.

Once you have experienced your personal private moment, then you can create a private moment for your character using the exact same guidelines as previously described. You will discover that everyone, no matter who they are, has feelings and vulnerabilities that they don't want anyone to find out.

LOSS AND BETRAYAL

This involves journal work and is based off Emotional Recall Exercise #2 found in CHAPTER 4. Follow the exercise I described but specifically aim it at your character. Follow those directions and allow yourself to take your character back to a time when they felt loss or betrayal. They can be at any age when this loss/betrayal event happened. Let them experience this moment truthfully.

After they have fully experienced that memory, allow them to write in your journal regarding that experience. It should be a response to the memory. Maybe they are writing a letter, making a diary entry or drawing a picture. Let it happen naturally don't predetermine how they will express it. You should allow yourself 15 – 20 minutes for this journal work but can take longer until you feel you have completed the task then continue following the directions from that section and allow yourself to return back to your relaxed state of being.

CHARACTER ANALYSIS SHEET

Answer these questions as your character:

1. What part of my body do I lead from?
2. What is the base of my movement (fast, slow, connected, disconnected)?
3. Where is my center?
4. What is my weight (as in movement (light, heavy)? Be specific.
5. How do I move through space?
6. What is my status?
7. What do I want?
8. What's in my way?
9. What are my patterns of speech?
10. What is my occupation?
11. If I were a car, I would be:
12. If I were a flower, I would be:
13. If I were a smell/scent, I would be:
14. If I were an animal, I would be:
15. If I were a color, I would be:
16. If I was a food, I would be:
17. How would I describe myself?
18. Describe your character in the third person if you were to see them on the street?

CHAPTER 9: WORKING ON MONOLOGUES AND SCENES

Monologues Overview 286

Cutting and PastingCutting and Pasting...................287

Choosing the Monologue......................................293

Analyzing the Monologue 295

Marking the Monologue 296

Exploring the Monologue 297

Blocking the Monologue 300

Scenes Overview 304

Fair Verona...305

Preparing 306

Working with a Partner...307

Blocking a Scene 308

Using Props and Set...309

MONOLOGUES OVERVIEW

Finding a monologue can be a challenge. Most of the online play services that sell plays like Concord Theatricals formally Samuel French Company. And Dramatist Play Service (DPS) sometimes offer a preview of the script but sometimes that's not enough to know if you'll like the play or even know if there is a monologue in it for you to do. You can go to bookstores but many of them only have a small section of plays most of them classic, most are classical, and a few recent entries.

They usually have monologue books for you to buy, but again, sometimes it's hard to tell if the monologue from the collection is from an actual play or a stand-alone. I'll talk about that in the "Choosing a Monologue" section of this chapter.

If you go to an audition and hear a monologue you like, write it down and try to find it so you can learn it for a for a future audition. Your acting friends may have some ideas, as well as an acting coach. And finally, just go online and search for monologues and see what pops up. In any case, there are plenty of resources you can use to search and find monologues.

A resource you might find useful is **stageagent.com**. It doesn't have a huge variety to choose from but it's a great place to start. The other two web sites which I mentioned above are: **dramatists.com** and **concordtheatricals.com** (Formally Samuel French, Inc.)

Whatever way you find your monologue, know that it's going to take some time. But finding the right monologue that works for you is better than finding a mediocre one that sometimes works on occasions.

CUTTING AND PASTING

This term refers to taking a monologue and shortening it for the purposes of an audition or taking a scene between two people and removing the dialogue of one character to create a monologue. This is a standard practice for most actors, however, remember that this does not mean you can replace words that you don't want to say if it is in the lines you are keeping.

In the old days before computers were invented, actors would photocopy a monologue and literally cut out the sections of the monologue they wanted to use with scissors and paste it into their monologue book. This process was used primarily to shorten the monologue because a monologue should be no longer than a minute and a half, two minutes absolute maximum for an audition.

This phrase was used long before it was adopted by computer users. When cutting and pasting a monologue there are a few things to keep in mind.

1. Do your best to keep the arc of the monologue intact.
2. Be sure the ideas and a character's thought process make sense.
3. Anything that it is important for the character to say to move the monologue forward remains.
4. If, creating a monologue from a scene and there is a transition line that the other character says that is important for your character's monologue to make sense, simply have your character say that line as if they are repeating or commenting on that line and then continue with the actual lines you are keeping.

I'm going to give you two examples of the cutting and pasting technique with two monologues that I did with this method. The first is example is taking a scene and turning it into a monologue.

This is from the brilliantly funny play, *Noises Off* by Michael Frayne. Here is the scene:

***

Garry Don't worry about the words, Dotty, my pet.

Dotty Coming up like oranges and lemons.

Garry Listen, Dotty, your words are fine, your words are better that the, do you know what I mean? (To Brooke) Isn't that right?

Brooke ((her thoughts elsewhere) Sorry?

Garry (to Dotty) I mean, OK, so he's the, you know. Fine. But, Dotty, love, you've been playing this kind of part for, well, Jesus, you know what I mean.

Lloyd All right? So. Garry and Brooke are off, Dotty's· holding the receiver…

Garry No, but here we are, we're all thinking, my God, we open tomorrow night, we've only had a fortnight to rehearse, we don't' know where we are, but my God, here we are!

Dotty That's right, my sweet. Isn't that right, Lloyd?

Lloyd Brilliantly put, Garry.

Garry No, but we've got to play Weston-super-Mare all the rest of this week, then Yeovil, then God knows where, then God knows where else, and so on for God knows how long, and we're all of us feeling pretty much, you…9To Brooke) I mean, aren't you?

Brooke Sorry?

***

And here is the cut and paste version:

Garry Listen, Dotty, your words are fine, your words are better that the, do you know what I mean? (To Brooke) Isn't that right? (To Dotty) I mean, OK, so he's the, you know. Fine. But, Dotty, love, you've been playing this kind of part for, well, Jesus, you know what I mean. No, but here we are, we're all thinking, my God, we open tomorrow night, we've only had a fortnight to rehearse, we don't' know where we are, but my God, here we are! No, but we've got to play Weston-super-Mare all the rest of this week, then Yeovil, then God knows where, then God knows where else, and so on for God knows how long, and we're all of us feeling pretty much, you…(To Brooke) I mean, aren't you?

Notice, that the momentum of the dialogue stays intact, the character is still fully fleshed out, and it makes sense by itself. There was no need for me to say another character's line, I just used a pause to listen and see the other character's reactions before continuing the monologue.

The next example is taking a monologue and cutting it shorter. This is from the play *The Pillowman"* by Martin McDonagh.

Ariel Well, y'know, I'll tell you what there is about me. There is an overwhelming, and there is an all-pervading, hatred . . . a hatred . . . of people like you. Of people who lay even the littlest finger . . . on children. I wake up with it. It wakes me up. It rides on the bus with me to work. It whispers to me, "They will not get away with it." I come in early. I make sure all the bindings are clean and the electrodes are in the right order so we won't . . . waste . . . time. I admit, sometimes I use excessive force. And sometimes I use excessive force on an entirely innocent individual. But I'll tell you this. If an entirely innocent individual leaves this room for the outside world, they're not gonna contemplate even raising their voice to a little kid again, just in case I hear'em and drag'em in here for another load of excessive force. Now, is this kind of behavior in an officer of the law in some way questionable morally? Of course it is! But you know what? I don't care! 'Cos, when I'm an old man, you know what? Little kids are gonna follow me around and they're gonna know my name and what I stood for, and they're gonna give me some of their sweets in thanks, and I'm gonna take those sweets and thank them and tell them to get home safe, and I'm gonna be happy. Not because of the sweets, I don't really like sweets, but because I'd know . . . I'd know in my heart, that if I hadn't been there, not all of them would have been there. Because I'm a good policeman. Not necessarily good in the sense of being able to solve lots of stuff, because I'm not, but good in the sense of I stand for something. I stand for something. I stand on the right side. The child's side. The opposite side to you. And so, naturally when I hear that a child has been killed in a fashion . . . in a fashion such as this . . . You know what? I would torture you to death just for writing a story like that, let alone acting it out! 'Cos two wrongs do not make a right. Two wrongs do not make a right. So kneel down over here, please, so I can connect you to this battery.

And here is the cut version:

Ariel Well, y'know, I'll tell you what there is about me. There is an overwhelming, and there is an all-pervading, hatred . . . a hatred . . . of people like you. Of people who lay even the littlest finger . . . on children. I wake up with it. It wakes me up. It rides on the bus with me to work. It whispers to me, "They will not get away with it." I come in early. I make sure all the bindings are clean and the electrodes are in the right order so we won't . . . waste . . . time. I admit, sometimes I use excessive force. And sometimes I use excessive force on an entirely innocent individual. But I'll tell you this. If an entirely innocent individual leaves this room for the outside world, they're not gonna contemplate even raising their voice to a little kid again, just in case I hear'em and drag'em in here for another load of excessive force. Now, is this kind of behavior in an officer of the law in some way questionable morally? Of course it is! But you know what? I don't care! Because I'm a good policeman. Not necessarily good in the sense of being able to solve lots of stuff, because I'm not, but good in the sense of I stand for something. I stand for something. I stand on the right side. The child's side. The opposite side to you. And so, naturally when I hear that a child has been killed in a fashion . . . in a fashion such as this . . . You know what? I would torture you to death just for writing a story like that, let alone acting it out! 'Cos two wrongs do not make a right. Two wrongs do not make a right. So kneel down over here, please, so I can connect you to this battery.

As you can see from the original script the monologue is longer than two minutes. I simply cut out one paragraph to shorten it a bit. The main idea of the story stays in place, we lose nothing about the character, and there is still an arc to the monologue.

Of course, this was a simple example that just removed one paragraph to make it work, but some monologues might take some finesse and more extensive cuts in order to make it work and fit into a shorter monologue.

In this last example, you simply have to stop the monologue at a place that seems appropriate without cutting anything in between.
This is from the play *Thieves* by Herb Gardner. The bolded text is what I cut out to shorten it just a bit.

Martin First, Sally...first, I want you to know how much I appreciate the wonderful work you've done on our apartment here. How you've managed to capture, in only five short weeks, the subtle, elusive, yet classic mood previously found only in the Port Authority Bus Terminal. In addition, Sally, you have somewhat mystically, lost or forgotten the name of the moving and storage company with whom you placed nearly fifty-five thousand dollars' worth of our furniture. This, coupled with the fact that you disappeared eight days ago on what was ostensibly a trip to Gristede Brothers to buy some Strawberry Yogurt, and did not return until this evening, has led to a certain amount of confusion for me...all confusion, of course vanished with the arrival last week of this simple, touching, yet concise note from the Misters Morris, Klein, Fishback and Fishback---(pulls out crumpled letter and reads)---"We have been retained by your wife, Sally Lane Cramer, herein after referred to as 'Wife', to represent her in the matter of your divorce. Said wife having requested that her whereabouts remain unknown to you at the present, we therefore..." (Carefully folding letter into paper airplane) After eight days of staring into the air conditioner, wondering which Santini brother had my furniture, which Gristede Brother had my wife, and which Fishback owned my soul, a light began to dawn...or maybe one went out...and I realized that nobody was hiding you from me, that your whereabouts, as said wife, have been unknown to me for years...that you make a fine letter writer, a great decorator, and a perfect stranger. **You said you came back to talk about the divorce. You didn't mention it. Neither did I. And the habit, the habit of being together, began again. But I couldn't sleep. I couldn't sleep and I thought about it and tonight, Sally, I have decided to retire from the games. The Olympics are over, lady, the torch is out...and you are free. (He tosses the paper airplane.) Said husband, hereinafter referred to as 'gone', has had it.**

By following my examples, you can create a monologue form any script if it still makes sense after you've finished. But please note that not all monologues have the ability to be cut, either because of the way it's written or if there is too much dialogue in a scene that is important for the storytelling and wouldn't make sense for the other character to say it.

Choosing the Monologue

When choosing a monologue, the first rule is it must be from a play (Full-length, One-Act, 10-Minute). Monologues that do not come from a play or film are called a "Stand-alone". This means that it was written specifically as a self-contained monologue. There are many reasons why these types of monologues don't work at an audition,

1. Mostly expositional - You're telling a story rather than living in a moment.
2. No character development – Because it's only a monologue, it becomes harder for you as the actor to develop a character since there is no backstory. You have to create everything to find the given circumstances so you don't portray a generic character.
3. Harder to act – Since you don't have a backstory, you also have to create the situation so you can choose the right verbs so that you can make the story-telling active. That makes it even harder for you.

I can usually spot one right away, especially if the title of the play appears in the actual monologue, which turns me off as a director because I'm thinking, "Out of so many women monologues out there, why are they doing this one?".

There are mixed reviews about doing film monologues for stage productions, so if you absolutely feel compelled to do one, be sure to do one that is not iconic, i.e. Jack Nicolson in *A Few Good* Men, Sally Field's funeral speech in *Steel Magnolias*, Samuel M. Jackson in *Pulp Fiction*, Jodie Foster in *The Accused*, and Marlon Brando's classic speech from *On the Waterfront*, "I coulda been a contender" just to name a few.

Regardless of the type of monologue you choose it must be from a play or film.

When choosing a monologue try to pick one based on a character that you would cast yourself as. The roles you see yourself playing will help determine your age range. It frowned upon for young actors doing monologues that are clearly written for someone older and vice-versa. It is not wise to do a monologue by a character that you would never get cast as; the whole point of the audition is to see if you are right for a part, not to show off and say "You wish you could do this part."

As you start figuring out what age rage you are, you also want to think about what kind of roles you can do. This is called "type". A few of the common types are: The leading man, the ingénue, the best friend, quirky, uptight, easy-going, teacher, lawyer, doctor, and these are just a few. There are variations of type, as well. You could be typed in two categories or a combination but that is for you to figure out You can always ask people you know what they could see you playing or doing.

Now with that being said, there's no reason you shouldn't stretch yourself too. Have one of these "out-of-type" character monologues handy in case they ask to see something else. And also, you never know, you may grow into that part as you get older.

One thing that I find important are the words. If my mouth doesn't feel right saying the words or I don't connect to the character based on what they're saying, I will not consider that monologue. That is equally important, if you have to "act" to do the monologue than it's not the one for you.

Look to see if the monologue has something that speaks out to you that you can work with on stage. Sometimes, if the dialogue permits it, you can cut and paste a monologue using a two-character dialogue as I described in the previous section.

ANALYZING THE MONOLOGUE

Once you've chosen a monologue, it's time to analyze it. This can be the best part, learning about your character, figuring out what they want, how they are going to get, their personality, etc. You get this information by reading the play, if you haven't already. It is impossible to make choices about your character based on the monologue alone. Do not make that mistake.

If you don't have access to the entire play at home you can go to your public library, search online, ask your actor friends if they have a copy, or talk to a local theatre. On the other hand, if you are on a time constraint and don't have time read the play or simply can't find it, even reading the synopsis might give you some clues on the direction to go.

Many beginning actors skip this step, which is crucial for any monologue work. You must read the play to understand the character that you are portraying. The play offers insights to the character's wants, needs, emotions, and state of mind. You will discover how other characters feel about you and how the world of the play revolves around the character you've chosen.

Now it's time to analyze the monologue. Figure out what the intention is, what the tactic is. What words are important? How does the play relate to the monologue? What is the overall feeling of it? What is the personality of the character saying these words? Is there a dialect? Who are they speaking to? Seems like a lot to remember. Well it is. So how do you keep track of all this while working on your monologue. We put everything down on the script. This is called "marking" and is covered in the next section.

MARKING THE MONOLOGUE

With the analysis finished, we have to keep track of the choices we are making and the other factors that we discovered from analyzing the monologue. We do that by marking the script. We put down in the margins all the ideas that we have. Always write in pencil because ideas change.

We want to mark down as much as possible so we can see the path our character is taking. Here are some markings I use to keep track of what's happening and as I said in CHAPTER 4, "Make the intangible, tangible."

1. Circle the words that are important.
2. Mark your beats
3. Draw a square around the first word of a sentence and draw an underscore through that line to the margin to denote which tactic you are using.
4. Circle words or sentences and draw a line from it to the margin to give yourself notes such as "Think of my ex-boss", or "Don't push volume".

Whatever you want to remind yourself, put it there. No one else will see your monologue and if you have someone helping you, you give them a clean copy. These notes are your guide and should be kept a secret. No one should know what you use to get you where you need to be.

These marking will not happen all at once. As you begin, it will only contain what you've analyzed about it. But as you keep exploring the monologue you will add more and more: building that journey your character is taking with your ideas.

EXPLORING THE MONOLOGUE

After analyzing the monologue, read the monologue again. This time, doing a cold reading of it out loud, just to see where your voice and tempo naturally wants to go. Check to make sure you can say all the words. Also check on breath, to make sure you're not running out of air during sentences and the breath flows easily and correctly.

Break the monologue down and find the objectives, obstacles and tactics. Search for active verbs that you can work with your body. Also search within the text to see if anything can be said in a different light, i.e., something funny said sad, or something mad said sarcastic. Explore the piece thoroughly. Don't choreograph the monologue with emotion. Find what the character wants and find those tactics to get your character to reach their objective.

Look for the highs and lows of the piece. Mark your script for all the arcs that you find. A simple arrow curving up should be enough to remind you that the section coming up is an arc in the monologue. Remember that arcs can also indicate highly emotional response from a character whether positive or negative. Arcs don't mean you should get louder or to act bigger. It simply means your character is experiencing a heightened, emotional moment different from the previous moment or beat.

Allow your body to feel the words, see where it takes your character. Again I must emphasize, **do not set anything in stone.** Explore moving as you speak the words. Experiment with acting out what you are saying. Imagine saying your monologue to someone who is deaf or who doesn't speak English and you are trying to get them to understand what you are saying through your body movements. Don't hold back. Use the "Mud Exercise" from CHAPTER 7 to further examine the movement of your piece. Pick an action like washing a car, doing dishes or cleaning the house. As you speak your monologue how does your body react and what happens to the action that you are trying to accomplish.

It's also here that you look back at the vocal techniques you are using for the piece. Make sure you're using the range in your voice, changing tempos, and using your breath correctly. Explore saying the monologue in a complete whisper. Sing the monologue to an original tune. Try saying the monologue really fast or very slow. Practice saying it up and down a musical scale. Use every form of vocal musicality and expression that I have discussed in the CHAPTER 6 and registration from CHAPTER 5.

Even in a monologue you are still fighting for something. Always keep the character's needs organic. Keep it simple. If you over complicate it, the monologue will become out of focus and unclear and look manipulated which will lose the audience's interest...fast. Keep exploring.

EXERCISES FOR EXPLORING A MONOLOGUE

PARAPHRASE

Say a monologue or scene in your own words. Identify the meaning and listen to how your voice responds to your own ideas.

GIBBERISH

Say a monologue or scene in gibberish to discover the same impulses without written text. The words you say should not be recognizable as a real foreign language. They are pure nonsensical words.

BLOCKING THE MONOLOGUE

Blocking a monologue is one of the hardest things to do by yourself. Movement can refer to an action the character does or simply standing still. You don't move because you want to, you move because the character needs to.

Sometimes you will find clues in the monologue that will help you find the movement needed in the piece. Usually the playwright will include direction, other times a line might hint that the character is doing something. Be a script detective and find these clues.

Above all, let the movement be organic. Let it come from within yourself through instinct. Movement for the sake of movement will give your acting a lack of meaning and purpose. It will distract the audience and pull them out of the moment and you will lose their interest.

Explore the monologue by physically acting out all the verbs. Look at any directions the playwright may have included. Use your rehearsal environment to set-up the place where your character is located. Follow your impulses and see where it takes you. It's all right if you have too much movement in the beginning of this process. It will get pared down as you start to edit your blocking and use only the movements that help your character tell the story.

Remember that blocking comes from a character's intention, tactic, action and eventually, emotion.

FINAL LOOK OVER

Continue to explore and strengthen the objectives, tactics, and vocal flows of the monologue and keep preparing the piece. Check to make sure your blocking is natural and simple. Not too much, not too little. There should not be a presentational feel to it unless that is the style of the piece. Is your voice natural and free? Or does it sound manipulated and forced? Is your character saying the text or are you acting it? Even though you're portraying a character, you still want it to sound unrehearsed and not forced. You want people to believe that this could be you, because it sounds and looks natural.

Keep looking over your lines. It's easy to start paraphrasing the lines as you get further along in the process. Check in with your body. Is it relaxed and tension-free? Is your body telling the story with you? Is your breathing easy and flowing freely?

During this final stage of the monologue process, keep exploring. The monologue should be a living, breathing entity, and should continue to grow every time you perform it.

This is a monologue that I use for auditions from *The Lesson* by Eugene Ionesco. On this page is the unaltered version, without any markings. On the following page you will see the same monologue with the way I marked it. Please note, that this is a cut and paste version of the monologue taken from a scene.

The Professor - The Lesson - Eugene Ionesco

Tell me if you are not too exhausted, how many are four minus three? (Pause) I'm sorry, but I'm obliged to contradict you. Four minus three does not make seven. You are confused: four plus three makes seven, four minus three does not make seven...This is not addition anymore, we must now subtract. Look here. Here are three matches. And here is another one, that makes four. Now watch carefully - we have four matches, I take one away, now how many are left? Five? That's not it. That's not it at all, you always have a tendency to add. But one must be able to subtract too. It's not enough to integrate, you must also disintegrate. That's the way life is. That's philosophy. That's science. That's progress. Civilization. Let us take a simpler example. If you had two noses and I pulled one of them off...how many would you have? (Pause) What do you mean, none? You've not understood my example. Suppose you have only one ear. If I gave you another one, how many would you have? Good and if I gave you still another one how many would you have? Now, I take one away...and there remains...how many ears? Good. I take away still another one, how many do you have left? No, you have two. I take one away, I eat one up, then how many do you have left? Let's leave this for the moment. Let's go on to another exercise...

The Professor - The Lesson - Eugene Ionesco

Tell me if you are not too exhausted, how many are four minus three? (pause) I'm sorry, but I'm obliged to contradict you. Four minus three does not make seven. You are confused: four plus three makes seven, four minus three does not make seven... This is not addition anymore, we must now subtract. Look here. Here are three matches. And here is another one, that makes four. Now watch carefully - we have four matches, I take one away, now how many are left? Five? That's not it. That's not it at all, you always have a tendency to add. But one must be able to subtract too. It's not enough to integrate, you must also disintegrate. That's the way life is. That's philosophy. That's science. That's progress. Civilization. Let us take a simpler example. If you had two noses and I pulled one of them off...how many would you have? (Pause) What do you mean, none? You've not understood my example. Suppose you have only one ear. If I gave you another one, how many would you have? Good and if I gave you still another one how many would you have? Now, I take one away...and there remains...how many ears? Good. I take away still another one, how many do you have left? No, you have two. I take one away, I eat one up, then how many do you have left? Let's leave this for the moment. Let's go on to another exercise...

Annotations (objectives / "above" the text):

- To push forward
- To correct
- To enlighten
- To make my point
- I have to make her understand.
- As if revealing a magic trick.
- To keep control of my patience. I'm frustrated.
- To drill into her head. I can feel my patience slipping.
- I will make her understand.
- This is my fault. I'm not explaining this right.
- To pat her on the back.
- Walking on eggshells.
- To validate her worth.
- To explode.
- Take a breath. Regain composure.

Annotations ("below" the text):

- She answers 7.
- Don't get angry, she misunderstood
- She doesn't understand
- As if explaining to a foreigner
- Why does she keep adding?
- Take a breath. Let me start over.
- Psychological gesture
- She answers none.
- Psychological gesture
- Reinforce her ability to do mathematics.
- I'm getting through to her.
- I am talking to a brick wall.
- I'm a teacher. I can't lose my control.

OVERALL OBJECTIVE: TO PREPARE HER FOR HER DOCTOR'S ORAL EXAM AND TEST HER KNOWLEDGE ON SUBTRACTION.

303

SCENES OVERVIEW

Scene Analysis is handled the same way that you analyze and work with a monologue except that you are including the entire scene not just a monologue from it. When you are working on a scene, just as with a monologue, you should read the play to get as much information about your character.

The important thing to remember is that you are working with a partner or partners now and they are relying on you to give them your all. You should put as much work into the process of the scene as you would if you were preparing a monologue. The more you give them, the more they'll give you, and together you will create a seamless piece of scene work.

FAIR VERONA

I first heard the phrase "fair Verona" while I was studying Shakespeare at conservatory. In simplest terms it means what the audience knows at the beginning of the play. It comes from the opening soliloquy in *Romeo and Juliet* when the chorus comes out and sets up the play by telling the audience what has already happened and giving the audience all the information they need to know.

These days we rarely use exposition to set a play up for an audience. They learn about the show from how the stage is set and what the actors say at the beginning of the play.

When you first get your scene and read it, figure out what the audience will know from the first few lines of the play. Look at the way the characters speak to each other: Is their relationship clear? Go through the beginning with a fine-tooth comb. Any information that will help establish the scene should be brought forth to the audience.

Let's look at the opening of *Oleanna* and see what information the audience can gain from the opening moments of the scene. By the set we can tell that the play takes place in a school of some sort. John is a teacher and is on the phone talking to his wife who seems upset about a purchase of a house. We see Carol coming in with schoolbooks so we know she is a student. And by the few opening lines we find that she did not schedule an appointment but dropped in unexpectedly to discuss a problem that she is having with the class. We also know that it takes place in contemporary times from the way John and Carol are dressed.

With all that set in place, we have given the audience a good amount of "fair Verona" and information and they can now watch the drama unfold and be drawn into the world of the play. This also gives you, the actor, a great jumping point to begin your work on the scene and to run with it.

PREPARING

When preparing for your scene, you should read the entire play, analyze it, and do research. This should go without saying but, (as we get more in tune with our craft), we tend to forget this step or become lazy about it. Read it all the way through and do your best not to try and say your lines from the play or your scene.

If you haven't already done so, you should meet with your partner so you can discuss what is fair Verona and the given circumstances for the scene, including: the moment before, time, location, relationship, status, and anything you've uncovered through research. It is important to do this so that when both you and your partner are working alone on the scene, you will be working within the same parameters for both your characters.

You can always refer back to CHAPTER 8 to refresh your memory on character analysis before you start creating your character for the scene. You will be fleshing out your character throughout the process of scene study but you should have a basic understanding of your character before rehearsing with your partner for the first time.

Read your lines from your scene without an objective or tactic behind them. Let your mouth get used to saying the lines. Once you have done this a few times, figure out what you want in the scene from what your character says and what is said to them. Mark your scene with your initial, instinctual ideas of objectives, tactics, sensory feelings, "as ifs", arcs, and emotional tones for your character in your script.

As you start to identify your character through your character analysis, you will find that the lines will come easier to you and you can start using your preferred technique to memorize your lines. This is covered in the next section of this chapter. Once you are no longer dependent on the script, you will find that you can make newer discoveries about your character.

Note: Remember to always write in pencil…things change.

WORKING WITH A PARTNER

When working with a partner you must remember you are working together towards the same result: an engaging scene. Neither one of you should be calling the shots when it comes to blocking, acting, or voicing an opinion about the elements of the scene.

Do not, under any circumstances, tell your partner to do something differently when it comes to their acting. If you find that you are not getting what you need from them emotionally, you must tap into your resources as an actor and make it work for you. Do not give your partner acting notes any time during the scene study process. That is not your job or responsibility. Each actor has their own way of working and it may take someone longer or shorter, depending on their skill, to reach the place where they need to be. Respect their journey.

If they ask for an opinion, you can talk to them about it but don't make decisions for them concerning their character or actions. The same can be applied to you. You can talk to your partner about your character if you have questions but don't expect them to fill in the missing parts of your character or acting. Discussion is always a great way to discover new things without relying on someone to give you the answers.

There may be times when you get frustrated with your partner. You cannot let that affect the scene. Personal interference in the acting process will hinder your ability to give 100% to your partner. If you find that you have disagreements about the scene, talk to your teacher in private and tell them your concerns. Don't point fingers and say, "I'm right, they're wrong." State it something like "I'm having a problem connecting because I feel I'm not getting what I need from them." Your teacher will watch the scene, take notes, and give you and your partner constructive criticism. They will, most likely, pose questions regarding the characters and scene elements to help both of you make adjustments, leading you in the right.

BLOCKING A SCENE

As you rehearse your scene with your partner outside of class, let the blocking come organically through what you want, what you're hearing, how you're reacting, etc. Don't try to manipulate the blocking, let it happen naturally. Your director or acting teacher will make adjustments as necessary or they may block the scene for you.

There are two common mistakes I find among actors when it comes to blocking. The first is that they tend to want to move about on stage. They feel that moving is acting and will wander about the stage, or waver back and forth. This gives the impression of meandering without reason. The second is the opposite, not moving. They stand in one place, not letting their body move within the space. They seem unattached to what is happening in the scene and are not allowing the impetus to move affect them.

You must find the right blend of both. I always say that movement and/or action comes from what the character wants or needs. This is an important rule to remember. When you are blocking a scene try to ask yourself, "Am I moving because I'm bored or am I moving because the character needs to move?"

Sometimes it may not be movement that your character needs to do but an action. If the scene involves an action such as packing up boxes, polishing glass trinkets, making a drink, getting dressed, you might consider having your character perform that task during the scene or at the very least trying to accomplish that task.

You will find that when you are doing something on stage (with objective) other than waiting for your next line you will begin to live in the shoes of your character and create organic movement.

USING PROPS AND SET

When you are rehearsing or presenting your scene, use set pieces and props. Most acting classes will have basic set pieces such as chairs, blocks, tables, etc. Be creative and use these to create your surroundings. A couch can be made out of two chairs pushed together, a bed from four chairs: two chairs facing the audience and two chairs pushed with their backs to the audience. Whatever it is you need, use what you have and think outside the box.

Make sure you have all props that you need that are necessary for the scene. If you don't have what you need in the class, look for something at home that can be a substitute. Never mime something that you actually use in the scene. One reason is that it's not real and takes the audience member out of the scene and another reason is that most actors don't know how to mime an object correctly. They end up using their hand to create the "prop" as opposed to having their hand use the "prop".

To avoid this: find, make, or borrow the items you need for the scene. Most theatre classes have a prop room for students to gather props from and use in their scenes. Dress the stage as close as you can to where the scene is being placed. Now with that being said, don't overdress the set or use props that you absolutely don't need in the scene. Be judicious about your decisions and the set and props will add to your scene not detract from it.

CHAPTER 10: AUDITIONS

Auditions Overview 312

Scheduling an Audition (Agent Or Agency) 313

Scheduling an Audition (Casting Notice) 314

Preparing for the Audition 315

What to Wear 320

Headshots 324

Resumes 326

Arriving at The Audition 329

Entering the Audition Space 331

Presenting Your Pieces 333

Callbacks and Cold Readings 337

After the Audition 339

Self-Taping Overview 340

The Set-up 341

Following Directions 343

Readers 344

Slating and Performances 345

Costumes and Props 347

Staying Proactive Between Auditions 348

AUDITIONS OVERVIEW

Auditions. The word alone can strike fear into any actor. The idea of getting up in front of complete strangers and delivering a monologue or song to get a role in a show can be very scary. We worry about how we will look, how we will sound, what others will think of us. It's not uncommon to feel this way but can be prevented or at least alleviated if you prepare yourself beforehand.

Most actors learn about auditions from trade papers like Backstage (NY, CA), PerformInk (Chicago) or other newspapers from their cities. Nowadays, theatres post their auditions on their websites, social media, or other online venues. Some auditions are found by word-of-mouth and through casting agencies. Whichever way you learn about an audition, the best thing you can do is be prepared and know how to approach the process with the best tools in order to give the best impression.

I will also cover how to audition for film/commercials. When applicable, I will cover what to do for those types of auditions in the sections of this chapter that require it.

Remember, no matter if it's theatre or film, your audition starts from the minute you make contact with those holding the audition until the minute you walk out.

SCHEDULING AN AUDITION (AGENT OR AGENCY)

Casting notices for commercials, film and stage from agencies are usually screened through the agencies. If you are chosen for an audition, the agency will contact you and supply the location, time, date, and sides (the script to learn), if there are any. You should always ask the agency what they are expecting you to wear. Never call the production company regarding any question about the auditions. All questions should be directed to your agent or agency.

Write everything down or print out the email that your agent sends to you. This will ensure that you won't forget anything and you will be well prepared. When talking to your agent or agency have your personal calendar, production schedule or class schedule handy so you can make sure that the days and times of your audition won't conflict with any upcoming events. One of the worst things an actor can do is schedule a time for an audition and then cancel because of a previously scheduled conflict. This could reflect negatively on you and your agency, preventing you from being submitted for future projects.

If you have to cancel for any reason, contact your agency as soon as you can and explain your situation. Depending on the audition, you may be able to reschedule if the auditions are happening on multiple days.

SCHEDULING AN AUDITION (CASTING NOTICE)

Most casting notices have all the information needed for the audition. Pay close attention to the time, location and roles that are open for audition. Always have your personal calendar, production schedule, or class schedule handy so you can make sure the days and times won't conflict with any upcoming events.

If the casting notice requires you to call and make an appointment, call from your home. This will prevent any distractions or interference while scheduling your audition time. Calling from home will also allow you not to feel rushed while making the call. If you have any questions regarding the audition, now is the time to ask. Be sure that any questions you are asking have not already been answered in the casting notice. This is the information you should write down when scheduling the audition: time, place, persons conducting the auditions, and what is expected, such as monologues, songs, cold readings, or provided sides.

Should you need to leave a message for an audition, give as much information on the message without rambling on. Leave your name, phone number, the reason you are calling and the best time they can reach you. Do not leave any additional questions on the message, you can ask those when they return your call. If there is a possibility that you will not be able to answer your phone when they return your call, it is acceptable to leave one or two questions on the message.

If you have been called by a theatre to audition for a part, in addition to the items covered in the last paragraph, you should also ask about the name of the play, the role they want you to audition for and if there is something in particular they would like to see from you. They might tell you to bring a monologue or they may say that you are reading from the script. Make sure you get all information.

PREPARING FOR THE AUDITION

THE MONOLOGUE

Every actor should have a set of monologues that they use for auditions to show off their range, ability and type. Never use a monologue that doesn't fit into roles that you can be cast in. Know your type. Play to your strengths. Do what you do best and show it. We covered the subject of picking a monologue in CHAPTER 10.

Always have 3 - 5 monologues ready. The monologues should vary in length. Between 1 – 2 minutes, no longer. Having a wide range of styles is also recommended. Styles include but are not limited to comedy, drama, contemporary, classical, Shakespeare, stylized, absurdism, existentialism, etc. Pick a monologue from a play, either produced or original. Do not use self-contained monologues. These types of monologues usually aren't very well written; the characters aren't fleshed out, and generally frowned upon by directors. Self-contained monologues are mostly used in classroom situations only.

You should have 1 - 2 Shakespearean pieces in your set of monologues as well; this is good way to show off your ability to handle stylized language, both in voice and body. Amongst your Shakespearean pieces under your belt you should have comedy, tragic, verse, prose, and dramatic.

When choosing your Shakespearean piece **do not** use sonnets. They aren't very action oriented or emotionally driven. Sonnets are primarily used in acting schools or acting classes to train the actor and familiarize them with the Shakespearean verse.

In addition to choosing your monologues, you should vary the styles and consider the use of opposites. This will show your range as an actor by not showing the same emotional qualities, tempos, and acting styles in both pieces. Consider these opposites when choosing your monologues: Heavy/Light, Physical/Language, Straight/Quirky, Comedic/Dramatic, Ingénue or Leading Man/Character.

315

THE SONG

As with a monologue, you should have 3 – 5 songs in your arsenal when going to an audition. The songs you choose should show off your voice, style, and acting ability. Pick songs that show off your vocal/emotional range, the ability to tell a story through music. and your comfort with singing. These are all aspects that you should be aware of when choosing your songs. It is always the singer's responsibility to have the song in the correct key. Do not expect the accompanist to be able to transpose on the spot.

Usually you will be asked to perform one minute of a song or 16 bars of music. Know what they want ahead of time so you can cut your song for the best use of your time on stage and show off your singing ability within the time limit you are given. On occasion, you will be asked to sing a cappella which means to sing without musical accompaniment. If this is the case, make sure you are comfortable with the songs you have chosen and that they don't rely heavily on musical underscoring. Songs with long music breaks between lyrics is not a wise choice when singing a cappella.

Choose songs with different styles. The more styles you can sing, the more you'll be able to show the audition panel your range and castability. Among the songs styles you should have under your belt include legit, upbeat, ballad, comedy, rock, pop, Broadway, and many others. No matter which style you choose, it should represent the style of the musical and show off your voice and talent. Remember that many songs can fit into more than one genre.

Auditions are not the time to try new songs that you are unfamiliar with or songs that are out of your range. This will not give you a fair chance at the audition and you will look unprepared or seem unable to assess the songs you are capable of singing.

The next step is to organize your music into a 3-ring binder so it's easily accessible at the audition. The sheet music you put into the binder should be copies and not the originals. You should have both the

16 bar version and the full version of your songs in the binder. You never know when you will be asked to sing an entire song.

Put the sheet music back-to-back into non-glossy sheet-protectors so there are two pages per protector. You should have the sheet music in the right key, with the cuts already made. If your 16 bar cut is two pages, put them adjacent to each other so the accompanist doesn't have to turn the page. Do not mark cuts or notations on the actual music; instead, use dry erase markers to mark the sheet-protectors. Doing it this way will protect the music from constant pencil erasures and allow for quick changes to markings if you need to make them.

Put the music in alphabetical order, this will help you find songs quicker if they ask you to sing another song. One thing that you also might consider is to put two or three songs in the front of the binder that you're expecting to sing, so the accompanist won't have to search for them. If they ask for another song and it isn't in the three that you have pre-chosen, the alphabetical system is still in effect and you will be able to find the music easier.

SONG TERMINOLOGY

LEGIT
- More operatic
- More lyrical
- More tone
- Rogers and Hammerstein, Sondheim, Les Misérables, The Phantom of the Opera, etc.

BALLADS
- Slower
- More lyrical
- Sustained notes
- Sustained energy
- Emotional

UPBEAT
- Perky
- Syncopated
- Lively
- Energized
- Can be emotional

CHARACTER
- Older characters
- Cynical
- Quirky
- Only sing this type of song if you are auditioning for a character role or the director has asked for this type of song.

COMEDY/NOVELTY

- Usually upbeat
- Keep objective of song
- Don't sing it for the sake of being funny
- Tell the story
- Avoid these songs unless asked to sing it by the director or music director.

PATTER SONGS

- Fast paced
- Energized lyrics
- Sings almost every note
- Less sustained notes

ROCK

- Hedwig and the Angry Inch
- Hair
- Jesus Christ Superstar
- Spring Awakening
- Rent

COUNTRY

- Big River
- The Robber Bridegroom

GOSPEL

- The Wiz
- Godspell
- Porgy and Bess
- Sister Act

WHAT TO WEAR

What you wear at an audition is just as important as what monologue or song you choose. It represents how you see yourself and how you want to present yourself at the audition. The type of audition you are going to will dictate what you should wear.

COMMERCIALS AND FILM

When auditioning for a commercial or film, some agencies prefer to have the actors dress appropriately to the part they are auditioning for. If you are unsure about what to wear, ask your agent and they will tell you what the casting agency is asking to see. Dress as close as you can to the description they give you. Improvise your outfit as best you can if you don't have anything that resembles the look they are looking for. Be creative. An actor has many resources to fall on and it's their creativity that they fall upon when it's needed.

I remember when I was auditioning for the part of a leprechaun for a commercial and only had a day to prepare. I didn't have a leprechaun costume, it was after Halloween and there were no costume shops around with that costume available. I didn't have any money to buy fabric/clothes to make a leprechaun outfit. I had to improvise so I hemmed up a pair of black pants just below the knee, put on a white socks (pulled up to the knee), a green button shirt, black vest, and a pair of black dress shoes. This was my interpretation of a leprechaun and the best way that I could represent it under the circumstances. As long as you do your best, that's what counts.

STAGE

Stage auditions are different from commercial and film entirely. Usually the director does not want to see an actor in costume at the audition. They rely on your acting ability to convey that character for them. Therefore, it is important to dress appropriately for a stage audition. Wear something comfortable and bring a sweater in case it is cold in the green room or in the theatre area. Always dress neatly. Don't go dressed in wrinkled clothes. It seems almost juvenile to mention it but I have seen many people go to an audition with stains on their clothes, looking wrinkled and disheveled.

While what you wear isn't going to make or break your audition, it will leave an impression about you to all involved with the production, including potential people you might work with in the future.

MEN

Men should wear a nice pair of slacks or khaki pants. Appropriate colors for pants are cream colored or black. Jeans shouldn't be your first choice but if that's all you have, make sure there are no holes or rips in them. Do not under any circumstances wear overly baggy pants, parachute pants, shorts, jogging pants, or sweatpants. Basically avoid any overly casual attire.

Shirts should be a nice button down shirt, polo shirt, or solid pullover tee-shirt. Avoid shirts with funny slogans on them or brightly colored/loud shirts, i.e., Hawaiian shirts, tie-dye, tank tops, muscle tees, etc.

Shoes should be black and casual. Boots and tennis shoes aren't always first choice but if that's all you have, make sure they are clean, not brightly colored, and appropriate to move in. Character shoes are always acceptable at an audition. Actors should always have a pair of character shoes especially if they are auditioning for a musical since most musical auditions require a dance routine as part of the audition process. Shoes not appropriate for any audition are flip-flops, Birkenstocks, open-toed shoes, and old dirty shoes.

For those men who have long hair, keep it out of your face when you are auditioning.

WOMEN

Women should wear a nice pair of slacks or khaki pants. Appropriate colors for pants are cream colored or black. Jeans shouldn't be your first choice but if that's all you have, make sure there are no holes or rips in them. The pants women should not wear fall under the same restrictions as the men with the addition of leggings, leg warmers, tights (by themselves) and the like.

Dresses are also acceptable. Nothing too long or too short. The general rule of thumb is 1 – 2 inches above or below the knee. If you wear a dress to an audition, be sure to have a change of clothes if there is going to be a dance section to the audition. Learning a dance routine in a dress at an audition will limit you tremendously.

Women can wear blouses and solid tee-shirts. As with men, you should avoid shirts with funny slogans on them or brightly colored/loud shirts, i.e., glittery, sparkly, or tie-dye, etc.

Shoes should be black, casual, and low-heeled or flat. If you have women's character shoes those would be the best to wear. As with men, shoes that are not appropriate for an audition are flip-flops, Birkenstocks, open-toed shoes, old dirty shoes, or high heels.

Women should always have a pair of character shoes with heels, especially if they are auditioning for a musical since most musical auditions require a dance routine as part of the audition process.

Also, do not wear excessive jewelry, it will be distracting and also hinder any movement should there be a dance audition as well. Keep your hair pulled back and out of the face and no heavy make-up.

HEADSHOTS

Bring a recent headshot within 3 years. Don't make the mistake of bringing in one that is older and thinking you look the same. You don't. If you are not sure if your headshot is acceptable talk to your agent or someone you know that can be objective.

The headshot should be surrounded by a white border. Right, top, and left border should be about a ¼ to ½ inch. The bottom should be about 1 – 1 ½ inches. Your name should be printed somewhere on the headshot, preferably centered in the bottom border area. The font should be big so the name is readable. Do not use a fancy font. Keep it to standard fonts: Times New Roman, Arial, Palatino, Helvetica, etc. The name can be justified right, center or left. Someone will always have an opinion on where to place it. As long as it doesn't take away from the focal point of the photo, you can place it wherever you want.

Make sure your headshot looks professional. If you don't have headshots and are looking for someone to take them for you, don't be afraid to shop around. Check the web, Google photographers in your area, specifically those that specialize in headshots for actors. Ask to see their portfolio. Price around. Don't jump at the first one you look at. Make sure you get the right photographer at the price you can afford. Besides the web, you can also look at your fellow actor's headshots while at auditions or at agencies if the opportunity arises. If you like their headshot ask them who took their photos.

Note: You should <u>never</u> use an everyday photo unless you have no headshots whatsoever.

Your headshot should also depict the type of actor you are or your personality: Ingénue, leading man, character, guy/girl next-door, etc. If you have more than one look and/or more than one headshot, use the one that closely resembles the part you are auditioning for.

Your headshot should also look like you. Don't airbrush out wrinkles, freckles, facial discolorations, or anything that they will see when you are auditioning. The closer you look like your headshot, the better. Avoid using "character" or "costumed" headshots. This type of photo is gimmicky and might put off the director entirely, making them only see you in one way instead of keeping you open for other options.

RESUMES

Besides the headshot, the resume is the bread and butter for an actor. It has all the information that a director, agency or theatre needs. Your resume should contain all contact information and list of shows that you have done. The shows can be listed in chronological order or broken into categories: Commercials, Films, Theatre, Musical Theatre, Regional, International, Stand-up, etc. List all shows, films, and commercials, full-length student projects and understudy roles.

If you have to edit and remove shows, remember that professional shows outweigh non-professional shows and larger roles outweigh smaller roles. In other words, a smaller role in a professional theatre or production company outweighs a larger role in a community theatre or student film. At the bottom of the resume you should include all special skills that you have such as dialects, stage combat, dancing, singing and anything else you think might be useful for a director to know.

The resume should be easy to read. Use a font that is standard such as Times New Roman, Arial, Palatino, etc. Your name should appear at the top between 24 pt. – 36 pt., centered and underlined if you prefer. The statistical information such as height, weight, eye color, etc., should be smaller than the "Name font" but larger than the body font. Never list your age or your direct phone number. Always use your agent's phone number or a number that is only for professional purposes.

The credits for your resume should be set in three columns. The font for the body of the resume shouldn't be larger than 12 pt. and no smaller than 9 pt. The resume should be on 8"x10" paper and stapled to the back of your headshot. The staples should be horizontal not diagonal.

Everyone has a different way they format their resume. There is no one right way. As long as it is clear, presents the information needed in a neat and readable format, and fits on 8"x10" paper, you're good to go. If you need ideas for resume formats you can search the web or look at the resumes of your friends who are actors.

Name
Union Status

Height/Weight	Email address	Agency
Eye Color	Website address	Agency address
Hair Color		Agency phone number
Vocal Range		Agency email address

Films
Production	Role	Production Company/Director
Production	Role	Prod. Co./Director

Commercials
Commercial	Role	Prod. Co.//Director
Commercial	Role	Prod. Co.//Director

Theatre
Show	Role	Theatre or Director
Show	Role	Theatre or Director

Musical Theatre
Show	Role	Theatre or Director
Show	Role	Theatre or Director

International
Show	Role	Theatre or Director
Show	Role	Theatre or Director

Education
Grad School	Degree	Major
Under Grad School	Degree	Major
Vocational School	Degree	Course of Study

Special Skills
Skill 1	Skill 2	Skill 3
Skill 4	Skill 5	Skill 6

Arriving at The Audition

Now that you have your monologues and songs rehearsed, your clothes picked out, your resume and headshots updated, and your confidence in full swing, it's time to go to the audition. You should arrive 30 minutes earlier than the time you are called. This will allow you to adjust to the surroundings, sign in, and pick up any text that is needed.

When speaking to anyone at the audition, be polite. This means everyone: the receptionist, the monitor, the stage manager (if one is present), and the other actors auditioning. Make sure you have brought extra headshots and resumes in case they ask for more. Bring your calendar with you so you can mark any conflicts with rehearsals and performances dates on the audition form. Fill out all paperwork completely and to the best of your knowledge and, if you haven't already, find out who will be present at your audition.

Use your time to go over your monologue or scene. If you are given text for a cold reading and it's yours to keep, mark that text with any notes to help ensure a well-rounded and thoughtful audition. Make strong bold choices when marking your scene.

It is perfectly acceptable to practice your monologue quietly in the waiting area as long as you keep it to yourself and keep your blocking to a minimum so you aren't distracting to the other actors in the room. If it isn't feasible or you feel uncomfortable doing that, you may go outside to practice. If you must leave the area, make sure you let someone associated with the audition know, preferably the monitor or the person who checked you in. It is your responsibility to come back in time for your audition. It is not their job to come find you if they need you for anything.

While waiting for the audition to begin, it is very important to use this time to focus your energy into the task at hand, working your monologue, scene, song, or whatever you are doing for that particular audition. Don't wander around and be disruptive. Walking around aimlessly can cause other actors to lose focus and concentration.

Most importantly, don't listen to other actors who talk about what the director is looking for or put negative energy out. Most of the time they are saying or doing this to put the other actors on edge. Yes, there are actors out there that like to play mental games with other actors to make them nervous or throw them off. Don't fall victim to that. If you hear someone talking negatively to someone else, walk away. If they are talking to you, simply excuse yourself and walk away. Either way, avoid it as best you can.

If you know someone at the audition and you want to talk to them, go outside; don't talk where the other actors are. If the holding area is big and spacious, you may stay in the room and talk but keep your voice low so you aren't disturbing the other actors who are using their time to prepare for the audition.

Note: Most importantly turn off your cell phone.

ENTERING THE AUDITION SPACE

There are two ways auditions can be held, either you are brought into the room as a group or brought in separately. In either case keep these helpful tips in mind.

Enter the room with confidence. Don't slouch or walk timidly. This might be the first time the audition panel is seeing you and you want them to know you are there for the purpose of succeeding. Don't misinterpret confidence with cockiness or superiority. Often when I see an actor coming in with a "I'm better than all of these people" attitude, I'm put off and not impressed by their audition and will rarely call them back.

Be sure that you have all your audition material with you (songs, headshots, resumes, sides, etc.) Once you are in the room, do not write additional notes in your script or on your music. Pay attention to the actors auditioning. Show them the same respect you would want when you are on stage performing.

When you are called to audition, greet the people conducting the audition. If you are brought in as a group that is usually difficult to do, but if you are called in individually then the opportunity may present itself better. Make sure you shake their hand, look them in the eye and give your greeting with a smile. A simple "Hi, I'm...", "Nice to meet you", etc., is all you need to do.

Be prepared to talk. They might engage you in conversation. Use this time to tell them something interesting about yourself or possibly you might have something in common with one of them. This is a great opportunity to make a connection with them. Don't be afraid to talk but don't be overly talkative either. If they ask you questions that you don't feel comfortable answering, don't be intimidated into revealing that information.

If you feel you are not 100% confident about your audition due to being sick, nervousness, not prepared, etc., under no circumstances should you give a disclaimer prior to your audition. Don't tell them you aren't prepared because you only had a day to learn the lines. They don't want to hear excuses. You may think that they will be more sympathetic when you audition but it will have the opposite effect. They will think you are making excuses because you aren't prepared. Do not apologize for your audition.

Remember the 3 P's. Be positive. Be pleasant. Be professional.

Presenting Your Pieces

Once the introductions are over, or if in a group and introductions weren't possible, it's time for your audition. If they ask for volunteers, take the lead and go first. It shows confidence. When approaching the stage or the audition area, walk tall and in a nice steady pace. Face the audition panel and don't forget to smile.

Before presenting your piece make sure you have set the stage with what you need i.e., a chair, a small prop needed, etc. If you have music, bring it to the accompanist, go through the tempo with them by tapping your hand to the beat and singing softly to them so they understand how you want it. Make sure you go through all markings, cuts, etc., with them. If your song is following a monologue, write the cue line for the music to start in the music and let them know what the cue line is.

When presenting your piece, say your name, the character you are portraying, and the play it's from. You do not have to mention the author of the play with your introduction unless the monitors/people conducting the audition request it. When introducing your song, name the title and the show it is from. Whether you are doing one monologue, two monologues, a monologue and a song, two monologues and a song or just a song, the format is always the same when presenting your pieces.

When introducing yourself be sure to say "I'm 'your name' and not "my name is 'your name'". The reason being that saying "I'm" creates a personal connection and is friendlier. It's like a handshake while using the word "my" creates a separation between you and the people you are auditioning for and appears less personal. Below is the format I use when presenting my pieces.

ONE MONOLOGUE
"Good Morning, I'm John Smith. I'll be doing Big Daddy from 'Cat on a Hot Tin Roof'.

ONE MONOLOGUE AND A SONG
"Good Morning, I'm John Smith. I'll be doing Big Daddy from 'Cat on a Hot Tin Roof'. I'll be singing 'Guv'ment' from Big River."

TWO MONOLOGUES
"Good Morning, I'm John Smith. I'll be doing Big Daddy from 'Cat on a Hot Tin Roof' and The Professor from 'The Lesson'"

TWO MONOLOGUES AND A SONG
"Good Morning, I'm John Smith. I'll be doing Big Daddy from 'Cat on a Hot Tin Roof' and The Professor from 'The Lesson' by Eugene Ionesco. I'll be singing 'Guv'ment' from Big River."

ONE SONG
"Good Morning, I'm John Smith. I'll be singing 'Guv'ment' from Big River."

TWO SONGS
"Good Morning, I'm John Smith. I'll be singing 'Guv'ment' from Big River and 'Mr. Cellophane' from Chicago."

As you introduce the pieces you are presenting, it is perfectly acceptable to look at the people conducting the audition in the eye. Speak clearly, enunciate and use proper projection. Don't forget to smile.

After the introductions of the pieces, take a moment to ready yourself and then begin. Take a small breath, a small step forward or back, whichever you like and start or if you prefer, turn your back to them, take a breath, turn around and start your opening moment. Do not take a long time to begin your audition after you finish your introduction of the piece or pieces you are presenting. The monitors do not want to see you "preparing" to act; they want to see what you can do.

During your audition, do not look at the monitors. Find a spot against the back wall if the person you are talking to is in front of you or at a slight angle. If you look at the monitors you give the impression that you are looking for a response from them. This will make them incredibly self-conscious. They are not there to be included in your piece; they are there to assess your ability.

Speak with projection and clarity. Let your character think. Lead them through the character's thought process like leading someone through a maze of ideas. String your lines together with thoughts. Carry and push through the ends of lines or thoughts with energy. Be aware of your transitional lines, the objectives of your character and the reactions from your "invisible partner." Allow this to feed your character as you are presenting your monologue. Remember at the audition you are not only acting as the character you are portraying, you are also the other person you are talking to, the environment, your surroundings, you are representing everything.

Keep your movements sharp and clean. Don't walk through your movements and thoughts. Complete them. If you are grabbing something in the monologue really grab, if you're jumping really jump. Commit yourself to the movements required to present the monologue. Don't muddle your thoughts by wandering around on stage with nervous energy. Stay focused.

When you've finished your first monologue take a short breath and begin the next piece. If you are singing a song at the end of your monologue and you do not have a cue line for the accompanist, give a slight nod to them. If you have your last line marked in the music, he'll know to start playing. If the accompanist doesn't start after the cue line, simple look at them and give a slight nod.

After you are finished with your audition, take a short beat to show that you are finished, say thank you, and wait a few seconds to see if they have anything to say. They may ask you to sing another song or do another monologue. If they don't say anything or if they simply say thank you, take your music from the accompanist, thank them and take your seat or leave the audition space, depending on the situation.

Sometimes after an audition they will let you know if you are called back. They will also tell you the callback time. If you don't get feedback after you've finished your audition that does not mean they didn't like your work or that you weren't called back. It could be that they are taking notes and deciding whom to call back after they have seen everyone. They may post callbacks at a later time or they may tell you to call the theatre to find out if you were called back or cast in the show. In any event, you presented yourself in the best light. When you walk back into the waiting room, do not say anything about your audition. As you leave, be sure to thank the person or persons involved with checking you in - that is the finishing touch to your initial audition.

CALLBACKS AND COLD READINGS

It is rare that an audition would only have you do a cold reading but it does happen. Cold readings usually happen at a callback when the director wants you to read for a specific role.

Whether you are asked to do a cold reading for an audition or a callback, the procedure is always the same. You are given a script and little time to prepare. Use whatever time you have to look over your script and make strong, bold choices. Sometimes you may have only 30 seconds from your seat to the stage to look over the script and make your choices; sometimes you may be given 5 minutes. Try to come up with three choices for the scene or monologue that you have been given. You may be asked to do it more than once. No matter how much time you have, use it wisely.

With any of the choices you make, justify your choices through the dialogue and actions of the character. Be as true to the script and the character as you can. Avoid wandering around on stage or standing completely still while reading. Breathe life into your character and always do the reading in a manner that is comfortable with you. And remember: follow your impulses.

When you first present your cold reading, you shouldn't ask the director for their interpretation of the script or how they want you to do it. Present it with the choices you have made and do it with confidence. After your cold reading, they may ask you to do it again with an adjustment, or if they didn't, you can do it with another choice you made.

Don't hold the script close and cover your face. Hold the script extended with the arm that you don't favor. In other words, if you're right-handed, hold the script with your left hand and vice versa. Keep your thumb on your next line and try to say as much of the line looking out before looking back at the script.

Sometimes the cold reading will involve a scene partner. Involve them as much as you can when performing the cold reading. Try to make a connection with them, make eye contact or physical contact if the script calls for it. Try to do as much of the blocking that is written into the script as you can. Make adjustments if your partner forgets to do something physically called for in the script. Under no circumstance should you correct them or tell them to do that action. Stay in the moment.

After the cold reading if no adjustments are asked for or required, say thank you. Hand the script back to the stage manager or director and go back to your seat or leave the audition area, depending on the situation, and wait for further instructions.

After the Audition

Waiting is the hardest part after the audition and every actor goes through that process. It's best to forget about the casting process and keep moving forward as if you didn't get the part. Waiting by the phone is not going to make it happen.

Do not, I repeat, <u>do not</u> call the production company or director to find out if you've been cast or if any decisions have been made <u>unless</u> they gave specific instructions to do so. If you haven't heard from them within the time frame they gave, odds are you didn't get the role. If you auditioned through an agent, call them to find out any additional information.

No matter the outcome, go on to your next job or audition. Don't be demoralized or discouraged. Many good actors don't get a role or called back because they don't fit what the director is looking for at that time. Don't take it personal. Keep pushing through and keep auditioning.

SELF-TAPING OVERVIEW

This information comes from a webinar I attended with a top-ranked L.A. casting director through SAG-AFTRA. So, this is the latest at the publishing of this edition.

Self-taping is becoming part of the standard practice when auditioning for film and commercials. Usually if you have an agent they will film you at their office. However, if you do not have an agent or find that you have to do it yourself, this will set you up for success and help you make the best impression.

There is an expectation that the clients of casting directions are looking for in actors. This includes being able to follow directions, knowing how to handle equipment, and how to upload files. There are several sites that you can use to upload your finished audition. The most popular ones are WeTransfer, Dropbox, and G-Drive. For G-Drive be sure you have permissions turned off, it doesn't require a password and be sure the links don't expire.

If you must use YouTube and send them a link to your audition video, be sure it is marked as unlisted and not private to ensure that we will always have access to your video. The other way they may request your file, is sending it directly to them from your phone.

Please remember these four important rules when auditioning with a self-tape:
1. Be prepared
2. Be on time
3. Be professional
4. Don't take the audition for granted

Self-taping will become more common practice and agencies might not have the talent come in to film them directly. If this is the case, and you don't feel comfortable or lack the technological know-how for a self-tape, inform your agent immediately.

THE SET-UP

You don't have to spend a lot of money to create a home studio for self-taped auditions but it should be a space that is your own and you feel comfortable in. Ideally, it should be big enough to get most of your body in the frame without being completely against the wall. All you need is a backdrop, good lighting, and a decent camera or phone, though a camera is much preferred.

The backdrop can be any number of things; collapsible, seamless background paper, a plain wall, or an ironed sheet. The best color for your backdrop should he gray-blue, this shows off everyone's skin tone the best. Whatever color you use, you shouldn't blend into it making you hard to see.

The camera should be placed far enough away that the wide shot gets all if not most of your body. Your camera should be on a tri-pod. This will ensure there is no shaking in your video audition. Even if you have someone taping for you, use a tri-pod. Under no circumstance should you do a selfie-angled audition, unless it is specifically asked by the casting director or production company. The brand of camera is not important as long as it has great resolution and a good mic for picking up sound. If you are using Zoom as your means for self-taping remember that what you see in the frame, they see unless you edit the video to remove the unwanted scenery.

The video itself should be 720p when converting it. They don't need anything bigger and if it's too small they won't be able to see you clearly.

Quality of picture and sound are just as important as the audition itself. The more professionalism and care you take in your self-tape, the more likely you are to impress those you are auditioning for. They want to watch you and not be distracted by poor shaking, out of focus, low quality video and sound, or bad lighting.

I'm putting an emphasis on quality because the first impression is the quality of your audition not the performance. They need to know that the actor is confident and can hold themselves. This is done through your self-tape.

Lighting yourself for a self-tape is not as difficult as it may seem so don't over-complicate it. They are looking for natural lighting, not lighting for a stage production or that spotlights you. A popular lighting apparatus is the ring light with adjustable light temperatures. There are some good and inexpensive ones out there so shop around before choosing one. Another way to light yourself is using the natural sunlight through your window. Be sure that it isn't too strong. It should be flat and light you, not cause you to wash out on film.

Microphones are also very important to self-taping. Lavaliers are the best. CD's don't mind seeing a lavalier but it can also be hidden on your body out of sight. The mic you use must give you good sound quality. After you do a taping, watch and be sure it sounds clear and there isn't an echo or tinny sound.

A simple rule to remember is this: if you don't have the proper equipment to do the audition, don't do it.

Following Directions

Casting directors and production companies send out casting notices to agents who, in turn, contact their talent with the details. These details include character, a description, the copy, and the requirements for filming the audition. The copy is the dialogue that you will say during your audition. When you are self-taping be sure to read everything and know what is required for your audition including how they want the slate, how many takes they want, possibly a way they would like the delivered. Each casting notices may require something different so read everyone with specificity.

Casting directors look for actors who can take direction even if it's from a piece of paper. The casting notice may contain directions on what they are looking for including tone, character, specific blocking needed for the audition, and how many takes they want. Always follow the instructions of the casting director. Always. If you are unsure of something contact your agent for clarification. If you don't have an agent and you are unsure of what the production company or casting director want, you can contact them but be sure the information isn't on the casting notice or it is unclear to understand what they are requiring.

Casting notices will also include what type of frame they want for the audition. It's usually a full body shot for the slate and a medium shot from the waist up so your hands can be seen. An example of not following directions would be this: they ask for a close-up but you feel more comfortable with a medium shot and shoot your audition the way you want, they will take notice of that and probably won't even look at your audition.

When you are framing yourself with your phone, be sure to always have the camera positioned horizontally. It is very rare that they will want it in the vertical position unless they specifically ask for it.

READERS

The reader is the person who is reading the other parts of the dialogue for you. The reader is there to help you, not to outshine you. The reader's voice should be quieter than yours and not try to out-act you. The casting directors are interested in your audition not theirs.

The readers are always off-camera so they are not seen. If you do not have anyone to read with you live and your set-up permits it, you can have them read from a video call. They won't be seen in the audition tape and still serve the same purpose.

Not everyone has access to a reader and in that case there are apps you can download that will say the lines that need to be said. Remember, the audition is for you. They don't care if the reader is a computerized voice.

As long as the reader doesn't take focus away from your audition, you're good to go.

SLATING AND PERFORMANCES

The slate refers to what you say before your audition. Look at this as a way to introduce yourself. You should look directly into the camera when giving your slate. Your personality should shine through. Think of the slate as a handshake. Make it warm, friendly, inviting. Don't be overly friendly, be natural. The slate will usually include your name, height, agent, location, and role you are auditioning for.

The performance of your audition is the star of the show. Just like preparing a monologue you must do your homework. Look up how to pronounce words, dress for the role you are auditioning for, your hairstyle should match the character, use any props necessary for your scene, if needed, and of course, analyze the copy you were given.

Unlike the slate, for your actual audition do not look into the camera. Look at a slight angle as if the person is opposite you in the film. You may have the urge to do it profile as if they are next to you, this is not good. Instead, think of the shot as an over-the-shoulder from the other character's perspective. Consider these situations to help you decide where you are going to look. Are they sitting across from you at a table? Are they coming into a room? Are there multiple people you are addressing in the scene? Where you look don't make it straight on into the camera, a harsh angle, or profile.

Do as many takes that are needed until you are happy with your performance. Actors have a hard time watching themselves perform but you are going to have to get over that if you want to produce the best work you can do. No matter how many takes they want, you will put your slate and your audition clips into one file. The slate being first and then the audition clips following that. If your second take is better than the first, then use that first when you are combining the video clips into one file.

Sometimes you may be required to use a prop in the audition. When this happens, make sure the prop doesn't block your face. It should always be to the side of you or below your head. Practice using your prop and your blocking prior to filming.

The casting notice should tell you how to label your audition file. In case it doesn't, it should be labeled like this: FIRSTNAME_LASTNAME_ROLE.

COSTUMES AND PROPS

An actor's wardrobe for costumes should match the roles they constantly audition for. Your costume wardrobe should be separate from your normal clothes. While this is not set in stone, it would be a tragic thing if you wore your favorite sweater for an audition, only to ruin it and lose it. Therefore, your audition wardrobe is a safety net for you, as well.

You should also have a collection of basic props for your auditions. These are also important to have, they may ask you to bring props due to safety and health reasons. The props should be kept in a prop box. Your prop box should have your basic props and necessities should you be asked to film in-person or if you book the role. Your prop box should include: a coffee cup, straws, masks, gloves, hand sanitizer, lipstick, eye glasses and anything else you might consider a basic prop. You most likely will bring your prop box with you if they ask you to.

STAYING PROACTIVE BETWEEN AUDITIONS

You won't be auditioning every day, so during the time you have off, invest in your future. Stay supple. Spend an hour a day concentrating on your craft. Practice your audition skills in front of the camera. Gather costumes and props for your wardrobe and prop box. Work on your recording studio. Practice your auditions in front of your friends.

To stay warm and always ready for a self-taped audition, challenge yourself to do a self-taping for 30 days. The more you practice the more you will get better. But above all, don't become complacent. Practice. Practice. Practice.

The more you practice and stay in control of your craft the less variables will interfere with you being cast. It will always come down to look, voice, or chemistry but if you are prepared and practice daily, you will know it was because of those factors and not because you were unprepared and unprofessional.

Lastly, once you submit your audition, it becomes the property of the production company. They paid to have the talent audition, therefore your audition belongs to them. Don't fret over this as it may be to your advantage. You may not have been right for one role but you may be right for another. They may keep your audition as a future reference and call you back for a different audition. However, if you are a member of SAG-AFTRA and you see your audition online, contact SAG-AFTRA immediately.

CHAPTER 11: REHEARSALS AND PERFORMANCES

The First Read-Through 350

Making Choices..352

The Rehearsals 353

The Role Of The Director...354

Working With A Director..355

The Role Of The Stage Manager 357

Tech Week 358

The Performances...359

THE FIRST READ-THROUGH

Being cast in a show is exciting but now the real work begins. It's time to put everything you've learned into practice. Most theatres hand out the script at the first-read through. This will most likely be the first time you will see the script unless you are already familiar with the play you are performing in.

Don't be late. Manage your time and plan on arriving 15 minutes early. This will ensure that you will not be late due to traffic, unexpected delays or anything that might spring up at the last minute. When you arrive, check in with the stage manager to let them know that you are there. They will give instructions on what to do next.

At the read-through, you will meet the other actors in the show, as well as the production team. They will go over policies and procedures including late policies, rehearsal schedules and conflict dates. The director will talk about the vision of the show and may talk about the set and what the production will include. Everyone will introduce themselves so be prepared to talk about your previous experiences. If you don't have any experience, that's okay, everyone has to start somewhere.

Once introductions are over, you may have to fill out some paperwork, so be sure you bring a pen. After all the official business has been taken care of, they will hand out the script and you will begin reading the script. The director may want the actors to read it full out to hear what the actors are bringing to their characters. The director may take notes as he is hearing the script out loud for the first time. Try to make eye contact with the other actors you are reading with so you can form a connection while reading together.

After the read-thru, the director or stage manager will go over the next week's rehearsal schedule again to make sure everyone is on the same page. If you have any questions, ask. Don't be shy if you are unsure about something. Once the read-thru is officially over, try to meet the other actors in the show. This will be a great way to start forming the "family" bond that happens when a cast rehearses a show together.

MAKING CHOICES

After making any initial choices regarding your character from the read-through, you must do research (CHAPTER 10). With the research done, take your initial choices a step further. Figure out what your character wants, only this time it's not just for a monologue or a scene it's for the whole script. Start off with your super objective for your character in the scope of the entire play. What do they want?

Look at the relationships that your character has with all the people in the play. Find the dynamics with the way the dialogue is written between characters. This will greatly inform you about objectives, tactics, relationship, status, and everything I have covered in the previous chapters. Look at how the playwright describes your character when they first make their entrance or during the play.

Continue reading the play, marking your script with initial arcs within scenes, objectives and tactics. These might change during the course of the rehearsals but at least you will have a starting point to work from. You don't want to go to your first rehearsal without giving the director something to work with. A director wants to see what an actor is bringing to the table. It's not his responsibility to tell you how to act but help you bring out the choices you are making or help guide you in the right direction if you stray off course.

THE REHEARSALS

This is where it all starts. You will block out scenes and work with the other actors for the next 5 – 10 weeks, depending on how long the rehearsal schedule is. During these rehearsals, try new things and make discoveries. You will be holding the script in your hand so you may find it hard to fully give 100% to your acting but give the most you can.

Be prepared not to be rehearsing your scenes for the entire period you are in rehearsals. You may have to wait, which happens a lot. Use this time to read your script, go over your lines, etc., but try not to be disruptive by talking on your cell phone, texting, playing games, and so on. If you have to leave the rehearsal space be sure to let the stage manager know.

The first rehearsals you attend will be focused on blocking. Once blocking is finished with the show, the following rehearsals will be concentrating on working the scenes, fleshing out ideas, and making the characters come to life. As a general rule, once you have blocked a scene, start to memorize your lines. You are not expected to be off-book for usually 3 – 4 weeks from the first rehearsal but don't try to memorize until after a scene has been blocked.

While you rehearse the show at the theatre, it is your responsibility to continue to work on building your character at home. You should be continuing your research, exploring your character, working on memorizing and marking out your text.

Rehearsals will become easier as you learn your lines and get off-book. Once you are completely memorized, you can really play with your character and have fun.

THE ROLE OF THE DIRECTOR

The director is the one with the vision of the show. They cast the show the way they see the characters, they have the ideas that they would like for the set, lights, costumes, and sounds. They will have all the answers. If you find you are having difficulty with your character you should talk with them. Don't come at them with a lot of questions but if there are one or two concerns you have, ask for help or clarification.

The director is there to edit the show. They see the overall picture and know how the final result should look. They have a lot on their plate. They aren't only dealing with the actors. They're dealing with the production team, theatre managers, and others involved in the production process. Understand and respect that. If you have a question that can be answered by the stage manager, direct it to them.

The director will give notes after every rehearsal, usually when you start running the show. Have a piece of paper and pen handy to write down any notes you receive. A director hates to give a note twice so work hard to adjust to the note they have given.

Once the show has opened, the director technically is no longer in charge of the production, the stage manager is. Occasionally, a director will give notes after an opening night to tighten or adjust one or two things. Do not let that distract you. Remember, just because you open a show doesn't mean you stop learning, growing, and discovering on stage.

WORKING WITH A DIRECTOR

There are three types of directors: the one that choreographs your every move, the one that uses organic blocking, and the one that uses a combination of both. I prefer using the third with emphasis on organic blocking. This allows the actors to be creative and allows me to shape and create what they are giving me. For me, this is the ideal type of director. They have ideas for how the play will look but also want the actors to be involved in the process.

If you are lucky enough to work with a director who uses the third style of directing be thankful and use it to your best advantage. The director will have ideas for scenes and specific blocking for parts of scenes but will allow you to bring your own ideas to the table. Bring all your ideas to the stage. Try new things. The director may or may not like it but they are there to shape and edit. Take any adjustments that are given. You and the director will be working together creating the life on stage.

You may on occasion work with a director that only uses organic blocking. Often the blocking changes at every rehearsal so it is difficult to keep track of blocking and can get confusing or frustrating for the actor. The actor is given free reign in moving and expected to allow everything on the stage to happen organically. The director may simply let the actors run the scene and allow the blocking to happen through the actor's own impulses. The actor may not get any feedback from the director. While this is great for the actor in being creative it is not beneficial because the actor thrives on being directed. If you are an actor that isn't comfortable with not being told what to do or where to go, you may not enjoy this process much.

The last, and in my mind, the worst of all styles is the director that choreographs everything. You will run across many directors who use this style. I do not like this style at all. The director will dictate every move you make on stage. They will tell you when to stand, when to sit, when to pick things up, put them down. They will justify your actions, give you line readings, basically taking all the creativity away from the actor and leaving them left with simply justifying their choreography. This will leave the actor feeling empty and unfulfilled as an artist. However, since you are an actor you must prevail and make it work and do the best you can under those circumstances. The one choice in the process you will be able to make, is deciding if you want to work with that director again.

I will usually avoid those directors at all costs even if it means not auditioning for a dream role. Why would I want to have a dream role where I had no decisions in the process?

No matter which type of director you work with, you must remember it is their show, their vision, their baby. They will always have the last say and our role in the process is to make their vision come true.

THE ROLE OF THE STAGE MANAGER

The stage manager or SM is the right-hand man to the director. They know everything the director knows. Usually the stage manager will run the rehearsal as far as gathering the actors, calling time, and letting actors know what is going on. Show the SM the same respect that you would show the director.

Besides being the time manager, the SM keeps track of all blocking of the show by marking it down in their script. If you forget your blocking or need clarification about movement, go to the SM first before going to the director. The stage manager will usually give any sound cues that are needed and read lines for the actors missing from rehearsals.

The SM will never give notes until the show is in production runs. When the show opens and the director steps away, the SM is in charge of the show to keep the vision, clarity, and direction of the director. They will call time when the house is opening and your time for places for the show. Whenever you are told a time, such as "15 minutes to places", respond with "Thank you 15" or whatever the call was announced. This lets the SM know that they were heard.

TECH WEEK

This is probably the least creative part of the process for the actor. Tech week involves putting all the technical elements together: lights, sound, props, costumes, make-up, special effects, etc. It can be long and arduous. Expect a lot of waiting around.

Tech weeks usually begin 5 – 6 days prior to opening night. Each night of tech, a new element will be introduced to the actor. The first few nights are usually dedicated to lights. Be patient. There will be a lot of stopping and starting. If you are on stage and you hear the director or stage manager say "hold", stop what you're doing. Don't start talking to the other actors. Remain focused. If you aren't on stage, look over your lines or read a book. Keep yourself occupied.

Over the next few nights you will add props, costumes, and make-up into the equation. With each addition, you may find yourself forgetting lines or feeling a bit overwhelmed. Don't let that effect you. It's all part of the process of tech week.

During tech week, the stage manager will show you where your props are being kept. They will also walk you through the set to show you where everything is and any potential hazards such as nails, screws, sharp edges, electrical outlets, etc.

As the week progresses, you will start running the show, getting further along before someone calls "hold". If you do have to stop, don't get frustrated. Just wait until they tell you to go again. Hopefully, the last two nights of tech before opening night will be full run-throughs without any stops. There have been times when a full run of the show happens on opening night. It can and will happen. That's the thrill of the theatre.

The Performances

This is the moment you've been working towards. Opening night is always exciting but don't let your nervous or excited energy be disruptive to the other actors in the show. Focus your energy. You should arrive at the theatre at the pre-designated call time. Usually, it is an hour or an hour and a half prior to the show starting.

When you arrive at the theatre, sign in if there is a call sheet. Once you have signed in, go to your dressing room or the assigned area for the actors. You can begin to prepare for the show: warming up, putting on make-up, etc. There may be a company warm-up that everyone must attend. Also, there may be a fight call involved if there is stage combat in your show. A fight call involves running all stage combat in the show to keep it fresh and to make sure everything is running smoothly.

After the warm-up, the SM will instruct you to check props. It is your responsibility to make sure your prop is where you need it. The SM will have a table or area where the props are stored. It is not their responsibility to place the prop where you need to have it. Do not touch another actor's prop under any circumstances.

Once you have set your props, you may return to the dressing room or actors' area and continue getting ready for the performance. Remember, to say "Thank you 'call time'" whenever the SM gives you one. At places, go to your beginning entrance space and wait until the show starts. Do not look through the curtain to see who is in the audience while you are backstage. This is unprofessional. A general rule of thumb – "If you can see them, they can see you." You should not talk while backstage. If you have to talk, use a very low whisper.

There may or may not be a curtain speech, once the curtain speech is finished, the show will start. So take a deep, relaxing breath and remember to have fun.

After the show the SM may have notes for you. Take them as you would take if the director had given them to you. Make sure to clean up your area after you get out of make-up. Hang up your costume neatly. Throw out your trash. Leave the place as neat as when you arrived. The stage manager and other crew members of the show are not your mother or cleaner-uppers.

Congratulations! You have completed your show.

CHAPTER 12: SHAKESPEARE

Shakespeare Overview 362

Rhythmic Patterns 363

Scansion 367

Script Detective 368

Exploring Shakespearean Verse...............................369

Learning To Scan The Text 371

Physicalizing the Text 378

SHAKESPEARE OVERVIEW

Gale Fury-Childs was my first professor to open my eyes to Shakespeare while I attended the Pacific Conservatory for the Performing Arts. She taught me to embrace it, love it, and relish the words that were written. It's because of her that I have a greater appreciation for Shakespeare and his text. I write this chapter with dedication to her inspiration and passion.

Now, Shakespeare is one of those subjects that one chapter couldn't possibly cover. So, look at this as an introduction to the wonderful world of Shakespeare. This chapter will cover the bare basics of understanding and deciphering Shakespearean text.

In Shakespeare, there are two types of monologues: soliloquies and set speeches. A soliloquy is a monologue that is performed when no other characters are on stage while the character is speaking. A soliloquy can be seen as a private moment for the character. They never lie and will always reveal their true thoughts when they speak a soliloquy. Think of a soap opera character when they have a voice-over for their own thoughts or when they are speaking to themselves.

A set speech is when a character is speaking a monologue in public and can be heard by the characters on stage. It is not a private moment for the character, which in turn means, what they are saying, can either be the truth or a lie. This is usually the standard for monologues these days in the contemporary theatre. Because a set speech is spoken in public it can be filled with more influencing rhetoric than a soliloquy.

Rhythmic Patterns

The unique feature of Shakespeare's writing as well as other contemporaries of his time was the style of writing. It was a combination of verse and prose. Verse is written in rhythmic fashion and prose is not. Each line of a verse contains a set number of syllables called a meter. Shakespeare uses patterns of stressed and unstressed syllables to create the rhythm of the meter. The unstressed syllable is marked with a ‿ and the stressed is marked with a /.

Shakespeare primarily wrote ten syllables (or five sets of two syllables) for his metrical lines. When a meter is written with five sets of two syllables, or ten syllables in total, it is called a pentameter. Each pair of syllables is called a foot. This means that there are five feet in every pentameter. Each foot in the pentameter contains two syllables. The placement of the stressed and unstressed syllable in the foot will dictate what kind of rhythmic meter it is. Let's take a look at the basic kinds of rhythmic patterns Shakespearean verse can have.

IAMBIC

When all five feet in a pentameter contain an unstressed syllable in the first foot and a stressed syllable in the second foot we call that an iambic pentameter. This is the rhythmic structure of which all of Shakespearean verse is based. Let me reiterate: an iambic pentameter is when the first part of the foot is unstressed and the second part of the foot is stressed.

In order to figure out what kind of rhythm is being used, we mark the text with the stressed and unstressed symbols. We call this scansion. The rhythm of iambic pentameter looks like this with the scansion.

‿ / ‿ / ‿ / ‿ / ‿ /

da-**Dum**/da-**Dum**/da-**Dum**/da-**Dum**/da-**Dum**

Here is an example of an iambic line from Henry V.

Once **more**/unto/the **breach**/, dear **friends**/, once **more**;

The line fits perfectly into the natural rhythm of the iambic pentameter but as with anything, rules can be broken.

FEMININE ENDING or DOUBLE ENDING

One rule that we break is adding an extra ½ foot to the ending of a normal iambic pentameter. This is called a feminine ending. We mark a meter with a feminine ending with a ★. The rhythm of an iambic pentameter with a feminine ending looks like this:

da-**Dum**/da-**Dum**/da-**Dum**/da-**Dum**/da-**Dum**/da ★

Here is an example of an iambic pentameter with a feminine ending using Hamlet's beginning line from his famous speech.

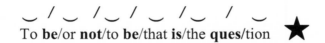

To **be**/or **not**/to **be**/that **is**/the **ques**/tion ★

You'll notice that the added ½ foot "tion" gives the iambic a sense of unfinished business. Usually a feminine ending marks a strong emotional feeling for the character saying that line.

TROCHEE

When a stressed syllable is followed by an unstressed syllable in a foot we call that a trochee. It doesn't matter where the stressed and unstressed foot happens in the line and how many there are in the pentameter. If it's there, it's a trochee. The rhythmic pattern would look like this:

$$\smile \ / \ \smile \ / \ \ / \ \smile\smile \ / \ \smile \ /$$
da-**Dum**/da-**Dum**/**Dum**-da/da-**Dum**/da-**Dum**

You'll notice that the third foot in the meter contains the stressed and unstressed syllables. Here is an example of a trochee using a line from Hamlet.

$$\smile \ / \ \smile \ / \ \smile \ / \ \smile \ \smile \ / \ \smile \ /$$
And **by**/op**po**/sing **end**/them. To/**die** to/**sleep** – ★

As you can see the trochee happens in the fifth foot of the meter "die to" and in the added ½ foot "sleep", giving it the feminine ending.

SPONDEE

The next rhythmic pattern we're going to look at is a spondee. A spondee is when one or more feet in the pentameter contains two stressed syllables. An example of the rhythmic pattern for a spondee looks like this:

$$\smile \ / \ \smile \ / \ \ / \ \ / \ \smile \ / \ \smile \ /$$
da-**Dum**/da-**Dum**/ **Dum** - **Dum** /da-**Dum**/da-**Dum**

You'll notice that the third foot in the meter contains the two stressed syllables. Here is an example of a spondee using a line from Hamlet.

$$\smile \ / \ \smile \ / \ \smile \ / \ \ / \ \ / \ \smile \ /$$
To **sleep**/per**chance**/to **dream**/– **ay**, **there's**/the **rub**.

Here you can see that the fourth foot in the meter contains the two stressed syllables "<u>ay, there's</u>".

PYRRHIC

The last rhythmic pattern we're going to look at is a pyrrhic. A pyrrhic is when one or more feet in the pentameter contains two unstressed syllables. An example of the rhythmic pattern for a pyrrhic looks like this:

⏜ / ⏜ / ⏜ ⏜ / ⏜ /
da-**Dum**/da-**Dum**/da-da/da-**Dum**/da-**Dum**

You'll notice that the third foot in the meter contains the two stressed syllables. Here is an example of a pyrrhic using the same line from Hamlet that we used for the trochee.

⏜ / ⏜/ ⏜ / ⏜ ⏜ / ⏜ /
And **by**/op**po**/sing **end**/them. To/**die** to/**sleep** –

Here you can see that the fourth foot in the meter contains the two unstressed syllables "<u>them. To</u>". Also because this meter contains two different rhythmic types: trochee and pyrrhic, it can be either of the two.

You now have the basic tools needed to mark the rhythmic types for Shakespearean verse.

SCANSION

Now that you understand the rhythmic values of different meter types and you know how to mark stressed syllables, unstressed syllables, and feminine endings, let's look at other scansion symbols that you will be using with Shakespeare.

Stressed word – to notate a stressed word use an underline. This is used when you are marking the words of a text that are important to conveying the point. Where the / is used to mark the stressed syllable, the underline is used to mark the entire word.

Caesura – This symbol is used to mark a pause (such as a comma, dash, colon, semi-colon, etc.) within, or at the end of a verse line. The symbol used can either be an arrow / or what I like to use "railroad tracks" // . They're called railroad tracks because you have to slow down at them.

Full End Stop – This is used to denote the end of a sentence such as a period, exclamation point, question mark, etc. The symbol for a full end stop is a Ø . Think of it as a railroad track with a stop sign.

Carry-over – This is used to show that the end of a verse line is carried over to the next meter. The symbol for this is ⊃ .

SCRIPT DETECTIVE

Just as we do research for contemporary plays, we must also do research for Shakespeare. But it's more than doing research, it's doing detective work; we have to figure out what Shakespeare has written. Shakespeare's text contains many words that are uncommon by today's standards, and for each word there may be more than one meaning depending on the context in which it is used.

You must look up every word to make sure that you are using it in the correct context. There are many books out there that help you decipher Shakespeare. I like to use the *Shakespeare Lexicon and Quotation Dictionary* by Alexander Schmidt. It comes in two volumes. It's well worth the price if you're planning on working with Shakespeare beyond this book.

Besides looking up the words, you must also figure out the type of literary style he is using to convey the meaning of the line, soliloquy, set speech, or scene. We will cover the various styles in a later section.

You must also go through and mark all your text with the scansion marks that I've talked about. It helps to figure out your character's emotions and thoughts.

You should also explore the themes within the play. Find the words within the play or monologue and write them down. After you do that, write down any general themes pertaining to the words that you have written down. There can be many themes within a play or monologue so try to explore and find as many as you can.

You will never do more script work in your life than you will do with the plays of Shakespeare. It can be a very daunting task but very rewarding in the end. You will notice that when you thoroughly analyze the words, verses, and phrasings, you will discover a wonderful and enriching language that is sure to capture and intrigue you.

EXPLORING SHAKESPEAREAN VERSE

Besides using variations of the iambic pentameter to express different ways a character feels, acts, connects, relates, and lives on stage, Shakespeare also uses many literary styles to add further depth to the play and its characters. Below is a short list of styles that he uses.

ANTITHESIS

The most dominant style of Shakespearean writing: setting the word against the word with opposition. This can be done within a sentence or between two sentences. Other forms of antithesis can include:

CONTRASTING PUNS

Using a word to mean two different things in a sentence and giving it a double meaning.

"Go, play, boy, play. Thy mother plays and I play too."

PHILOSOPHICAL

Using simple philosophy to make a point with two contrasting ideas.

"To be or not to be..."

RHETORIC

Using words or sentences in a way that proves to be very effective in influencing others on stage including figurative language of the times.

"Once more, unto the breach, dear friends, once more."

DOUBLE ENTENDRE

The art of saying one word but giving a different meaning behind it, usually sexual.

"Who <u>laid</u> him down, and bask'd him in the sun,
And <u>rail'd</u> on Lady Fortune in good terms."

STICHOMYTHIA

Quick repartee of wit back and forth by two characters using words like a Ping-Pong match.

Antony. No, Caesar, we will answer on their charge.
Make forth, the generals would have some words.

Octavius. Stir not until the signal.

Brutus. Words before blows, is it so, countrymen?

Oct. Not that we love words better, as you do.

Bru. Good words are better than bad strokes, Octavius.

Ant. In your bad stroke, Brutus, you give good words.

LEARNING TO SCAN THE TEXT

Now it is time to learn how to scan and mark Shakespearean text. Below is the prologue from Romeo and Juliet, Act 1, sc. 1.

Two households, both alike in dignity,

In fair Verona, where we lay our scene,

From ancient grudge break to new mutiny,

Where civil blood makes civil hands unclean.

From forth the fatal loins of these two foes

A pair of star-cross'd lovers take their life;

Whole misadventured piteous overthrows

Do with their death bury their parents' strife.

The fearful passage of their death-mark'd love,

And the continuance of their parents' rage,

Which, but their children's end, nought could remove,

Is now the two hours' traffic of our stage;

The which if you with patient ears attend,

What here shall miss, our toil shall strive to mend.

Before marking the text:
1. Read the play.
2. Re-read your text several times to understand its meaning.
3. Look at the objectives, obstacles, and tactics your character uses in the text.
4. Look up all the words as I mentioned in the script detective section.
5. Tap out the iambic pentameter of the text. Feel for the rhythm. Listen for any feminine endings that may occur.

Initial mark-up of text:
1. In pencil, split up the feet in the meter with a slash mark then using the unstressed and stressed symbols mark the text in iambic pentameter. Do not use any other rhythmic form yet. That is why you are using pencil. Note any feminine endings and mark those sentences.
2. After the text has been marked with the iambic pentameter and feminine endings, go through the text again and mark the trochee, spondee, and pyrrhic rhythms in the feet. Allow your instincts to lead you. Don't forcefully try to add rhythms. Let it happen naturally.
3. Now use the scansion marks (caesuras and end stops) to note all punctuation in the text, including periods, question marks, colons, semi-colons, etc.
4. Repeat again this time, marking any carry-over sentences.
5. Re-read the speech and notice if the character's objectives are clear.
6. Now mark the text for all the stressed words with an underline.
7. Re-read the text once again and notice how the scansion affects the way you understand the text.

After mark-up of text:

1. Write out the text in prose. Noting all the punctuation and thoughts. Remember prose is written how we commonly write today. Don't copy iambic pattern of verse.
2. Next, paraphrase the text in your own words. See if you can get the meaning across in today's use of language.
3. Pick words in each line that tell the story. A good way to do this is to think of a person learning to speak English for the first time, only picking the words that get the thought across.
4. Pick two or three words in each sentence to clarify the theme of the text.
5. Write down a list of the most important theme words.
6. Now make a newspaper headline to capture the audience's attention using three or four words from the list of theme words.

Congratulations! You have now completed your first scansion of Shakespearean text.

SCANSION EXAMPLE

I'm going to show you how I would use scansion and detective work to figure out the prologue from Romeo and Juliet.

WORDS TO LOOK UP

dignity

mutiny

civil blood

civil hands

unclean

misadventured

piteous

overthrows

death-mark'd

strife

traffic

attend

toil

men

LITERARY STYLES

<u>Antithesis</u>

ancient grudge/new mutiny

civil blood/civil hands

forth the fatal loins/lovers take their life

death mark'd love/parents' rage

continuance/remove

two hours traffic/patient ears

<u>Contrasting Puns</u>

break/makes

Philosophical

Rhetoric

both alike/two foes

Double Entendre

Stichomythia

STRESSED WORDS

households, alike, dignity

Verona, lay, scene

ancient grudge, new mutiny

blood, hands, unclean

fatal, loins, foes

lovers, take, life

misadventured, overthrows

death, bury, strife

death-mark'd, love

parent's, rage

children's, removed

traffic, stage

patient, ears, attend

toil, strive, mend

IMPORTANT THEME WORDS

households

dignity

grudge

mutiny

blood

unclean

loins

foes

lovers

overthrows

death

bury

strife

death-mark'd

love

rage

children

remove

patient

toil

strive

mend

THEMES

love/hate

life/death

peace/rage

lovers/foes

NEWSPAPER HEADLINE

Grudge Bury Lovers

Two house/holds, both/alike/in dig/nity, //

In fair/Vero/na, where/we lay/our scene, //

From an/cient grudge/break to/new mu/tiny, //

Where ci/vil blood/makes ci/vil hands/unclean. ∅

From forth/the fa/tal loins/of/ these/two foes ⤵

A pair/of star-/cross'd lo/vers take/their life; //

Whole mis/adven/tured pi/teous o/verthrows ⤵

Do with/their death/bury/their par/ents' strife. ∅

The fear/ful pass/age of/their death-/mark'd love, //

And the/contin/uance/of their/parents'/rage, // ★

Which, but/their chil/dren's end,/nought could/remove, //

Is now/the two/hours' traf/fic of/our stage; //

The which/if you/with pa/tient ears/attend, //

What here/shall miss,/our toil/shall strive/to mend. ∅

PHYSICALIZING THE TEXT

This is a fantastic way to release the words and sounds of Shakespeare and get them into your body. Try these exercises to physicalize the text[1] and gain a better understanding of them.

Release the sensual and physical power of words by sounding them. Don't be delicate. Play with words as you did when you were a child. Trust your intellectual powers. Need and know the word physically, emotionally, and organically. After each exercise, return to the text you are working with immediately, before you think about it, and realize the difference.

1. **Speak the text with full voice.** Give it a full vitality; exaggerate the life of the words and the emotional power.

2. **Whisper the text.** This helps clarify thinking in the text. You reveal sensual qualities in the text.

3. **Intone or chant the text.** This is calming, cleansing, and will help you discover the length of thought and emotional intensity of sections of text.

4. **Speak the text while moving.** This releases the text, paces it, links the words, and underscores the physical process of speaking.

5. **Voice the first and last words of each line of text.** First, voice all the first words of each line, silently thinking and breathing the other words in line. Next, voice all the final words of each line. Note that the first words instigate the line, and final words complete each line.

6. **Voice the vowels only.** Connect to the breath of the whole word, and discover the emotional intensity of each word. Long vowel

---

[1] Handout from Rudd, Paul (Spring 2005). Shakespeare II. Actors Studio Drama School, New School University

sounds indicate open feeling, shorter ones contain or control; longer ones slow pace, shorter ones propel.

Build images in the text. Look for the pictures; see and communicate the sight in the text as you speak them so listeners identify them.

SUMMARY

This is only the tip of the iceberg when it comes to Shakespeare but I encourage you to use this chapter as a starting point to explore Shakespeare fully. There are so many aspects and nuances to Shakespeare's writing that one chapter cannot cover it all. Take my advice, read as many plays of Shakespeare as you can. If you want to learn more, read books about him, take a class, anything to help you pursue this often shrugged-off part of acting.

As you begin to unravel the complexities of his text, you will find that he is truly a writer to be relished and enjoyed, and the text a joy to perform.

CHAPTER 13: SUZUKI

Suzuki Overview 382

Using Text..383

Ich Ni Sum 384

Stomping 386

Shakuhachi 388

Ten-Te-Ke-Ten...390

The Walks 391

Statues And Jumping.....................................393

Speech And Fights.......................................394

SUZUKI OVERVIEW

Suzuki[1] is a Japanese art form used to create tension in the body. With Suzuki, you are able to strengthen your abilities of focus and concentration.

It is believed that when you performed Suzuki you were playing for the gods. All movement for Suzuki comes from the koshi. The koshi, is located three inches below your belly button. When doing Suzuki you should wear socks or be in bare feet, wear shorts, and a tee-shirt.

Neutral positions - All exercises have neutral positions. A neutral position is always the first position you take when beginning any exercise. Neutral positions will be described when an exercise is described.

When performing Suzuki exercises you are always facing an invisible opponent.

---

[1] Notes taken from Suzuki 1 and 2, P.C.P.A., 1993

USING TEXT

It is important when doing Suzuki that you use memorized text. This enables you to strengthen your mind as well as your body. Everyone involved in your Suzuki class should know the same speeches and songs. It is important. For all intents and purposes we will use the speeches I learned.

Speech A:

O, splendor of sunburst breaking forth this day,
Whereon, I lay your hands once more on Helen your wife.
And yet it is not so much as men think,
For the woman's' sake I came to Troy,
But against that guest proved treacherous
Who like a robber carried the woman away?

Speech B:

To sit in solemn silence on a dull dark dock
In a pestilential prison with a lifelong lock
Awaiting the sensation of a short sharp shock
With the chippy chippy chopper on a big black block.

Most often during the exercises you will have to recite one or even both of the speeches while in a difficult position. No matter how hard it is to do, fight to do it. It will make you stronger.

ICH NI SUM

"Ich, Ni, Sum" means One, Two, Three in Japanese. This is a familiar phrase that will be heard throughout the Suzuki exercises. Usually a clap or the sound of a stick hitting a mat will be your cue to begin the exercise, followed by the instructor calling out "Ich", "Ni" or "Sum", depending on where you are in the exercise.

"O, splendor" will be used for this exercise.

1. Begin in the neutral position ( ) – Sitting up with legs pulled in and heels on the ground.

2. Ich position ( ) - Maintaining your balance and staying in the neutral position lift your feet and expose the soles to your opponent. Keep your heels on the floor.

3. Ni position ( ) - In this position the legs and feet are extended. Hands go out to the sides and are perpendicular to the floor, the body is kept in line, and you are maintaining balance.

4. Sum position ( ) - Remaining in the "Ni" position, spread legs open maintaining balance; you should feel a tightening in your stomach.

The pattern to this exercise is as follows:

> Neutral position
> (CLAP or MAT HIT)
> Ich position
> (CLAP or MAT HIT)
> Ni position then recite "O, splendor"*
> (CLAP or MAT HIT)
> Sum position then recite "O, splendor"**
> (CLAP or MAT HIT)
> Return to Neutral position

> * In beginning exercises, "O, splendor" will be said here.
> ** In later exercises, "O, splendor" will be said here.

STOMPING

BASIC STOMP

The movement comes from the koshi. Begin by standing in an upright position, legs together. Bend at the knees, your arms are at your sides. Imagine your hands are each holding a pole parallel to the ground. Do not stomp on cement or hard wood. This can cause damage to your knees. Perform stomping on a floor that has some cushioning and give to it.

The ultimate stomp should make you fall to the ground, of course you won't. Each stomp should have purpose and be just as strong as the last stomp. Knees should be brought up to waist level for each stomp.

Your focus should be on the infinite and there is no facial expression. Don't be surprised if you find yourself laughing when you first attempt to stomp. It is a very difficult thing to do at first.

SIDE STOMPING

Begin in the neutral position. On the word "Ich" and sound of the stick (clap) you will bring your right leg up in front of you (showing your enemy the sole of your foot) and circle it around and stomp it to the side.

Next, you will hear "Ni" and the stick. This will be your cue to slide your feet together. Your left foot will slide towards and meet the right.

"Sum" will indicate that you will do a grand plié. Hands will be over the knees.

"Shi" (four) - You will return to the neutral position.

After this, you will repeat the exercise, this time starting with your left foot.

KE GIN SO – A VARIATION OF SIDE-STOMPING

Ich - Bring leg up as if wrapping it around a pole, showing your enemy your foot.

Ni - Stomp foot to ground, then bring other leg up as if wrapping around pole, showing your enemy your foot.

Sum - Stomp foot to ground.

Continue this until the instructor in the class tells you to stop. If you are doing this by yourself, you can decide when to stop this exercise.

Note: Make sure you always show your enemy your foot. Make movements strong and clean.

SHAKUHACHI

This stomping exercise is done to music, preferably with traditional upbeat Japanese music using a Shakuhachi: a Japanese woodwind instrument.

When the music begins, stomp (the energy comes from the koshi) in a circle counter clockwise. You should cover the entire area of the room in which you are working in. Remember when you are stomping to keep your focus on the infinite and arms at side. You should have no facial expression and there should be no tension in your body, especially in your shoulders.

There will be a point in the music when you will stomp to one side of the room. The music will stop and you will fall to the ground. Use this time to focus your energy on the next part of the exercise.

A different Japanese tune will begin. This will lead you into the exercise known as "Waking from a Thousand Year Sleep". You will slowly wake up and stand up in a neutral position. Take your time when waking and standing up. It is not a race to stand up. Be aware of your body as you are moving in the space.

After you have stood up and assumed the neutral position you will walk toward the front of the room. Everyone will form a line. It is important that you get to the ending point and be in the neutral position before the music ends.

Be focused and aware of the "god" you are playing to. You can choose different levels when you are walking to the front of the room.

BACKWARDS SHAKUHACHI

Beginning at the front of the room. The music will start and you will proceed to move backwards, with the same focus. Imagine running a movie backwards, that's the effect you are achieving. The movements should be fluid. Keep the energy of moving forward as you do this exercise. When the music ends, fall to the ground. What happens next is dependent on what you want to do next: you may stand in a neutral position to do a standing exercise or remain collapsed on the ground and perform the "Waking from A Thousand Year Sleep" exercise.

FREESTYLE SHAKUHACHI

Same as first Shakuhachi only you are free to move anywhere in the room and your hands and arms can be anywhere in the space. They must remain in the same position and not move. Everything else is the same. You must get to the end of the room before the first part of the music ends.

TEN-TE-KE-TEN

SLOW TEN-TE-KE-TEN

This exercise is for moving in space without changing the position of the body. When done correctly, it should appear that you are floating in air if someone was watching only your upper body and not your hips and legs. They can do this by placing their hand in front of their face so that their hand blocks your lower body while they watch you.

Usually this is done with two lines facing each other about 20 – 30 feet apart. When the music starts, walk in a continuous motion towards the opposite end of the room where the other line started. As soon as the music changes, slowly turn around (towards the audience) and face the other direction. When the music starts again walk slowly towards where you began. When you reach it stay in neutral until the music stops. Come down.

With arms – move your arms and then freeze them. With your arms in this position do the "Slow Ten-Te-Ke-Ten" walk. When you reach the end of the room and turn around, change your arm positions. Allow your arms to be expressive.

FAST TEN-TE-KE-TEN

This is the same as "Slow Ten-Te-Ke-Ten" except it is at a quicker pace. Imagine the music is your heartbeat. Your arms should be moving in all directions, even backwards. When you hear the stick hit the mat, freeze. Hold on to your center and your balance. When the stick hits again, continue with the "Fast Ten-Te-Ke-Ten" movement across the floor.

THE WALKS

WALKING DOWNSTAGE

STOMPING

Walk forward to the front of the room with a stomp. With the same intensity and verve as with Shakuhachi.

KNOCK-KNEED

Walk around the space with your knees together, imagine your thighs are holding a piece of paper. Your feet and toes should be pointing inward, slide your feet one in front of the other, heel to toe, in sharp movements as you move down to the front of the room.

RICKSHAW

Walk around the room on the outside edge of your feet. Lean your upper torso forward as if pulling a rickshaw. Use a quick motion. Continue to push energy into the ground as you walk.

TIPPY-TOE

Walk around the room on your toes with your heels off the ground. Make sure you keep your center and balance. Slide feet across floor. Push the energy through the floor.

SIDEKICK

This is almost the same as "Knock-kneed" except your knees aren't together. Lift through your hip. Show opponent heel from the side.

HALF-MOON

Keep your feet on the floor. The sides of your feet should be touching. Move the right foot over to the left side of your left foot and stop. Make sure the sides are touching. Now move the left foot to the left side of your right foot and stop. Make sure the sides of your feet are touching. Bend down at the knees. Stand back up and continue the walk until you reach the end of the room.

SILENT STOMPING

With toes raised, bring knees up and move foot to side and bring down sharply. There should be no sound when your foot hits the ground. Do not slide your feet.

NOH WALK

Hold your arms out like holding a giant egg. Bend at the knees. Your feet should be planted on the ground. Slide your feet quickly along the ground.

COCKROACH

Start in a sitting crouched position. Your arms are outstretched like you are holding eggs. Your heels should be off the ground and your toes supporting your weight. Slide feet forward. Move as quickly as you can. As you are walking, keep your center and stay focused.

STATUES AND JUMPING

STATUES

For statues, the neutral position is when you are crouched down, your feet flat on the ground and your tailbone is close to the ground.

When the stick hits the mat, hit a pose. Hold a pose that changes your center. When the stick hits the mat again, return to a neutral position. When the stick hits the mat the third time, hold a new pose with a new center and recite one of the speeches. When you are finished, hold position until stick hits mat again then return to neutral position.

JUMPING

Get into the neutral position as in the exercise "ICH NI SUM." When the stick hits the mat, jump up and return to the neutral position.

SPEECH AND FIGHTS

SPEAKING THE SPEECH

Start in the "ICH NI SUM" neutral position. Begin your speech. As you are speaking it, slowly rise up on your toes and stand up. By the end of the speech you should be on your tippy-toes and your hands should be behind your head.

Return to the neutral position, saying the same speech and ending in the neutral position by the end.

You can also do this with a short song (2 minutes).

O, SPLENDOR FIGHTS

Begin the same as "ICH NI SUM" coming downstage. Then add "SHI" raising your pole parallel to the body. Your arm should be next to your ear. The pole should be touching the forearm. On "GOH" side stomp. Poles come down, parallel to the floor. "ROH" Finish up the side stomp and bring feet together. Do a grand plié. Back to neutral and bring feet in.

CHAPTER 14: STAGE COMBAT

Stage Combat Overview 396

Rules of Stage Combat 397

Hospital And Non-Hospital Zone Chart..................399

General Guidelines 400

Knaps 402

Pushing...403

Stumbles, Trips, and Falls Overview 405

Stumbles...406

Tripping..408

Falling 411

Kicks 414

Punches/Slaps...417

Grabbing And Choking 420

Running into Walls and Other Objects 423

STAGE COMBAT OVERVIEW

The art of stage combat[1] is often misconstrued as easy and fun. Although it is fun, it is not easy. Stage combat is like a dance without music, and like a dance, it must be choreographed and rehearsed. Both parties must be alert and focused. Without focus, concentration, listening and visual skills, it is easy for one of the actors in the fight sequence to get hurt. That's why it's important to always follow these rules before doing any stage combat moves.

WARM-UP

As with anything that you do in the theatre, warming up is the most important. Make sure to spend 15 to 20 minutes warming up the body and muscles along with your brain. This will loosen your muscles and add flexibility in your movements. Incorporate all safe stretching procedures when warming up. Don't strain yourself. Don't hurt yourself.

---

[1] Notes taken from Stage Combat 1 and 2, P.C.P.A., Jack Greenman, 1992-93

RULES OF STAGE COMBAT

COMMUNICATION

It is important to talk to your partner about the moves you are going to be executing. Talk through everything thoroughly. If, for any reason, something changes in the stage combat choreography, inform your partner immediately. Accidents can happen in stage combat at any time but 90% of the accidents are caused by miscommunication between partners. If you always communicate, there is a lower chance of being injured.

SPACING

There should always be a good amount of space between you and your partner. If you are too close you could actually hurt yourself or the person(s) you are performing with on stage.

SPEED

Whenever you rehearse stage combat, start at ¼ speed. Increase the speed as you feel more comfortable with the moves. Under no circumstances should you ever perform any stage combat move at full speed. I repeat:

Note: Never perform stage combat at full speed. It should be performed at ¾ of real time speed.

EYE CONTACT

Making eye contact is the best way to communicate with your partner when doing stage combat. It lets your partner know that you are ready and focused. Failure to make eye contact could result in injury due to miscommunication and unawareness. Always make eye contact.

HOSPITAL AND NON-HOSPITAL ZONES

This refers to the areas of the body that are safe or unsafe to hit. You want to avoid any hospital zones on the body. Hospital zones (H) are the head, neck, lower back/spine, groin and shins. Non-hospital zones (NH) are chest, stomach, thighs, quads, and calves.

Arms and legs can either be H or NH zones depending on the actions you take. Always be careful and discuss all moves with your partner before trying them.

On the next page you will find a diagram for the Hospital and Non-hospital zones of the body.

HOSPITAL AND NON-HOSPITAL ZONE CHART

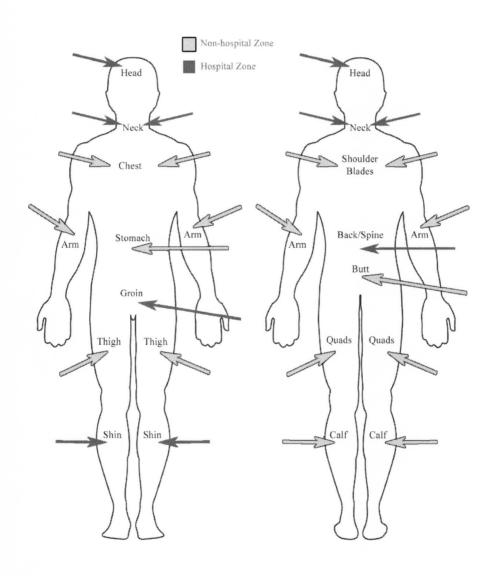

General Guidelines

CENTER OF GRAVITY
Always be centered. With one leg grounded, you should be able to move your other leg forward, back, left, right, up, and down without losing balance.

STAY IN CONTROL
Don't let the adrenaline get the better of you during the combat. Don't let the fight speed up. If you feel it is getting out of control or going too fast, say, "Stop" and start again.

STAY FOCUSED AND AWARE
Be aware of all surroundings. Always give your partner and the fight your undivided attention. Do not let outside influences distract you. Focus on the task on hand. Do not let your mind wander.

REACTION MATCHES ACTION
The reaction to being hit, tripped, and punched, etc., should match the intensity of the action. Under or overplaying will make the combat look false.

FORWARD FORCE AND PULLING BACK
When performing any form of stage combat involving a punch or kick, remember this important factor. The initial forward motion into the body can be quick but should slow down prior to making contact with your knap then pulling back with a faster speed. With a punch like a cross, uppercut, or hook, after the knap, continue through with the punch and pick up speed to finish the movement.

All kicks and some punches, like jabs, do not continue forward, instead the person giving the punch or kick sells the combat by pulling back with a quick, sharper movement. This gives the illusion that you performed this combat move at full speed.

POSITIONING

When doing a punch to someone, always check the safe distance by putting your thumb on your chest and extending your pinky out. The person with the longest arms puts their fist next to the pinky. That is the distance from the body part that you will be aiming for when performing a punch.

KNAPS

A knap is the sound you make when you want to simulate the sound of being punched or kicked. There are three different knaps: slip knap, slap knap, and body knap. When working on stage combat, pick the knap that is most appropriate for the punch or kick, as well as the best for concealing it from being seen by the audience.

SLIP KNAP

The fist you are using to punch your opponent opens up and connects with the other hand. After creating the knap sound, your punching hand returns back to a fist.

The hand that makes the knap can be placed on the shoulder before receiving the knap from the other hand. This is usually used for right and left uppercuts.

SLAP KNAP

The hands are kept low towards the center of the torso about 2 inches apart. Make the knap by slapping hands in one up and down motion Slap right hand against left hand (like hitting two cymbals together). The right hand will go up and the left hand will go down.

BODY KNAP

Make the knap sound by hitting a non-hospital zone on the body with an open fist and pulling away sharply.

PUSHING

There are two types of prep that I like to use for pushing: The "Lean-in" and the "Pull-in". These preps depend on the type of situation that the push is happening. It is important to remember that the force of the push has to be matched by both combatants so it looks real. In both cases, there should be a slight push felt but not actually pushed unless the one choreographing the fight has indicated that they want you to do it. Just be careful if a real push is required that you don't actually push someone off-balance.

THE LEAN-IN

For this prep we are going to assume that Actor A, the pusher is facing stage left and Actor B, the one being pushed is facing stage right. You should be a little less than an arm's length away.

To prep, Actor A will have their left foot in front and the right foot behind. Actor B will have their left foot between Actor A's feet and the right foot to the side of Actor A's right foot and slightly back from their own left foot. It should look something like this –

ACTOR B

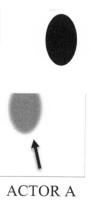

ACTOR A

Actor A will lean in while maintaining the level at which they are standing and put their hands on Actor B's chest, if it is a woman you will place your hands to the side slightly below where the clavicle and shoulders meet. Then with the force that you and your partner agree on, Actor A will push by leaning back into place, outstretching the arms to give the illusion that they are pushing and bring the left foot even with the right foot. Actor B will take a step back with the left foot and then continue with a stumble or fall. Adding some sort of sound as you are pushing and being pushed will also help sell it to the audience.

THE PULL-IN

For this prep, Actor B is a bit closer to Actor A. The same rules apply as to where your hands and feet are. Actor A will grab Actor B's shirt just above the chest and below the shoulders. Actor A will pull Actor B towards them as Actor B leans in. When Actor A pushes, they will simply step back with the left foot so it is even with right foot while extending their arms and giving a sound to accompany the push. Actor B will react accordingly by taking a step back with the left foot and then following through with a stumble or fall.

PUSHING FOR THE BACK

The two differences with this push are that since it is from the back and Actor B can't see you and Actor B has their left foot forward and their right foot slightly back. Because Actor B can't see Actor A, it is important to make a sound so actor B knows when you are going to push them. When actor B is pushed, their right foot goes forward and then the follow through with a stumble or fall.

STUMBLES, TRIPS, AND FALLS OVERVIEW

Before getting started on this chapter it is important that you take extra precaution. As I stated in the preface to Stage Combat, it can be dangerous if you are not careful, disciplined and observant of your surroundings. I would recommend rehearsing any type of pratfall with a gymnasium mat or a stable but cushioned area. Do not under any circumstances rehearse falling where there is not give to the floor such as cement, plaster, tiled, etc. I would also advise that you wear kneepads and wrist guards when practicing stumbling, falling, and tripping.

I started doing pratfalls when I was attending conservatory. It came to me naturally. I could fall out of trees, run into walls, fall down a flight of stairs, you name it, I tried it. My classmates would always ask me to do falls when they were around. They challenged me to trip over basketballs, get hit by a broom, crash into doors, and fall off the end of the stage.

Over the years, I perfected the art of pratfalls by observing those who knew how to do it and asking questions. I also watched and learned from the great physical comedians of my time: John Ritter, Carol Burnett, Lucille Ball, and Mel Brooks, just to name a few.

These are the ways that I fall and am imparting my knowledge on how I do it. If you want to learn professionally how to do pratfalls or stage combat look for a class taught by a certified instructor.

STUMBLES

Stumbling is the easiest of the "pratfall" techniques. The idea behind stumbling is that you've lost your balance. This type of pratfall can be a set-up to falling and tripping. Stumbling can be used to portray a drunk person, someone who has lost their equilibrium, someone about to faint, being on an imaginary plane that has lost its balance, pretty much anything that requires you to not be balanced on stage but NOT fall or trip.

First, place your center at your shoulders and allow that to be the first part of your body that leads in the space. Allow your right shoulder to be heavy in weight and both your feet assigned a light value in weight. If you do not know the principles behind Leading and Weight refer to CHAPTER 7.

In a neutral stance, allow your shoulders to move to the right with the heavy weight assigned to it. As you lean to the right, allow your left foot (which has been assigned the light weight value to move in front of your right foot to catch yourself. Quickly bring your right foot behind the left foot and try to place it in a neutral position (parallel to your shoulders). The right foot should have a heavier weight than the left, creating the illusion that you are trying to catch yourself. As your foot lands on the floor, allow your shoulder to continue to the left and your left foot repeats its action of moving to the right. If you repeat this process across the floor you should be able to give the appearance of a stagger to the right.

Once you have practiced that a few times, reverse direction and go the other way. This time the heavy weight is in your left shoulder. Your feet have the same weight value as before. Your left shoulder moves to the left, your right foot crosses in front of your left foot, your left foot crosses behind the right with a heavier weight value given to it and tries to position itself in a neutral position but the right immediate crosses in front of the left. Continue this pattern until you have reached the other end of the room. This will give the appearance of a stagger to the left.

Keep in mind that in order to create a realistic looking stagger you must allow your body to move freely in space without the appearance of controlling the movement. Allow the shoulder to lead in the direction to go. When you are about to lose balance, that's when you move your feet. You should not actually lose balance or be in any danger of losing balance when performing a stagger.

To create an off-balanced back and forth stagger, simply allow yourself to stagger to the right only once or twice and then immediately try to adjust by shifting the weight to your other shoulder and repeating the movement in the opposite direction. This will give an appearance of being drunk. Remember, the trick to pulling off being drunk on stage is fighting not to appear drunk. A drunk person doesn't want to appear drunk, they want to remain in control at all times, even though their equilibrium is off. It is one of the harder things to do on stage convincingly.

To stagger forward, shift the lead position to your nose or forehead, giving that part of your body the heavy weight value and allow your body to move forward. Your feet will move as if walking but with a slight lean so that the feet are never actually parallel to each other. One will always be in front of the other.

To reverse a forward stumble, place the lead to the back of the head with the heavy weight value assigned to it and allow your body to move backwards with the same foot movement as described for a forward stagger.

Once you have mastered all directions of staggering and stumbling, try to add twists, turns, and spins to your body for other staged effects such as being "controlled" like a puppet, being disoriented, or becoming incredibly dizzy.

TRIPPING

TRIPPING OVER FEET

The next level after learning to stumble is tripping. The idea is a pretty simple one to grasp. Your foot will catch on an object causing you to jolt forward and then you can go into a front stumble if you want. The basic trip is done like this:

First, decide which foot will be the one that causes the trip. This foot will also be the one that you use to catch yourself so you don't fall. Let's use the right foot for now. As you are walking, your right foot comes forward to take your next step. You are going to let it slightly catch onto the back of your left foot. As you do this you will automatically begin to lurch forward. With the same foot that you used to hitch on the back of your foot, bring it forward to stop yourself from falling. There you go: a trip.

To facilitate the trip more effectively, when you catch your foot and you lurch forward, allow your shoulders to lead the forward movement. Practice walking and tripping: first with your right foot and then with your left.

It should appear real and not rehearsed. You will need to practice this many times. At first it will look awkward and choreographed, but once you understand the concepts behind tripping, and trusting that you will to catch yourself, you will become more adept at the art of tripping over your feet.

TRIPPING OVER OBJECTS

Tripping over an object can be a bit more dangerous especially if the object moves: like a ball, skateboard, roller-skate, etc., Here is the basic rule to remember: walk through the trip you want to do. Go through it slowly and meticulously. First let's focus on a stationary object.

Just like tripping over your feet, the stationary object will be the source of the fall. Let us use stairs as our tripping source. Decide which foot you want to use, for this exercise I will describe it using the right foot. As you walk up the stairs let the top of your right foot (toes) catch onto the edge of the step, this will cause you to lurch forward like you did over your feet. Again, the foot that catches the step is the same foot that is going to catch you before you fall. Continue to practice tripping over a step. When you've mastered that, find another stationary object and try tripping over that one. Don't forget to walk through it first so your body can get used to the movement.

A moveable object is our next goal. Find something round like a ball. Choose a small ball at first, like a baseball or golf ball. After you learn to trip over those, you can move onto larger, round objects. Place the ball in the middle of the room and make sure there are no objects around that you can fall into, on the off-chance that you actually do fall.

Place the foot that you will be catching yourself with on the ball. Allow the ball to move under your foot so you can understand how the ball will move when you trip over it. Once you understand how the ball will move, take a few steps back and walk towards the ball, let your foot go on top of the ball and continue to move forward, allowing the ball to be moved backwards by the motion of your foot. As the ball moves under you, the foot on the ball lurches forward to catch yourself. After your foot leaves the ball, bring your other foot forward to regain your balance, or fall, depending on what you want to do. Ta Dah!: tripping over an object.

Keep practicing with different types of moveable objects, always checking to see how the object will move under you. Remember to be safe and wear your protective gear.

FALLING

Now we come to the most difficult and possibly dangerous one of all: the fall. Falls can be initiated by a stumble or a trip, which relies on your feet or an object. They can also be initiated by being pushed, missing a step (going downstairs), a punch, or anything that uses force (either by motion or gravity)

To fall correctly, follow this pattern: lean forward and bend at your knees. Your right leg or whichever leg is the upstage leg will move forward as if taking a step. Continue to bend your knee and lean forward, eventually you will need to fall to the ground. Try to get as close to the ground as you can so that you won't fall too far from it.

For this first fall, as you are about to succumb to gravity. Allow your hips to turn so that when you fall, you will land on your thigh and not on your knees. As you fall, your arm should extend forward so that you will catch yourself. Do not over-extend your arms too far. You are not reaching or stretching. Make sure your arm is almost parallel to the ground. You do not want your arms to be perpendicular to the floor because that would mean your hands would be bent at the wrist as you land. If this happens, you have a chance of putting pressure on your wrists as you catch yourself and could injure your wrist. You should slide forward when you land.

Do this fall slowly at first, getting used to how your body is supposed to move and slightly increasing the speed at which you fall. If you find yourself getting hurt, which is very common when learning how to fall, return to the speed that you did not hurt yourself and continue to practice. Eventually, with enough practice, you should be able to fall at a relatively normal speed without hurting yourself.

A variation of this fall is to fall forward using your knees but I do not recommend this practice. Without the right knowledge or protection you could injure your knees.

FALLING DOWNSTAIRS (STANDING)

To fall downstairs you are going to add the stumble that we worked on earlier in this chapter. Walk down the stairs and figure out which stair and foot you want to fall on. Use your hand on the wall or handrail to "try" and balance yourself. This will add to the credibility of the fall.

Once you figure out the logistics of your fall. Go to the top of the stairs and slowly walk down the stairs. Trip yourself, which will lead you into a stumble. Hold onto the rails as if you're trying to get your balance, and then either, end with gaining your composure at the bottom of the stairs or falling to the ground using the principles of the previous section "FALLING".

FALLING DOWNSTAIRS (TUMBLE)

To actually fall downstairs as in tumbling do the same set-up as falling downstairs while standing. When you fall down the stairs, you are going to fall as you learned in this chapter's section "FALLING", as you do this, let your shoulders land on the staircase and allow yourself to roll down them. You want your body to roll to the side so that the back of your shoulder and thighs are making the initial contact to the stairs so they can take the brunt of the force.

You will not be falling with your full weight. Try to cushion yourself by using your hands if you can to guide yourself down. This is a bit tricky and I would practice this many, many, many times slowly so you can see how your body will move. Kneepads are highly suggested.

FALLING BACKWARDS

Using the same principle as falling forward, falling backwards requires you to land on your butt since that is the most padded part of your body. Usually, falling backwards comes from being pushed by someone else or running into a wall with the recoiling force pushing you backwards. With your body in a neutral position take a step back and start to bend at your knee with the foot you are using.

As you are bending your knee continue to allow your butt to get closer to the floor. Eventually gravity will take over and you will fall to the ground. When you do, try to give yourself a little push with the leg that is bending so that you don't fall directly on your butt. Instead, you want to try to make it slide into the floor. As you land, you will have to use your arms to catch your fall. Be careful as you do this, because if you use your hands, your wrist will be bent and you could injure your wrists. You want to brace the fall with your forearms if at all possible. Wear elbow pads if you have them to protect your elbows from taking any damage from the brunt of the fall.

Continue to practice the backward fall until you feel comfortable and able to do it at a relatively normal speed. As you continue to get faster it will be easier to fall because, when we fall at a slow rate, we have a harder time trying to keep our balance.

KICKS

Note: When doing a kick, start in ¼ real time. Also, make sure you and your partner are ready. Give eye contact and give a good prep moment, either visually or verbally.

STANDING

1. Actor A stands with hands cupped at chest level about 8 - 12" from the chest. Palms facing down towards floor.
2. Actor B places foot into the cupped hands. Repeat until completely comfortable where hand will be and where to place the foot.
3. A kicks B with foot landing in cupped hand. B reacts to the force of the kick.

KNEELING

1. A is on ground with either one knee up or both knees on ground. Hands are cupped in the same position as the "standing kick."
2. B places foot into the cupped hand. Repeat until completely comfortable where hand will be and where to place the foot.
3. A kicks B with foot landing in cupped hand. B reacts to the force of the kick, falling backwards. This kick is used to simulate being kicked in the face.

DOUBLED-OVER KICK

1. A leans over, making sure balance is good and knees are slightly bent.
2. B places foot into the cupped hand. Repeat until completely comfortable where hand will be and where to place the foot.
3. A kicks B with foot landing in cupped hand.
4. B reacts to the force of the kick, usually stumbling backwards.

STANDING KICK TO THE STOMACH

1. A and B stand parallel facing each other.
2. A places B's foot in the stomach NH Zone.
3. B continues to place foot in the NH Zone that A designated.
4. B kicks A with foot landing in NH Zone, (the kick can be a forward kick or sideways kick.)
5. A reacts to the force of the kick. The result of this kick would result in the victim doubling over or falling backwards.

Note: The actual kick should never be stronger than a hard tap.

STANDING KICK TO STOMACH WITH KNEES ON GROUND

1. A is either on two knees or on all fours.
2. A places B's foot in the stomach NH Zone
3. B continues to place foot in the NH Zone that A designated.
4. B kicks A with foot landing in NH Zone. A reacts to the force of the kick. The result of this kick would be the victim falling to their side or on their back.

Note: This kick is approached from the side and should never be stronger than a hard tap. This kick can be prepped by running. Make sure body slows down before initiating the combat kick.

STRAIGHT ON KNEE TO GROIN

1. Feet shoulder width apart
2. B targets inside of A's thigh
3. A and B make eye contact
4. B makes knee to thigh contact with A.

Note: Cue is stepping back for kick.

FOOT OR HEEL TO GROIN
1. B is holding A from behind.
2. B has legs open, wide enough for A's leg to go through.
3. A kicks between legs and hits butt or thigh.

LAYING DOWN KICK TO GROIN

1. B kneels on one leg over A.
2. Depending on height, A kicks B with heel or knee
3. Contact made with thigh muscle only.

STANDING OVER LAYING VICTIM

1. B is standing over A
2. B kicks A inside of thigh with inside of foot

LAYING UNDER STANDING ATTACKER

1. B is standing over A
2. A kicks into B's inner thigh or butt

PUNCHES/SLAPS

PUNCH IN STOMACH
1. Target NH Zone of stomach.
2. Use strong force but pull back
3. Use flat part of fist (no knuckles or thumbs.)
4. Come straight into stomach not an uppercut
5. Can use open fist to make knap, hitting NH Zone with palm.

HAMMER PUNCH (IN THE BACK)
1. A marks NH zone of B's back (shoulder blade area).
2. A clasps hands together.
3. A hits NH zone with open fist, palm down.

PUNCH IN GROIN
1. A marks the NH hospital zone above or below B's groin area. (below the stomach or the thigh).
2. A uses flat part of fist.
3. A hits victim in the inner thigh or lower stomach.

RIGHT or LEFT CROSS/SLAP
1. A marks area of face they are aiming for.
2. A takes a slightly wide stance
3. A swivels pelvis when executing punch.
4. Cue: Wind-up
5. A and B make eye contact before the cross or slap happens.
6. Straight line to chin/jaw (remember the safe zone)
7. Slip knap
   a. Open hand and make knap, quickly closing hand into fist and following through
8. Follow through

Left Cross – Right leg will be in front of left leg.

Right Cross – Left leg will be in front of right leg.

RIGHT OR LEFT HOOK
This is the same as a cross, except you are curving into the area being punched.
1. Eye contact,
2. Wide stance
3. Swivel pelvis when executing punch
4. Cue: Wind-up
5. Curve punch to chin/jaw (remember the safe zone)
6. Slip knap
7. Follow through.

Other variations of making the knap.
1. Grab shirt before making knap
2. Hold shoulder before making knap.

UPPERCUT
Same as the Cross-punch except:
1. Palm of hand is at opponent's chest level, 1 foot away.
2. Body comes down as fist goes up.

JAB
1. Clap knap
2. Two jabs at a time
3. Cue: Elbow back
4. Curve arm, arc arm
5. Aim for chin or mouth
6. Pull back after each knap

BACK-HANDED PUNCH/SLAP

1. A marks area of face they are aiming for on side of face.
2. A takes a slightly wide stance
3. A swivels pelvis when executing punch/slap.
4. Cue: Wind-up
5. A and B make eye contact before the cross or slap happens.
6. A makes a straight line towards area of face.
7. B makes a clap knap
8. A follows through with slight diagonal direction towards the ceiling.

Right-handed – Right leg in front of left.

Left-handed – Left leg in front of right.

GRABBING AND CHOKING

HAIR PULL
Attacker –
1. Palm on head, mesh through hair
2. Move counter clockwise once
3. Snap wrist

Victim –
1. After attacker snaps wrist, grab attacker's wrist
2. Follow lead of attacker
3. To let go, bring victim down, then up. Release

GRABBING CLOTHES
1. Grab clothes of victim
2. Victim puts hand over attacker's hand.
3. Follow lead of attacker
4. To let go, bring victim down, then up. Release

BACKWARD CHOKE HOLD
1. Put left or right hand on shoulder with the other arm around the neck leaving plenty of room between arm and neck.
2. Victim grabs attacker's bicep and wrist
3. Victim puts neck on attacker's arm and sells the idea of being choked.
4. Follow lead of attacker. Victim is always in control.

FRONT CHOKE

1. Victim puts hands on attacker's wrists or covers their attacker's hands.
2. Victim puts chin on hand
3. Follow lead of attacker. Victim is always in control.

COMBO #1

1. A Jab, jab
2. B Stumble
3. A Right hook
4. B Stumble, stumble
5. B Right backhand
6. A Really stumble
7. B Right hook but
8. A Ducks
9. A Right cross
10. B Down for the count

COMBO #2

1. A Push
2. B Push
3. A Grab arm, turn partner around
4. B Push
5. A Fall, start to get up
6. B Grab hair, pull
7. A Travel with partner (on all fours)
8. B Face kick, push to ground, walk away
9. A Side swipe, under leg
10. B Fall
11. A Get up
12. B Get up
13. A Hit on back
14. B Kick in stomach 2 x
15. A Walks away

Running into Walls and Other Objects

This is my favorite thing to do and when I was in conservatory I was often asked to do this on any given day by my fellow classmates. As with any pratfall, you must first rehearse what you are going to do slowly and then build up speed.

To run into a wall, you will walk or run towards it. As you get about 3 feet from the wall, turn your head slightly as if getting distracted. Continue to walk towards the wall. As you get about 10" – 12" from it, turn your head back and lift your right or left hand up and place it just in front of your face. As you are about to hit the wall, allow your foot or hand to hit it to make the sound and allow yourself to stumble backwards or stumble and fall depending on what you want to achieve. Your face should never actually touch the wall.

Any stationary object can replace the wall. You can use a door, the side of the car, a chair, really anything. If you are running into something like the side of a desk, where your torso is the point of contact, use your thigh or foot to make the contact sound with the object and allow yourself to lurch forward slightly over the object.

As you practice more and more with the different things you can fall over, you will learn how your body naturally moves and make them more believable.

Running into walls or falling over objects are difficult stunts to do, so be careful. Once I was doing a variation of this with a tree limb and I missed my timing and ran my lip into my hand. Yes, I got a fat lip and it hurt. So always be careful and know that there is always a chance you can get hurt.

CHAPTER 15: GAMES AND EXERCISES

Yes/No 427

The Slug 427

Go 428

Pass the Ball 428

Mirror 428

Space Aliens 429

Alphabet Game...429

Count-Off..430

L.A. Tag 430

Fairy Tale in a Minute 431

Stunt Double..431

Aselephant/Asephalan 431

What's in the Box? 433

Environment Game (10'x10' room)..............................433

New Names 434

Four Rooms 434

Circle Dance..434

Body Parts 435

I'm Afraid, Will You Protect Me 435

Four Men in a Raft 435

The Board Meeting 435

Dinner Out 436

The Machine/Build a Robot 436

Word Association with Clicks 436

Add a Freeze 437

Three Poses Scene 437

Opposites Game 437

Guess the Word 438

Telephone 438

Essence Machines 438

One Word at a Time 438

Two Truths and a Lie 439

Gibberish Interpreters 439

This is a collection of games and exercises that you can use in your theatre class. Feel free to find variations to the games.

YES/NO

Purpose: To strengthen your choices as an actor.

Set-up: Pair off students. Each one stands 20 – 30 feet apart. Assign each pair "A" and "B" labels. "A" can only say "yes" and "B" can only say "No."

Object: With only saying Yes or No, the actors must convince their partner to leave their space and come over to them.

Things to remember:
Find different tactics
Vary your pitch
Increase your stakes
What's at stake if you don't get them to come over?
What is it important that your partner come to you?

THE SLUG

Purpose: To become body aware or your movement.
Set-up: Choose partners. One person lies on the ground. The partner then touches "the slug". The slug moving slowly tries to cover up the part of their body that was touched. Before the slug can fully protect that area, their partner touches another body part of "the slug" and the process continues.

Object: To observe how the body moves and to see how the muscles react when moving in slow motion.

GO

Purpose: To bring awareness to listening and communication skills.

Set-up: Actor A points to Actor B. Actor B says Go. Actor A moves to Actor B's space. Actor B points to Actor C. Actor C says go. Actor B moves to Actor C's space, this continues until someone messes up the sequence or if another actor makes it to the different space.

Object: To move to your space before the other actor reaches you.

PASS THE BALL

Set- up: One actor tosses an imaginary ball to another actor. The "ball" is tossed with a sound. The actor catching the ball repeats the sound as they catch it. Then the actor with the ball, changes the ball and throws it to a new actor with a different sound. Repeat this sequence until all actors have thrown the "ball".

MIRROR

Set-up: Split the actors into pairs. If they are working on scenes, scene partners should work together. Assign an Actor A and an Actor B. The partners look each other in the eyes and concentrate, focusing on their teammate. Partners bring their hands up in front of them, palms out. Their hands should be close but not touching. Actor A moves his hand and Actor B follows. After a few minutes have them switch. Now actor B continues moving and Actor A follows.

Once a clear connection has been established, challenge them to move around, slowly. They should always be able to see their partner as if looking into a mirror.

It is not about making the other person unable to follow but about creating a connection that makes it almost impossible to know who is leading the movement.

SPACE ALIENS

Purpose: To think outside the box.

Set-up: You are space aliens that have landed on Earth to gather information on them by the objects in their world. They are to explore the outside world and bring back one object. "Aliens" are not allowed to speak to anyone outside of the room. Aliens must return to the theatre space at a set time limit, usually 10 – 15 minutes.

Object: Using as much detail as possible, describe the object you found and how it is used. The object cannot be used its normal way. Example, a shopping cart turned over is a form of protection that the earthlings crawl into when they are in danger.

ALPHABET GAME

Purpose: To think on your feet while staying in character.

Set-up: Two actors perform a scene. They must speak in alphabetical order. Actor A's first sentence must start with A. Actor B's response must start with B. This continues until they have reached the end of the alphabet.

An alternate version is to start at a different point of the alphabet, starting with J and ending with I.

Note: Remind them to use their location, relationship, and objective to help them if they get stuck.

COUNT-OFF

Purpose: To bring awareness through observation.

Set-up: Count from 1 to the number of students in your class. Each student may only say one number only. Start back at the beginning if two people say the same number at the same time. Once they have successfully done this, challenge them by doubling the number. This time each student can only say two numbers and not back-to-back. Students may not give looks or gestures for someone to say a number. When starting a sequence over, no person may say the same number they said the previous round.

Object: To complete the sequence of numbers without a mistake.

L.A. TAG

This is a tried and true exercise that everyone has fun with. Usually better with larger numbers.

Set-up: Two actors go up and start a scene. They should use various movements, not standing still. Let the scene start. When an actor or the actors are in an interesting shape, someone yells "Freeze". That actor takes the exact position of another actor. The replaced actor sits down and the actor who replaced them starts a new scene, not a continuation of the previous scene. The actor who replaces another actor ALWAYS starts the new scene. Continue until everyone has gone or after a set time limit. Encourage everyone to participate and not to let scenes go on too long before yelling "Freeze".

Object: To think quickly and justify a new scene based on the frozen body position.

FAIRY TALE IN A MINUTE

Set-up: Divide the actors into groups. Give them 10 – 15 minutes to come up with a fairytale and act it out in 5 minutes. After everyone has gone, reduce the time to 3 minutes and have them act out the same fairytale. Repeat it one more time giving them only 1 minute to act out the fairytale.

Object: To find the important parts of a story that must be told.

STUNT DOUBLE

Set-up: Two actors go on stage. Assign two different actors to be a stunt double. One for Actor A and one for Actor B. During the scene, the actors create a situation that requires something physical to happen, i.e. drinking something nasty, dying, showing a dance move, etc. Before the actor in the scene does the physical action, yell, "Stunt Double" and the stunt person, steps in, replaces the other actor and does the action. Once it is completed, the stunt person goes back to the side lines and the other actor returns and the scene continues.

An alternative is once the physical action is completed, the stunt person becomes the actor in the scene, and the other actor they did the stunt for becomes the stunt double.

ASELEPHANT/ASEPHALAN

Purpose: To focus on what you have to do and not let anticipation get in the way of concentration.

Set-up: Have everyone sit in a circle, either on chairs or on the floor. You will need a pencil and a pen. If you do not have a pen and pencil handy, any two objects that are similar but different will do. Explain that the pencil is an aselepant. You will then demonstrate the exercise by holding the pencil out with your right hand to one of the actors in the circle. The actor receiving the "pencil" may not take it until the dialogue is complete. The pencil is always passed to the right and the pen is always passed to the left. Teach them this dialogue for passing the pencil.

Dialogue for passing the pencil: (passing to the right)
Actor 1: This is an aselephant.
Actor 2: A what?
Actor 1: An aselephant.
Actor 2: An aselephant?
Actor 1: An aselephant.
Actor 2: An aselephant.

Note: Do not add or subtract to the dialogue.

Once the dialogue is complete the actor takes the pencil and then turns to the person to their right and continues the same dialogue.

After the pencil has made it way around the circle. Show the pen to the group and explain that it is an asephalon. With your left hand, hold it out to a different actor and begin the dialogue. Since the dialogue is the same except for the word "asephalon", you shouldn't have to teach them what to say.

Dialogue for passing the pen: (passing to the left)
Actor 1: This is an asephalon.
Actor 2: A what?
Actor 1: An asephalon.
Actor 2: An asephalon?
Actor 1: An asephalon.
Actor 2: An asephalon.

Now that the pen and pencil have made been passed around. Do the exercise again using both objects. Complete the dialogue for passing the pencil to the actor on your right, and then immediately start the dialogue for passing the pen to your left. The pen and pencil are now going around the circle at the same time.

When the pencil and pen cross paths, the actor receiving them must be able to receive and pass the objects at the same time. This is where it becomes tricky and focusing on the task at hand becomes difficult. Remind them to breath and focus on what they have to accomplish, even though they are passing and/or receiving at the exact same time.

Object: To pass the objects around the circle without faltering.

WHAT'S IN THE BOX?

Set-up: In the middle of the room is a box. Inside the box is something that you want/are afraid of. Be specific. React to the object. You may take the "object" out of the box. We should be able to tell what it is based on your reaction or how you handle the object.

ENVIRONMENT GAME (10'X10' ROOM)

Actors should be split up and arranged facing the wall of each side of the room. Each side of the room is a different location. Have them create a room in their mind and explore the room. Actors are not working together. Each actor will create their own room. In addition to the room, have them create an environmental condition: cold, windy, hot, etc. Remind them to be specific in their surroundings and to interact with it if they can while experiencing the weather/temperature. Things you can have them think about as they are exploring their room or location are: Where are you? What surrounds you? How do you feel about this place? How does the weather/temperature affect you and your relationship to the room?, etc. After they have explored their room thoroughly, have them switch and move to the wall next to them. This will be a completely new location with a new environment/weather condition. Repeat until they have been to all the walls.

NEW NAMES

Give new names to common objects. Don't think about it. Just say it.

FOUR ROOMS

Set-up: This is the same set-up as the Environment Game except weather/temperature are not used. Instead, once they have established their room or location something goes wrong. How do they deal with it?

CIRCLE DANCE

Purpose: Move your body to the music. Express how you are feeling at that moment through movement. Do not dance.

Set-up: Arrange everyone in a circle. One at a time, you will call a person and they will go to the center of the circle. They will move their body to express how they are feeling. The others around the circle will copy the person in the center. It is about experiencing another person's emotion through your body. Try to match them as close as you can. After 5 minutes or so, call another person and they will take the center and the other person will move back to the circle. Repeat until everyone has gone.

Note: Use music that doesn't inspire dance but creates mood. Actors in the center shouldn't dance nor tell a story through their movement. They should merely reflect how they are feeling or what they have experienced throughout the day.

BODY PARTS

Set-up: Choose a favorite body part, give it lower rating. Choose a least favorite body part, give it higher rating. Move around and interact with other people in the room. What do you experience?

I'M AFRAID, WILL YOU PROTECT ME

Set-up: Actor chooses someone they like. They then choose someone they don't like. The object is to stay close to the person you like while avoid the person you don't like.

FOUR MEN IN A RAFT

Status game using cards. The value of the card determines your status. The raft is sinking and the four people must decide who is thrown overboard in the shark-infested waters. Give them a time limit and if no one is picked they boat will sink and they all get eaten by the sharks.

THE BOARD MEETING

Set-up: Same as the above scenario except the four actors must decide who is going to get fired. Give them a time limit. If no one agrees to be fired before time is up, they are all fired.

DINNER OUT

Set-up: Three actors. Two have no money and must convince the other actor to help them out but the other actor has only enough money for one of them. They must resolve the situation. Raise the stakes to make the other person choose you. The actor must choose one person to help.

THE MACHINE/BUILD A ROBOT

Set-up: The actor goes up one at a time and creates a movement with a sound. Actors join in, adding to the one of the movements. This continues until everyone has joined in.

The internet has plenty of resources for games. Here are a few games I found at Stagemilk.com founded by Andrew Hearle.

WORD ASSOCIATION WITH CLICKS

This game is played by professional theatre companies.

Set-up: Get your group into a circle. Teach them the rhythm which they will make with their bodies: thigh slap, clap, then click (right hand), click (left hand). Get the group comfortable with this rhythm.

Object: Choose the direction you will be going Start the rhythmic pattern. The first actor will say a word when clicking their left hand. The person next to them will say that person's word while clicking with their right hand and then a new word that associates with that word when clicking with the left hand. The next person in the circle (work in a clockwise motion) must do the same. They must repeat the last persons word with the right click and then think of a new word when they click with the left hand. Continue this until you have done a few successful laps around the circle.

The thigh slap and clap give the game a steady rhythm.

ADD A FREEZE

Set-up: Get the students into pairs. Student A must create a pose (a frozen image with his or her body). Student B must then, without thinking about it too much, create their own pose that compliments Student A's pose. For example, Student A may have posed doing a karate chop, and student B may then freeze in a scared/defensive pose. Student A then unfreezes and creates a new pose that compliments

Student B's pose that they are still holding. This then continues in the same way until you feel the group begin to tire. I have noticed that it works very well with high-school kids and older.

THREE POSES SCENE

Set-up: Split your group up into three. It doesn't matter the size of each group. Instruct each group to come up with three poses or "statues" which portray a story. The three poses should represent a beginning, middle and end of a story. Give each group around 5 minutes to prepare. Get the class to reform and let each group perform. Then get the rest of the class to explain what the story was about.

OPPOSITES GAME

Set-up: Get the students to walk neutrally around the space. If you say stop, the students must go and vice versa. Do this a few times to get them warmed up. Then teach the kids the swap of jump with clap. Then do this with the students a few times. Now freely change between all the options, trying to catch them out.

GUESS THE WORD

Set-up: Split the group in half. If you have an uneven number you may have to take part. Once everyone has lined up get them to pick a partner. Gather one half in and give them a word. It is best to use emotions for example, passion, love, anxiety. The goal is for the students to express that word to their partners simply using their bodies for expression. Try to keep the two groups in two lines opposite each other so people aren't running into each other. The listening group then has to guess the word. Go through each person in the listening group and see if they have got it right. Change groups and repeat using a new word.

TELEPHONE

Set-up: Get your group into a circle, either seated or standing. Start by whispering a short sentence into the ear of the person next to you. Let the sentence travel around the circle in this same manner and see if it comes back to you the same as it started. The goal is to get it back intact, but it can provide some great fun when it goes horribly wrong.

ESSENCE MACHINES

Set-up: This is based off of the Machine/Robot exercise only they are creating a repeating scene. Name a topic and give the participants a few moments to think of a repeating sound and action linked to that theme. For example, if the theme was "shopping" a participant could mime taking money out of a purse to give to a shopkeeper, whilst saying "I'll have two of those, please." As soon as someone has an idea, ask them to step into the center of a circle to begin their repeating sound and movement. Ask if somebody else can think of a suitable way to add in their own idea. Gradually, more and more people join in the activity. Some may be linked to existing parts of the "machine", whilst others may be separate. To continue the example above, someone could join the action by becoming the shopkeeper and saying "Shall I wrap them for you?", whilst somebody else could be a cleaner in the shopping mall.

ONE WORD AT A TIME

Set-up: Have your students stand on stage in a straight line, the story is started, with each person in turn adding one word. It usually starts with 'Once - upon - a - time'. The idea is to keep your thoughts free flowing, so that you don't try to guess what is coming or force the story in a particular direction. It is not always easy to maintain a logical flow for the story, although it is always amusing. If the group is too large, break into smaller groups.
This ensures that people are more attentive; although you should make sure everyone is included.

TWO TRUTHS AND A LIE

Set-up: Highly recommended for getting to know each other in a new group. Tell your partner three things about yourself - two of which are true and one of which is a lie. For example, you might tell your partner about your hobbies, your work, where you live, your family or where you have travelled. Afterwards, your partner tries to guess which was the lie. You might choose to tell three everyday facts or three more unusual things - but remember - only one of them should be a lie. Make sure each person listens carefully to what their partner says!

Now introduce your partner to the rest of the group and see if they can guess which was the lie.

Alternatively, tell your partner three true things about yourself and then swap over. Now the whole group makes a circle. Each partner introduces their friend to the group - they tell the group two of the true things and make up one lie about their partner.

GIBBERISH INTERPRETERS

This is a good character development game. It also requires extraordinary teamwork.

Set-up: Two students sit side by side in chairs facing the rest of the class. One is the gibberish speaker, a dignitary from some foreign or imagined place who's been asked to give a speech to the assembled crowd. The other person is their interpreter. Invent a scenario for these two "guests," e.g., a Russian ballerina who's come to the United States to plead for money to buy her dancers new shoes; an alien giving a lecture on life in the Pleides; a student from Lower Slobovia talking about bobsledding in the Huge Mountains, etc.). The gibberish speaking student must offer sentences about his subject, but only in a made-up language. The interpreter must interpret them as best he can for the audience. Make each "lecture" short, around 2-3 minutes and invite the audience to ask questions after the initial presentation.

A FINAL WORD

The world of theatre and film is ever changing and our job as actors to is too keep up with those trends and changing protocols. We should constantly be training ourselves, keep our instrument honed and ready for our next audition or production. We can't guarantee to be cast but we can do everything that is needed to do the best that we can.

The world is changing because of our new "normal". Additional precautions are being taken on stage and film to ensure the health and safety of the actors, crew, production staff, house managers, theatre patrons, and movie goers. Theatre doesn't stop, it evolves just like us as artists.

Your journey as an actor is a unique one. No one follows the same path to reach their goals. Sometimes you reach that goal and sometimes you don't. That's the nature of the business. But that shouldn't stop you from dreaming, studying, practicing, auditioning, performing, and growing.

Every day you should do something to keep your skills active: learn a new monologue, practice a technique, read a book or article on acting, attend webinars, take classes or workshops. Don't let yourself get rusty and don't take anything for granted.

I really hope this current revision of *The Portable Acting Coach* helps you achieve your dreams and inspires you to be the best and do the best that you can. We are the only ones that can make our dreams a reality, no one is going to hand it to us. We have to live through successes and failures, the ups and downs, the good times and the bad ones. No matter what happens, be the warrior that you need to be. Stand tall, be proud and confident of your work. Believe in yourself the way you want people to believe in you.

I don't know you but I believe in you because you bought this book and are taking the steps necessary to improve yourself and your skills. When the business gets you down, when the rejection seems never-ending, when the process of acting becomes a challenge, remember that you will always have someone in your corner, rooting you on and hoping you succeed.

I hope that one day I run into someone who read my book or had taken my classes and achieved what they set out to do. I will be flooded with a sense of joy and pride that they achieved their dreams and, in turn, I will have succeeded as well because I was a part of it.

Until we meet again, explore the possibilities!

Break a leg!

Bibliography and Sited Works

Albee, E., *Who's Afraid of Virginia Woolf?* (1962)

Barton, J., *Playing Shakespeare* (1984)

Blakemore, E.G., *The Riverside Shakespeare* (1974)

Cameron , J., *The Artist's Way* (1992)

Eagleson, R.D., *A Shakespeare Glossary* (1986)

Fletcher, P., *Classically Speaking* (2008)

Frayne, M., *Noises Off*

Grahame, K., *The Wind in the Willows*

Haber , M., *How to Get the Part without Falling Apart* (1999)

Hagen , U., *A Challenge for the Actor* (1991)

Hagen, U., *Respect for Acting* (1973)

Harder P. and Steinke G., *Music Theory: A Programmed Course* (1991)

Hearle, Andrew, *Stagemilk.com*

Ionesco, E. *The Lesson* (1958)

Linklater, K., *Freeing the Natural Voice* (1976)

Mamet, D., *Oleanna* (1993)

McDonagh, M., *The Pillow Man*

Manderino, N., *All About Method* (1985)

Meisner, S. and Longwell, D., *Sanford Meisner on Acting* (1987)

Moore, S., *The Stanislavsky System* (1984)

Morris, E and Hotchkins, J., *No Acting Please* (2002)

Post, D., *The Wind in the Willows* (1992)

Schmidt, A., *Shakespeare Lexicon and Quotation Dictionary* (1971)

Shakespeare, W., *Hamlet*

Shakespeare, W., *Henry V*

Shakespeare, W., *Richard III*

Shakespeare, W., *Romeo and Juliet*

Shurtleff, M., *Audition* (1979)

Silverbush, R. and Plotkin, S., *Speak the Speech!* (2002)

Simon, N., *Lost in Yonkers* (1991), *Thieves*

Skinner, E., *Speak with Distinction* (1990)

Stanislavsky, C., *An Actor Prepares* (1948)

BIBLIOGRAPHY AND SITED WORKS

Stanislavsky, C., *Building a Character* (1964)
Stanislavsky, C., *Creating a Role* (1961)
Williams, T., *Cat on a Hot Tin Roof* (1954)
Williams, T., *The Glass Menagerie* (1945)
Lagasca, T., Thuman, T., Fury-Childs, G., Kjennas, P., Leban, C., Barbour, K., Paulson, L., Coffin, *Notes and Handouts*, Pacific Conservatory of the Performing Arts (1991-1993),
Lagasca, T., Rudd, P., Thomas, N., Buhl, K., *Notes and Handouts* – Actors Studio Drama School New School University (2002-2005)

INDEX

A

Acting
  animal work 272
    animal to character 275
    animal to human 274
    character's animal 275
      character to animal......... 276
    exploring an animal 272
    loss and betrayal 274, 275
  arcs.. 109
  emotional
    chart.. 108
    tones.. 107
  emotional recall 123
  endowment.................................. 114
  if, the magic 99
  listening, how to.........................73
  moment before, the 101
  moment-to-moment................. 104
  objective/intention......................46
  obstacle...49
  overview..44
  relationship 66
    status..66
  sense memory 119
  slice of life exercise.................. 270
  status 69
  substitution 116
  terms...183
  trust...71
Action...78
  example
    Bad Seed, The 78
  primary and secondary 78
Analyzing monologues.................. 295
Animal work.................................. 272
Antithesis...........................170, 369
Arcs.. 109

breaking down the process 112
emotional tones, using.............. 110
example
  Wind in the Willows, The 111
Arriving at the Audition 329
Arsenic and Old Lace
  trust.. 71
Articulation................................... 153
  warm-up 158
auditions
  resumes..326
Auditions..312
  after the......................................339
  arriving at the............................329
  audition pieces
    introducing your...................334
    presenting your.....................333
  audition, scheduling an
    agent..313
    casting notice.........................314
  callbacks......................................337
  cold readings 337
  entering the audition space.....331
  headshots 324
  overview 312
  preparing
    the monologue.......................315
    the song 316
  resumes..326
    example 328
  song terminology......................318
  what to wear
    men..322
    women......................................323
  what to wear for
    commercial and film............320
    stage...321

B

Bad Seed, The
    action example 78
Barbour, Karen
    trust exercise 71
Beats
    counting out 166
Beats and Pauses 86
Before You Step on Stage 34
Bio
    character 82
Blocking a Scene 308
Blocking the monologue 300

C

Caesura 367
Callbacks 337
Carry-over 367
Cat on a Hot Tin Roof
    substitution example 116
Center stance (neutral position) . 133
Lines 36
Character Analysis
    from a play 261
    nine questions, the, Uta Hagan 265
    not from a play 263
    overview 258
Character analysis sheet 284
Character Bio
    example 82, 78
    given circumstances 82
Character observations 267
Choking 420
Choosing monologues 293
Circumstances 82
Cobra, The 253
Cold readings 337
Costumes and Props
    self-taping 347
Cutting and Pasting
    removing dialogue example
    Noises Off 287

removing lines example
    Pillowman, The 289
    Thieves 291

D

Definitions
    acting
        subtext 76
    action 78
    arcs 109
    articulation 153
    beats 86
    emotional recall 123
    emotional tones 107
    endowment 114
    example (patterns of speech). 170
    given circumstances 82
    if, the magic 99
    inner monologue 80
    justification 88
    laban 231
    leading (movement) 225
    listening 73
    lists (patterns of speech) 170
    making a point (patterns of
        speech) 172
    matter of fact (patterns of
        speech) 169
    Moment Before, The 101
    moment-to-moment 104
    movement 224
    obstacle 49
    pauses 87
    phonation 143
    positioning 140
    posture and alignment 135
    qualifiers (patterns of speech)
        171
    registration 149
    relationship 66
    relaxation, voice 132
    resonance 151
    respiration 140

rhythm (speech) 166
sense memory 119
Shakespeare
    antithesis 369
    caesura 367
    carry over 367
    contrasting puns 369
    double entendre 370
    double/feminine ending..... 364
    full end stop 367
    iambic 363
    philosophical........................... 369
    physicalizing the text........... 378
    pyrrhic..................................... 366
    rhetoric.................................... 369
    scanning the text................... 371
    set speech 362
    soliloquy.................................. 362
    spondee................................... 365
    stichomythia........................... 370
    trochee..................................... 364
  stepping stones (patterns of
    speech) 170
  substitution 116
  support, voice 146
  tactic 51
  telling a story (patterns of
    speech) 169
  tempo (speech) 166
  trust..71
  Vocal Gesture.............................55
  voice... 130
  weight (movement).................. 227
DeWitt, Margaret D....................... 175
Dialects
  neutral, standard,regional....... 217
  reference guide 220
Director
  role of the................................... 354
  working with the 355
Directors, three types of 355
Double endings (Shakespeare) ... 364

Double entendre (Shakespeare
    literary style)................................370

E

Emotional chart 108
Emotional Levels
  example
    Wind and the Willows..........111
Emotional recall..............................123
  exercise
    loss and betrayal..................126
    residue from 126
    when to use...........................126
Emotional Recall
  exercise #1 125
Emotional tones...............................107
Endowment
  exercise 114
  Glass Menagerie, The 114
Entering the Audition Space........331
Essence, using an
  substitution................................117
Example (patterns of speech) 170
Examples
  action
    Bad Seed, The 78
    character bio............................ 82
  if, the magic
    Richard III 99
  inner monologue........................ 80
  moment before, the
    Oliver Twist............................101
    Who's Afraid of Virginia Woolf?
   101
  moment-to-moment
    Lost in Yonkers....................104
  research 260
  Shakespeare
    scansion................................374
  status
    Glass Menagerie, The.............. 69
Exercises
  acting

meet your ancestor...............277
acting
    animal work
        animal to character.........275
        animal to human..............274
        character's animal..........275
            character to animal....276
        exploring an animal........272
        loss and betrayal.............275
        loss and betrayal animal274
    emotional recall #1...............125
    emotional recall #2
        loss and betrayal.............126
    endowment...........................114
    justification
        mud exercise 90
    listening................................74
    moment before, the.............103
    moment-to-moment.............106
    sense memory 119, 120
        substance...........................121
    substitution 117
    subtext..................................77
acting
    portrait exercise 279
    private moments 281
    loss and betrayal..................283
    monologues
        paraphrase..........................299
        gibberish..............................299
Acting
    animal work...........................272
    slice of life 270
movement
    bacon sizzles 234
    blowdarts...............................234
    breath....................................234
    chest isolations....................234
    leading...................................225
    mud exercise, the..................227
    pelvic clock...........................233
    physical centering.................233
    Psoas muscle stretch............253

stretching and limbering....233
sundog salutaion...................252
warm-up
    variation #1 - relaxtion.235
    variation #2 - stretching241
    variation #3 - relaxation
        and voice.......................245
    variation #4 - thirty minute
        warm-up 249
mud exercise....................................90
observations.....................................267
relaxation
    part 1 - relaxing.........................94
    part 2 - green light...................97
speech
    pitch
        Let your tone hum down
       175
    pitch and drills 174
        practice sentences...........174
    pitch range, finding the.......175
    rhythm.......................................167
    singing the text 173
    tempo..168
tactic...53
tactic exercise #2............................54
voice
    articulation
        consonants on "ah".........154
        consonants, voice and
            unvoiced.......................154
        licking ice cream..............153
        lip and tongue flutters ...153
        pinky press 153
        tongue sighs 153
        tongue snaps....................153
        tongue teasers 155
    gasps..141
    nasal breathing.........................142
    phonation
        jaw massage 144
        jaw shakes.........................144
        jaw shakes with sound ..144

moans.............................. 145
sighs................................ 144
sound gatherer................. 145
posture and alignment
arm lock............................ 137
arms swings 138
garden walk down the spine
.... 135
garden walk up the spine
.... 135
head rolls.......................... 137
marionette stretch 135
neck stretches.................. 138
noble posture assessment
.... 135
ragdoll.............................. 138
railroad chicken............... 136
shoulder rolls................... 137
side stretches................... 136
six-sided box.................... 139
tennis swings................... 139
registration
piano scales...................... 150
siren.................................. 149
voice
hoo 149
yodels 149
zah 149
relaxation
deep breathing................. 133
fire breathing................... 134
lava................................... 132
neutral position 133
tense and relax................. 133
resonance
face stretch, jack o'lantern
.... 152
hum (resonance) 151
hum into cup.................... 151
jack o'lantern face stretch
.... 152
pummel and rib hug........ 152
vowel work....................... 152

respiration and positioning
altoid breathing............... 142
breathing on counts........ 141
kah 142
lung vacuum 140
picking grapes.................. 141
snake, the.......................... 140
spelling name................... 148
wall coloring..................... 148
support
hello joe............................ 146
move object with breath 148
painting the room 147
panting 146
rib breathing..................... 147
suspension, breath 147
umbrella............................ 148
warm-up structure..................... 233
Exploring the monologue 297

F

Fair Verona............................. 305
Falling
backwards.......................... 413
downstairs 412
Forward 411
Falls Overview...................... 405
Fletcher, Patricia................... 211
Following Directions
self-taping......................... 343
Four Rules to Remember................. 24
don't compare 24
keep your secrets.............. 24
never apologize 24
permission to fail 24
Freeing the voice through singing
.... 173
Full end stop......................... 367
Fury-Childs, Gale................... 227, 362

G

Games................................... 425
Add a Freeze..................... 436

Alphabet Game 429
Aselephant/Asephalon 431
Body Parts 435
Build a Robot 436
Circle Dance 434
Count Off 430
Dinner Out 435
Environment Game 433
Essence Machine 438
Fairytales in a Minute 431
Four Men in a Raft 435
Four Rooms 434
Gibberish Interpreters 439
Go 428
Guess the Word 437
I'm Afraid, Will You Protect Me
.... 435
L.A. Tag 430
Mirror 428
New Names 434
One Word at a Time 438
Opposites Game 437
Pass the Ball 428
Space Alien 429
Stunt Double 431
Telephone 437
The Board Meeting 435
The Machine 436
The Slug 427
Three Poses Scene 437
Two Truths and a Lie 438
What's in the Box 433
Word Association with Clicks . 436
Yes/No 427
Gibberish Exercise 299
Given Circumstances
    character bio 82
Glass Menagerie, The
    endowment 114
    status example
Grabbing 420
Green light exercise
    Kemp, Elizabeth 97

H

Hagan, Uta
    Nine questions, the 265
    Respect for Acting 265
Headshots 324
Honing Speech
    listening skills 165

I

I am going to (Ultimate Verb List,
    The) 57
I want to (Ultimate Verb List, The)
    57
Iambic (Shakespeare) 363
If, the magic 99
    example, Richard III 99
Inner Monologue 80
Intangible object
    endowing an 115
International Phonetic Alphabet . 211
    vowel placement 215
Introducing your audition piece
    auditions 334

J

Journal, keeping a 26
Julius Caesar 370
Justification
    example
        Oliver Twist 88
    mud exercise 90
Justification and action 88

K

Keeping a journal 26
Kemp, Elizabeth
    Green light exercise 97
    warriors 22
Kicks 414
    doubled-over 414
    groin kicks 416
    kneeling 414

standing.. 414
stomach... 415
Koshi (Suzuki)................................. 382

L

Laban... 231
Leading (movement) 225
Leibman, Ron....................................23
Lesson, The
  monologue analysis example . 302
Lines
  memorizing 36
Linklater, Kristen
  thirty-minute warm-up 249
Listening 73
  relationship 67
Listening skills, honing speech.... 165
Lists (patterns of speech)............. 170
Loss and betrayal............................ 283
Lost in Yonkers
  moment-to-moment example 104

M

Making a point (patterns of speech)
.... 171
Marking The Monologue............... 296
Massages... 254
  ironing out the back.................. 254
  polarity.. 255
Matter of fact (patterns of speech)
.... 169
Meet your ancestor........................ 277
Memorizing
  changing lines.................................36
  techniques.......................................39
    cover up.......................................39
    perform an action 41
    vocal recording.......................40
    write out 39
  techniques
    through blocking.......................41
Memorizing Lines 36
Moment Before

example
  Who's Afraid of Virginia Woolf?
 101
  exercise 103
Moment before, the........................101
Moment-to-moment
  objective..104
Moment-to-Moment
  example
    Lost in Yonkers.......................104
  exercise 106
Monologue Overview 286
Monologues
  analysis example
    Lesson, The............................302
  analyzing.......................................295
  blocking...300
  choosing...293
  cutting and pasting....................287
  exploring..297
  Marking...296
  memorizing
    cover up.. 39
    vocal recording 40
    write out.. 39
Movement
  Laban..232
    eight basic efforts 232
  leading..225
  leading exercise)........................225
  massage
  overview 224
  psoas stretch 252
  warm-up
    variation #1 - relaxation.....235
    variation #2 - stretching.....241
    variation #3 - relaxation and
      voice 245
    variation #4 - thirty minute
      warm-up 249
Mud Exercise.................................... 90
Music Terms......................................183
Musical terms in Sheet Music.......176

451

N

Neutral American speech..............217
Neutral position.................................133
Nine questions, the, Uta Hagan....265

O

Object, endowing a...........................114
Objective/Intention..........................46
　finding the.......................................47
　moment-to-moment...................104
　super; main....................................46
　non-playable verbs......................46
Observations, character.................267
Obstacle..49
　example...49
　the six types.................................49
Oleanna
　fair verona....................................305
　objective example........................46
　tactic example.............................52
Oliver Twist
　justification example....................88
　moment before, the example ..101

P

Paraphrasing a monologue exercise
　..299
Patterns of speech, Utilizing.........169
Pauses..87
Performances, the............................359
Peter Piper...156
Philosophical (Shakespeare literary
　style)...369
Phonation..............................143, 287
Objective..46
Phrasing an Objective.....................46
Physical centering...........................233
Physicalizing the Text
　shakespeare..................................378
Pitch exercises..................................174
Portrait exercise..............................279
Positioning..140

Posture and alignment...................135
Preparing for a Scene......................306
Preparing for the audition............315
Presenting your pieces...................333
Primary Action.................................281
Private moments..............................281
Props and Set for Scenes...............309
Psoas Muscle Stretch......................252
Punches..417
Puns, contrasting (Shakespeare
　literary style)...............................369
Pushing
　pull-in, the....................................404
Pushing
　lean-in, the....................................403
Pyrrhic (Shakespeare)....................366

Q

Qualifiers (patterns of speech)....171

R

Readers
　self-taping.....................................344
Regional American speech.............217
Registration......................................149
Rehearsals and performances
　director, role of the....................354
　director, working with the......355
　first read–through, the..............350
　making choices.............................352
　performances, the.......................359
　rehearsals......................................353
　stage manager, role of the.......357
　tech week......................................358
Relationship..66
　defining a..66
　listening...67
　status..69
　working with tactics....................66
Relaxation
　voice..132
Relaxation Exercise, Part 1..............94
relaxation, voice..............................132

Research.................................. 259
Research example..................... 260
Residue
    emotional recall 126
Resonance 151
Respiration and positioning......... 140
Resume example 328
Resumes.................................... 326
Rhetoric (Shakespeare literary style)
.... 369
Rhythm...................................... 166
Richard III
    the magic...................................99
Romeo and Juliet....................... 371
Running into a Wall..................... 423

S

Scansion
    example................................ 374
    shakespeare
        learn to scan text.................. 372
Scansion (Shakespeare)................ 367
Scene Partner
    working with a 307
Scenes
    blocking a scene........................ 308
    fair Verona.............................. 305
    memorizing lines
        cover up....................................40
        get a friend 41
        memorizing through blocking
       41
        vocal recording........................40
    preparing................................. 306
    overview.................................. 304
    using props and the set........... 309
    working with a Scene partner 307
Schmidt, Alexander 368
Secondary Action..................... 281
Self-Taping
    costumes and props.................. 347
    following directions.................. 343
    readers..................................... 344

set-up, The............................341
slating and performances 345
staying proactive......................348
sense memory
    sight....................................121
    taste....................................121
Sense memory.............................119
    exercise 120
    sound...................................120
    touch 120
Set and Props for Scenes.............309
Shakespeare
    exploring Shakespearean verse
   369
    literary styles 369
    rhythmic patterns...................363
        double/feminine ending.....364
        iambic..............................363
        pyrrhic 366
        spondee 365
        trochee..............................364
    Romeo and Juliet.....................371
    scansion 367
        learn to scan text...............372
    script detective.......................368
    set speech.............................362
    soliloquy................................362
Shakespeare overview...................362
Shakuhachi (Suzuki)....................388
Singing
    compared to speaking...............130
Skinner, Edith.............................211
Slaps..417
Slating and Performances
    self-taping.............................345
Speaking
    compared to singing 130
Speech
    dialects
        neutral, standard,regional..217
    dialects reference guide...........220
    Inernational Phoenetic Alphabet
    (I.P.A.)...................................211

International Phonetic Alphabet
(I.P.A.) chart 212
musical terms in sheet music..176
neutral american..........................217
patterns of..169
principles of speaking, the.......166
regional american.........................217
removing a regional dialect.....219
rhythm...166
singing
    freeing the voice through....173
singing the text 173
standard american.......................218
tempo...166
utilizing patterns of...................169
Spondee (Shakespeare)................365
Stage
    diagram of 29
    moving on............................... 30
    terminology............................. 30
        ad-lib.................................. 30
        beat...................................... 30
        blocking.............................. 30
        business.............................. 30
        counter................................ 30
        cross.................................... 30
        cue.. 31
        delivery............................... 31
        dialogue 31
        gesture 31
        hand prop............................ 31
        kneeling 31
        off-book............................... 31
        pace....................................... 31
        pause..................................... 31
        pick up cue.......................... 32
        pick up pace........................ 33
        positioning.......................... 32
        projection............................ 33
        prop....................................... 33
        set 33
        set piece............................... 33
        turn out................................ 33

upstage 33
Stage Combat
    chart, hospital and non-hospital
        zones 399
    punches
        jab... 418
Stage combat
    basic combo #1 and #2............. 422
    choke hold
        backward 420
        front..................................... 421
    falling
        backwards 413
        downstairs............................ 412
        forward................................. 411
    grabbing
        clothes.................................. 420
        hair pulling.......................... 420
    guidelines, general 400
        center of gravity 400
        focus/awareness................. 400
        forward force/pulling back400
        positioning 401
        reaction 400
        stay in control 400
    hospital and non-hospital zones
        397
    kicks
        doubled-over........................ 414
        groin
            knee to................................ 416
        kneeling................................ 414
        standing................................ 414
            to stomach 415
            to stomach with knees... 415
    knaps
        body knap 402
        making 402
        slap knap.............................. 402
        slip knap............................... 402
    punches................................... 417
        back-handed 419

cross 417
groin 417
hammer punch..................... 417
hook, right or left 418
stomach................................ 417
uppercut............................... 418
pushing 403
rules of 397
communication..................... 397
eye contact 397
spacing.................................. 397
speed..................................... 397
running into walls 423
slaps 417
stumbles 406
stumbles, trips and falls overview
.... 405
tripping
over feet............................... 408
over objects.......................... 409
warm-up................................... 245
Stage combat overview................. 396
Stage diagram............................... 29
Stage directions 28
Stage manager
role of the 357
Stage terminology......................... 30
Standard American speech........... 218
Stanislavsky
Building a Character................. 258
singing................................... 173
Status... 69
example
Glass Menagerie, The 69
relationship............................ 69
tactic 69
Staying Proactive
self-taping 348
Stepping stones (patterns of speech)
.... 170
Stichomythia (Shakespeare literary
style) 370
Stomping (Suzuki) 386

Stretches
movement
cobra, the............................253
psoas muscle 252
Stumbles....................................406
Stumbles Overview......................405
Substitution...............................116
essence, using an..................117
example
Cat on a Hot Tin Roof...........116
exercise 117
when it doesn't work.............117
Subtext.................................... 76
Sundog Salutation 252
Support....................................146
suzuki
ich ni sum 384
Suzuki
fights, O Splendor................394
jumping 393
Shakuhachi..........................388
backwards.......................389
freestyle..........................389
speaking the speech..............394
statues 393
stomping.............................386
ke gin so..........................387
side stomping 386
ten-te-ke-ten
slow/fast 390
using text
speech A..........................383
speech B..........................383
walks, the............................391
cockroach........................392
half-moon........................392
knock-kneed....................391
noh walk.........................392
rickshaw.........................391
side kick.........................391
silent stomping................392
stomping.........................391
tippy-toe.........................391

Suzuki overview................................382

T

Tactic 51
   adding to the verb...................... 53
   choosing the verb....................... 52
   changing..................................... 52
   exercise #1:................................. 53
   exercise #2:................................. 54
   status... 69
   working with objectives 52
Tech week 358
Technique
   understanding the use of............ 23
Telling a story (patterns of speech)
  169
Tempo 166
Text
   physicalizing the.........................378
   using with Suzuki......................383
Theatre Terms.................................183
Thomas, Nova 130
Tongue teasers 155
Tripping...408
Tripping Over Objects.....................409
Trips Overview.................................405
Trochee (Shakespeare)...................364
Trust.. 71
   Arsenic and Old Lace.................... 71

U

Ultimate verb list
   intention and tactics 57
   vocal gestures
      suggested 65
Using text with Suzuki 383

V

Verb list
   see ultimate verb list 57
Vocal Gesture................................... 55
Voice 130
   articulation.................................153

musical instrument.................... 130
phonation................................... 143
Posture and alignment............. 135
registration................................ 149
relaxation 132
resonance 151
respiration and positioning 140
support, voice 146
tongue teasers
   amidst the mists.................... 156
   betty botta............................ 156
   Culligan................................. 157
   grip top sock 157
   mommala poppola 157
   peter piper............................. 156
   red leather............................. 157
   rubber baby 157
   rugged rocks.......................... 157
   she clasps the asps................ 156
   she sells seashells 157
   sit in solemn silence............. 156
   they giggled and scribbled. 156
   tip of the tongue, the 157
   tweedle battle....................... 157
   what-a-to-do.......................... 155
   whether the weather 155
   will you walk 155
   you need New York............... 155
warming up the...................... 131
Voice overview............................ 130
Vowel Placement
   international phonetic alphabet
  215

W

Warming up the voice 131
Warm-up
   articulation................................ 158
   stage combat.............................. 245
Warriors
   Kemp, Elizabeth 22
Weight
   movement................................... 227

What to Wear
commercials and film................ 320
Who's Afraid of Virginia Woolf?
moment before, the 101
Wind in the Willows, The

arcs, using...................................... 112
example text
speech, patterns of................ 172
Working with a Scene Partner..... 307

The Portable Acting Coach

Made in the USA
Columbia, SC
20 June 2020

11569477R00276